africa speaks, america answers

THE NATHAN I. HUGGINS LECTURES

africa speaks, america answers

modern jazz in revolutionary times

robin d. g. kelley

HARVARD UNIVERSITY PRESS

Cambridge, Massachusetts, and London, England

2012

Library of Congress Cataloging-in-Publication Data

Kelley, Robin D. G.
Africa speaks, America answers : modern jazz in revolutionary times /
Robin D. G. Kelley.
p.   cm.—(The Nathan I. Huggins lectures)
Includes bibliographical references and index.
ISBN 978-0-674-04624-5 (alk. paper)
1. Warren, Guy, 1923–2008.   2. Weston, Randy, 1926–   3. Abdul-Malik,
Ahmed.   4. Benjamin, Sathima Bea.   5. Fela, 1938–1997.   6. Jazz—African
influences.   7. Jazz—1951–1960—History and criticism.   8. Jazz—1961–
1970—History and criticism.   9. Jazz musicians—Biography.   I. Title.
ML3508.K44   2012
781.65′7296—dc23   2011039028

For LisaGay

Mpenzi wa roho yangu

Contents

Preface

Africa Speaks, America Answers originated several years ago as the Nathan I. Huggins Lectures sponsored by the W. E. B. Du Bois Institute at Harvard University. When Professor Henry Louis Gates Jr. graciously invited me to deliver the lectures in the spring of 2003, I was hard at work on a biography of the jazz pianist and composer Thelonious Monk. I suppose I could have lifted three lectures from my book-in-progress or used the occasion to rethink or reassess previous work. I chose to do neither. There was nothing in my biography of Monk I could have easily culled without duplicating the contents of the book, and I was too ensconced in jazz studies to suddenly shift analytic gears. So rather than turn down this extraordinary invitation, I made the imprudent decision to come up with something completely new: to explore a series of encounters between jazz and modern Africa through an examination of four artists—pianist Randy Weston, drummer Guy Warren (Kofi Ghanaba), bassist Ahmed Abdul-Malik, and saxophonist Kippie Moeketsi.

It seemed like a great idea at the time. Preparing the lectures allowed me to dig deeper into the lives and works of these extraordinary and—with the exception of Weston—largely unknown musicians. They also had something in common: each of these men was linked to Thelonious Monk. Weston and Warren befriended Monk, Abdul-Malik played in Monk's band for well over a year, and although Moeketsi never met him, he adored Thelonious and introduced his music to fellow South African musicians. But the critical element connecting each of these artists was not their association with Monk; rather, it was their connection to Africa. Although their links to modern Africa and to the jazz world varied, each one identified with Africa's struggle for liberation and made music dedicated to, or inspired by, the demands for independence and self-determination. The lectures, in short, were a set of ruminations on how the inexorable movement for African freedom in the 1950s and early 1960s influenced the work of four jazz musicians and composers on both sides of the Atlantic.

Though quite provisional, the lectures were well received, and the major conclusions have survived significant revision and expansion. I spent the next seven years tapping additional archives, combing through a wide range of primary sources and contemporary publications, and conducting several more interviews. Randy Weston has been particularly generous with his stories, time, and personal papers. His memoir with Willard Jenkins, *African Rhythms* (2010), has also been enormously valuable. In 2004, I traveled to Accra, Ghana, to conduct extensive interviews with Kofi Ghanaba and to examine his personal archives. I also met the remarkable South African vocalist and composer Sathima Bea Benjamin and decided to include her in the book. She had been living in exile for most of her professional life and, during the early part of her career, lived in the shadow of her husband, pianist Abdullah Ibrahim. I had initially viewed her role as emblematic of the challenges facing South African artists in exile, especially in the postcolonial era when the struggle against apartheid seemed like Africa's final frontier in the fight for freedom. Carol Ann Muller, the leading scholar of the life and work of Sathima Bea Benjamin, has emphasized the part that exile played in shaping her politics and aesthetics. But as I shifted focus to her formative years in South Africa, I realized that her unique identity as a jazz singer and her struggle for visibility owe a great deal to her experiences as a woman in a masculine world, as well as to her own creative choices.

I continued to rework this material and deliver substantially revised versions of these lectures to colleagues all over the world, from

Seattle to St. Louis, Toronto to Belfast, Oxford to Okinawa. Every discussion opened new horizons, raised fresh questions, and led to additional research. *Africa Speaks* also benefited from several books whose core themes dovetail with my own work—particularly Ingrid Monson's landmark study, *Freedom Sounds: Civil Rights Call Out to Jazz and Africa* (2007). Monson brilliantly reveals how Civil Rights, Black Power, and the struggle for African independence shaped the music and the musicians, inspiring political activism as well as aesthetic developments in jazz. Likewise, Penny Von Eschen's illuminating *Satchmo Blows Up the World: Jazz Ambassadors Play the Cold War* (2006) sheds light on how the U.S. State Department deployed (and employed) jazz musicians to win over newly independent African nations, Eastern bloc countries, Latin America, and the Middle East, inadvertently politicizing musicians as well as generating opportunities for cultural exchange. And then there has been an explosion of new writing on jazz in South Africa—Gwen Ansell's comprehensive *Soweto Blues: Jazz, Popular Music and Politics in South Africa* (2005); Michael F. Titlestad, *Making the Changes: Jazz in South African Literature and Reportage* (2005); Carol Ann Muller, *Focus: Music of South Africa* (2008) and, with Sathima [Benjamin] Ibrahim, *Musical Echoes: South African Women Thinking in Jazz* (2011); not to mention David Coplan's substantial revision of his classic study, *In Township Tonight! South Africa's Black City Music and Theater* (2008). In general, the scholarship on South African jazz has been quite substantial, and throughout this project I have benefited immensely from the work of Christopher J. Ballantine, *Marabi Nights: Early South African Jazz and Vaudeville* (2004), and the late Hotep Idris Galeta. Because so much has been written on jazz in South Africa since 2003, I chose to eliminate what would have been a chapter on alto saxophonist Kippie Moeketsi and the Jazz Epistles, although they figure prominently in the chapter on Sathima Bea Benjamin.

Consequently, *Africa Speaks, America Answers* is a bigger, more nuanced, and hopefully better book than I had originally conceived. At the same time, it is neither comprehensive nor definitive. Just over the last half-century, literally hundreds of musicians have navigated the musical currents on both sides of the Atlantic, promoted transnational dialogues and developed innovative fusions, and found in such intercultural exchanges insurgent political and cultural voices. The more notable figures include Art Blakey, Max Roach, Yusef Lateef, Pharaoh Sanders, the Congo's Joseph Kabasele, Nigeria's Zeal Onyia and Bayo Martins, dozens of South African artists, and more recently David Murray, Rene McLean, Craig Harris, Graham Haynes, Steve Coleman, and Neil Clarke—and this is just the tip of the iceberg. While some of these musicians appear in the following pages, I decided that a collective biography, bounded by the period of decolonization, would allow me to examine particular trans-Atlantic journeys with greater depth and complexity.

My hope is that *Africa Speaks, America Answers* offers a model for writing transnational histories of modern music, sheds light on the vexing relationship between art, politics, and spirituality, and contributes to a more global interpretation of jazz history.

africa
speaks,
america
answers

Prelude

Jazz, America's own music, is a happy gift which
Negroes have given to the whole world. We can be
right proud of our musical present wrapped up in
the rhythms of Africa that have now gone around
the world, refashioned, and back again.
—Langston Hughes, quoted in the *Chicago
Defender*, 1955

The October 19, 1962, issue of *Time* magazine ran an
unsigned editorial titled "Crow Jim" admonishing a new generation
of jazz musicians for embracing black nationalist politics. The essay
described a coterie of "angry young men who are passionately involved in the rise of Negro nationalism. Jazz compositions these
days bear titles like *A Message from Kenya* (Art Blakey), *Uhuru Afrika* (Randy Weston), *Africa Speaks, America Answers* (Guy Warren),
Afro-American Sketches (Oliver Nelson). Max Roach's *Freedom Now
Suite—We Insist* includes tunes like 'Tears for Johannesburg,' a lament for the Africans shot down in the Sharpeville massacre."[1]

Most of these artists were not self-identified black nationalists,
nor were they all "American Negroes." One, Guy Warren, was from
Ghana, and he was incensed over being thrown in with the lot. In a
long, unpublished letter to the editor, Warren made a point to distance himself from the other musicians and insisted that his album,
Africa Speaks, America Answers, in no way shared the politics or aesthetic sensibilities of the artists included in the article. He took them
to task for jumping on the "African bandwagon" and credited himself
with bringing African music to American jazz. He recalled how he
had introduced African rhythms when no one was interested. Then
"the miracle happened! Africa began to stir from her deep sleep, and
to stretch out her strong hands. The Black giant was ready to take her
place in world affairs . . . the flame of freedom began to burn through

everything and anything that stood in its way . . . suddenly AFRICA BECAME THE THING! It became the gimmick in the trade, and every s.o.b. jumped on the wagon to MAKE MONEY . . . So Max Roach, Art Blakey, and many other musicians started to play their so-called African music, and to give such aggressive titles to their music." Warren dismissed all of this music as "racial and prejudicial," "hollow," and "meaningless." And he was unequivocal in declaring that "IT IS NOT AFRICAN MUSIC."[2]

An African drummer committed to fusing jazz and African rhythms, Warren had spent the previous seven years struggling for recognition and fighting to get his unique brand of music heard. By 1962, he found himself competing in an overcrowded field. And yet, there is no denying that Africa had become "THE THING." It was the age of African independence, the Sharpeville Massacre in South Africa, Egyptian president Gamal Abdel Nasser's unprecedented stand against imperialist power, Patrice Lumumba's tragic assassination, the era of Bandung and the rise of the Third World—events and movements that profoundly shaped the politics and the music of the period. On the other side of the Atlantic, Africa's descendants were embroiled in their own freedom struggle, from Montgomery to Memphis, Birmingham to Brooklyn. But even as U.S. struggles for racial justice and equality intensified, for many black activists and artists their vision of a liberated future included Africa. African nationalist leaders visited the United States and made pilgrimages to Harlem while African Americans formed liberation support committees and looked to the continent to blaze a more hopeful future for the diaspora. Consequently, during the era of decolonization we witness an explosion of jazz recordings bearing African themes. Besides those already mentioned, the list includes Buddy Collette, "Tanganyika"; Sonny Rollins, "Airegin"; John Coltrane, "Liberia," "Dakar," "Dahomey Dance," "Tanganyika Strut," and "Africa"; Max Roach, "Man from South Africa," "All Africa," and "Garvey's Ghost"; Horace Parlan, "Home Is Africa"; Lee Morgan, "Search for the New Land"

and "Mr. Kenyatta"; Cannonball Adderley, "African Waltz," to name but a few.[5]

Although anticolonial movements and a nostalgic conception of Africa as a lost homeland inspired musicians to compose paeans to the continent, identification with Africa was hardly universal among black leaders and artists during this period. The force of Cold War anticommunism and the ongoing quest for full citizenship compelled many prominent African Americans to close ranks with U.S. nationalists and distance themselves from Africa and the struggles of colonized people. Whether motivated by a genuine belief in the conceits of the American Empire's democratizing project or a genuine fear of Cold War repression, a parade of black leaders bent over backward to prove their loyalty and membership in the American "family." Roi Ottley, Walter White, Adam Clayton Powell, and many others praised the material abundance and liberties African Americans enjoyed and, while acknowledging inequities and the persistence of prejudice, argued that America at its best still offered a beacon of freedom against the tyranny of communism. When Congressman Adam Clayton Powell attended the historic meeting of nonaligned nations in Bandung, Indonesia (without support or sanction from his own government), he defended his country against allegations that the persistence of segregation rendered the United States a hypocritical freedom fighter, at best. "Second class citizenship is on the way out," Powell told his critics. "To be a Negro is no longer a stigma."[4] Powell had personal motives for painting such a rosy picture of race relations. Faced with the blacklisting of his wife, pianist and singer Hazel Scott, for her alleged communist leanings, he felt compelled to establish his loyalist, anticommunist credentials. But Powell's defense of the United States as a genuine racial democracy in the making cannot be dismissed as merely a cynical ploy. Powell was part of a chorus of voices promoting the idea of putting black progress on display through State Department–sponsored jazz tours. Musicians like Dizzy Gillespie, Wilbur de Paris, and Louis

Armstrong were designated "goodwill ambassadors," leading racially integrated bands to the world's "hot spots" in order to showcase American talent and mask racial turmoil at home.[5]

Even black intellectuals and leaders independent of U.S. diplomatic institutions often chose to close ranks with fellow Americans rather than see themselves as a part of what Malcolm X once called a "tidal wave of color" beating back global white supremacy. Indeed, in 1956 when Martinican critic Aimé Césaire characterized racism in the United States as an extension of colonialism in a speech before the Congress of Black Writers and Artists in Paris, several black Americans in attendance took issue. John A. Davis, a political scientist and founder of the American Society for African Culture (AMSAC), also brother of the distinguished anthropologist Allison Davis, vehemently rejected the analogy, insisting that America itself has a long and distinguished *anti*colonial history. James Ivy of the National Association for the Advancement of Colored People (NAACP) went even further, arguing that "The Negroes in the United States are the most quintessential of Americans," having more in common with Europe than Africa. Even James Baldwin, a sharp critic of U.S. policy, dismissed the colonial analogy; he, too, felt there was something exceptional about being an "American Negro" that resulted from living in a "free" country.[6]

Cold War liberalism, alongside domestic struggles for racial justice and international movements for independence (both national sovereignty and nonalignment), profoundly shaped the political climate in which artists engaged both Africa and America. Most of the African American musicians discussed in this book pushed back against the notion of a unique black American identity, choosing instead to identify with Africa. They also embraced the metaphor of family, but their family was global, universal, and it knew no boundaries of place or race—although it did privilege Africa. For someone like Guy Warren, however, America *was* exceptional. First, it was the heartland of the music he loved dearly, then a territory to conquer and revitalize with his African rhythms, and finally a place of corruption, commercialism, and crass exploitation—a crumbling, bankrupt empire whose black inhabitants proved too ignorant or self-absorbed to embrace the riches of African music and culture.

By exploring the work, conversations, collaborations, and tensions between both African and African American musicians during the era of decolonization, I examine how modern Africa figured in reshaping jazz during the 1950s and early 1960s, how modern jazz figured in the formation of a modern African identity, and how various musical convergences and crossings shaped the political and cultural landscape on both continents. This book is *not* about the African roots of jazz, nor does it ask how American jazz musicians supported African liberation or "imagined" Africa.[7] Rather, it is about transnational encounters between musicians, or what the ethnomusicologist Jason Stanyek calls "intercultural collaboration," and encounters between musicians and particular locations (such as Lagos, Chicago, New York, or Cape Town). In other words, it hopes to explain how encounters with specific places, people, movements, cultures, provided fertile ground for *new* music and musical practices.

As a nod to the great critic and poet A. B. Spellman, whose *Four Lives in the Bebop Business* (1966) serves as a model for this book, I focus on four artists and the various groups they led during the age of African decolonization (roughly 1954–1963). Two of these artists, pianist Randy Weston and bassist and oudist Ahmed Abdul-Malik, hail from the United States (or, more precisely, Bedford-Stuyvesant, Brooklyn); drummer Guy Warren is Ghanaian; and vocalist Sathima Bea Benjamin is South African. Each of these artists was propelled by the upheavals of the 1950s to seek new musical forms, new collaborations, new fusions across time and space. They shared neither a common agenda nor a common culture, though they recognized and often embraced cultural commonalities, "jazz" being one. Nor did they always succeed. On the contrary, they occasionally clashed with fellow artists, or bumped up against prevailing assumptions, the intransigence of the market, an oppressive state that viewed their music as a threat to order, or consumers whose own stereotypes made them incapable of hearing and appreciating the work.

Yet they all shared a vision of jazz as a path to the future, a vehicle for both Africans and African Americans to articulate and realize their own distinctive modernity while critiquing its Western variant. And, from their vantage point, standing at what appeared to be the precipice of freedom for Africa and black America, the continent represented a beacon of modernity blazing a new path for the rest of the world, but one tempered by deeply spiritual, antimaterialist values. Indeed, I suggest that African American musicians were seeking new spiritual and ideological alternatives to what they saw as a declining West that led them to a deeper exploration of African music and culture. Likewise, African musicians who were drawn to jazz as a particular idiomatic expression of black modernity also saw the need to infuse it with the music of their homeland. Echoing the late poet Aimé Césaire, in the atomic age, when colonialism and the Holocaust left the West spiritually wanting, Africa represented both an ancient, pristine past possessing a higher spiritual order and a modernizing force able to maintain its humanity precisely because it presumably would not relinquish the best elements of its traditional values.[8] This sort of Janus-faced modernism is key to understanding the nexus of jazz and Africa in the age of decolonization. As Veit Erlmann warns, we have to resist the easy binary of modernity and tradition, especially when the subject is music. "Modernity and tradition," he writes, "are not only the two most significant historical fictions here but also the tropes whose role in the Western discourse about itself and the others is reflected and configured in the very grammar of musical performance itself."[9]

Although some of the artists in this book approached African musics and cultures as a window onto the past, a reclaiming of ancient identity, spirituality, and cultural practices, it was that very window that enabled these artists to hear new sounds, create new modes of music-making, and envision a different future. It should come as no surprise, then, that many of the musicians and composers included here—Africans and African Americans—mined Africa, as well as Asia and the Middle East, for sources of new ideas for *experimental* music. They were modernists in search of radically different elements in harmony (the use of modal music), rhythm, and timbre. African music (not just West African but North, South, and East African music) offered richer possibilities for "freeing" the music from the prevailing harmonic and rhythmic constrictions of swing and bebop.

But there were also limits. Artists constantly bumped up against the claims of authenticity. Critics, fans, record producers, even the musicians policed the boundaries between what they believed was "real" (in other words, traditional) African music and "real" jazz. Self-proclaimed experts alike questioned whether African Americans were capable of mastering "traditional" drumming techniques, or if Africans could "swing" or play authentic jazz. Arab music aficionados questioned whether jazz musicians could play an Arabic scale, or *maqām,* correctly. The hybrid and global character of the music generated many questions about its authenticity that mingled issues of race, class, and politics. Is homegrown jazz in South Africa authentically "African," or is it merely an import foisted upon a people by the American Empire? Should we question the authenticity of popular music in West Africa, such as highlife, because it draws on so many styles and genres throughout the African diaspora and Europe itself?

Ironically, the very conditions that made these fusions possible and commercially viable—a brief commercial boom for all things African in the wake of decolonization—also constrained innovation and experimentation. The work of these artists appeared amid a flurry of recordings and performances of African music and dance, and other seemingly exotic commodities. Just as the British Invasion of the early 1960s profoundly shaped American music and style, the "African invasion" fueled a desire among Americans for the primitive, the unspoiled, the savage, even the sexually charged—images often radically different from the kind of music these artists sought to create.

The first chapter takes up the so-called "African invasion" by charting Guy Warren's sojourn to America. It examines the swift incorporation of African rhythms in jazz during the 1950s and early 1960s, the group of drummers, besides Warren, responsible for bringing African (as opposed to Afro-Cuban) drumming to jazz. At the heart of the matter is a story of authenticity—who can play "African" drums and who cannot. Warren not only combined West African drums and jazz, but composed music dedicated to collapsing the constructed boundaries of genre, style, culture, and nation. Unfortunately, the music industry found Warren's persona and his music too innovative; he quickly slipped from the critics' purview and was abandoned by record producers scrambling to find a more "authentic" African drummer.

Chapter 2 follows the musical, political, and spiritual journey of Randy Weston, the pianist-composer whose name is synonymous with bridging jazz and Africa. Weston's fascination with Africa begins in the Brooklyn neighborhood of Bedford-Stuyvesant, where a rich Pan-African culture flourished even as Africa writhed under colonial domination. He set out on a personal quest to know the continent's history and to study the accomplishments of his ancestors in order to counter the prevailing racist, colonialist stereotypes. He made history himself in 1960 when he composed *Uhuru Afrika,* a four-part suite dedicated to African independence. When he finally set foot on African soil expecting to find the traditional world he had read so much about, he discovered the vibrant, modern city of Lagos, Nigeria, and a group of African musicians deeply immersed in either modern jazz or fusions of music from the diaspora. Weston's various African sojourns deepened his understanding of its culture, enriched his work as a composer, and sharpened his political commitment to liberatory politics both in the United States and abroad.

One of Weston's best friends and collaborators was bassist, oudist, and composer Ahmed Abdul-Malik, the subject of Chapter 3. His life and work require that we shift our sights from the West African—U.S. nexus to North Africa and the Middle East and the black Islamic imaginary. A converted Ahmadiyya Muslim who claimed Sudanese ancestry, Abdul-Malik was unique in his efforts to fuse jazz and musics of Egypt, Sudan, Lebanon, Syria, and other parts of the Muslim world to create new music that is at the same time deeply spiritual and ancient, and deeply experimental and modern. The context is critical. On the one hand, we witness a political fascination with North Africa and the Middle East spurred by the Suez Canal crisis and the meteoric rise of Egyptian president Gamal Abdel Nasser. On the other, the United States experienced a national obsession with the music of the Middle East, marketed and sold in the West as exotic and hypersexual, if not pornographic. Abdul-Malik's experiments were in many ways a foil against the Middle Eastern craze and a celebration of the dignity and power Islam represented for the black world.

In Chapter 4, I examine the life and music of South African vocalist Sathima Bea Benjamin. Her story takes us to the final frontier in the struggle to overthrow formal white rule in Africa. A brilliant jazz singer deeply committed to Africa and to the jazz world, Benjamin has nevertheless experienced a sense of alienation from both. Like Guy Warren, she wasn't "African" enough for the market or "Western" (American) enough to be considered among the pantheon of great jazz vocalists. And as a woman Benjamin has had to live in the shadow of her more famous husband, pianist Abdullah Ibrahim, and work in a field where gender bias is commonplace. But the limits imposed by gender and racial essentialism must be understood in the context of Benjamin's own creative choices and the world that forged her musical and political imagination—namely, apartheid South Africa in the 1950s and early 1960s.

The diasporic, trans-Atlantic conversations of these artists were less about recovering an atavistic past than creating new music. Of course, their intentions were not simply to create new music; they ran much deeper. In a crucial moment when *freedom* was perhaps the most important word circulating throughout the African diaspora, these black artists sought out each other to find new modes of expression that spoke to what they often understood as a linked struggle. They searched for new methods to express emotion, new avenues for spirituality, new ways to generate solidarity and connection.[10]

Jazz is a music of innovation, experimentation, and new discoveries. It emerges often out of unexpected juxtapositions, even mistakes and miscommunication—what jazz critic A. B. Spellman calls "the Marvelous." This constant discovery and illumination of the "marvelous" can help us move beyond the academic imperative to impose order—on movements, events, and even cultural and artistic developments.[11] Nearly every musician who has ever talked about "breakthroughs" in their quest for freedom described chance encounters, moments of miscommunication, confusion, and mistakes as central to their process of discovery. In a practice that values not only improvisation but experimentation, this is bound to happen.

Obviously, we need to pay more attention to the way music is made, to how artists speak to one another across culture, language, and idiom. But we also need to follow the musicians' example and free ourselves from fixed notions of tradition and authenticity. African musicians did not exist to bring something ancient to African American modernism; rather, they were both creating modern music, drawing on the entire diaspora as well as the world, to do so. Indeed, perhaps with the growth of trans-Atlantic collaborations and dissemination of culture, we can no longer speak so confidently about jazz as an *American* art form, or render African jazz musicians outside the pale of the music's history. And we certainly need to go beyond listening to non-American artists for ways they incorporate "their culture" into jazz—whether we're talking about South African or Israeli jazz musicians. Jazz reveals that, even in the search for tradition, its chains do not always bind us, and the most powerful map of the New World is in the imagination.

1 | The Drum Wars of Guy Warren

> Jazz is new to the native African . . . and he has no
> ear for it. He may have heard it on records but it
> has no special appeal. He does understand drums,
> though. That, so far as I can see, is the only affin-
> ity between the African Negro and the American
> Negro.
> > —Wilbur de Paris, bandleader, on his visit to
> > Africa, *New York Times,* 1957

> I would like to confess here that in all my experi-
> ence in America, I never found one single drum-
> mer who could play drums.
> > —Guy Warren, *I Have a Story to Tell* (1962)

The Boy Kumasenu (1951), written and directed by the
British filmmaker Sean Graham, tells an archetypal story about a
restless boy anxious to escape his quiet, traditional life in a Gold
Coast fishing village for the big city of Accra. Kumasenu was first
enticed by the city while working in a local store known for traffick-
ing in smuggled goods. The smuggler, a lorry driver named Yeboah—
played by none other than drummer Guy Warren—epitomized modern urban life. And if his dark shades and hipster hat did not make
this apparent, the film's narrator drove home the point: "Here in this
little story, Kumasenu first met the 20th century. The lorry driver's
swagger told of the big town . . . and their tongues spoke a language
half foreign to Kumasenu." The storeowner then pulls out a phonograph and the men begin dancing to highlife music—with Warren
leading the way.[1]

Jump forward forty-two years. In 1993, Ethiopian-born filmmaker Haile Gerima released his critically acclaimed *Sankofa,* named
for the Asante Adinkra symbol of a mythic bird turned backward,

meaning "remember your past, return to your roots." In the film's opening scene, an African American model in a reddish-blonde wig is being photographed on the beach in Cape Coast, Ghana, beneath the shadows of the infamous slave castle. Interspersed are scenes of an elder, wrapped in white cloth and doused in white powder, playing a modified drum kit consisting of carved wooden drums—two placed on their side and played with foot pedals as bass drums, and at least four other drums on stands played with two long curved wooden sticks.[2] He is the Sankofa. A few minutes into the first scene, the Sankofa confronts the model, shouting in Akan, "Back to your past! Return to your source!" He reminds the young model and the tourists gathered around that they stand on the very site where enslaved Africans were taken to the Americas; it is "sacred ground, covered with the blood of people who suffered."[3] The part of the Sankofa is played by Kofi Ghanaba, formerly known as Guy Warren.

As the enlightened Kofi Ghanaba, he saw the contrast between his role in *The Boy Kumasenu* and *Sankofa* as a metaphor for his own cultural evolution. When someone from the British Film Institute showed him a still photograph of him dancing in *The Boy Kumasenu*, "I said, who is this darn idiot? . . . I was dancing the jitterbug. So I said, Jesus, I've been through this too? But then when you come to *Sankofa*, you can see how I, this character has changed, from his American bound imprisonment to his free African life. It's very interesting."[4]

Interesting, indeed, but to characterize Guy Warren's artistic development as an evolution from American imprisonment to African liberation oversimplifies Warren's complicated, vexed, often productive relationship with the United States and, specifically, the cultural worlds of postwar Chicago and New York, as well as those of West Africa and England. Warren entered the United States full of energy and hubris, ready to Africanize jazz and establish a place for himself in the annals of music history. By the time he returned to Ghana, he had lost interest in America, and the American recording industry had lost interest in him. But he left his mark on the music—a mark that has been severely overlooked by critics and musicians alike, and yet exaggerated by Warren himself.

African Dances and Modern Rhythms

Contrary to Warren's claims, he did not introduce West African music to the United States. It is an incontrovertible fact that African music and dance arrived in North America with enslaved Africans, but by the early twentieth century only a few anthropologists and folklorists thought the musical and cultural practices of "American Negroes" bore some resemblance to those of Africa. What came to be regarded as "authentic" African music and dance made its way to the mainstream U.S. stage in the 1930s with the arrival of Asadata Dafora, a dancer, choreographer, and drummer. Born in 1890 in Freetown, Sierra Leone, a colony founded by British abolitionists in 1787 to resettle freed slaves (his great-great-grandfather was part of a group of former slaves from Nova Scotia, Canada), Dafora's mother was a renowned concert pianist who trained in Europe and encouraged her son to study opera. He traveled throughout Europe as a professional singer, and over time he began to incorporate elements of African dance. In 1929 he moved to Harlem, where he began producing a series of dance-dramas employing African and African American dancers.[5] Some of his better-known productions, *Zunguru* (1940) and *Batanga* (1941), introduced African dance and music to fairly elite audiences in the United States, often staged by the African Academy of Arts and Research, founded by Kingsley Ozuombo Mbadiwe.

The African Academy organized annual festivals beginning in 1942 showcasing African music and dance. Its second festival in 1943, titled "African Dances and Modern Rhythms," not only brought together music and dance from Brazil, Trinidad, Haiti, and Cuba, but included American jazz with performances by pianist Mary Lou Williams and tap dancer Bill Robinson.[6] These AAAR concerts apparently influenced jazz musicians fascinated with African music, including Charlie Parker and Dizzy Gillespie, who "found the connections between Afro-Cuban and African music and discovered the identity of our music with theirs." Gillespie noted, "Those concerts should definitely have been recorded because we had a ball discovering our identity."[7]

Among the participants was Prince Efrom Odok, a revered master drummer from Nigeria. Born in 1890 in the Calabar region, he learned to play and make drums under his father's tutelage. In 1920, he left Nigeria for the United States, preceding Asadata Dafora by nine years, and opened a small center in Harlem where he taught African music and dance. As more and more Nigerians made their way across the Atlantic, he was able to organize an ensemble made up entirely of drummers from Calabar. By 1938, the group performed at the Dance International Festival, at the Rainbow Room, and at Columbia University, among other noteworthy venues.[8] Still, the number of trained drummers in the United States was exceedingly small. In 1943, Odok could count only "20 really expert African drummers in the United States."[9] As much as he appreciated jazz, for many years he never accepted an invitation to play in a jazz band, "being somewhat scornful of such comparatively primitive rhythms and tone effects on the drums."[10] Yet he frequently pointed to the affinities between jazz and African music, asserting that swing was "nothing but an imitation of native African music." One of his main objectives was to teach black New Yorkers "the music and dances of their forefathers."[11] Whether out of economic necessity or recognition that his stance on jazz was contradictory, he eventually chose to collaborate with jazz musicians. In 1945, he teamed up with trumpeter Frankie Newton and pianist Ray Parker to participate in "Primitive and Concert Jazz," a dance program choreographed by dancer Mura Dehn.[12]

Other dancers and choreographers followed suit—notably Katherine Dunham and Pearl Primus, who drew on dance forms from Africa and the African diaspora. Of particular importance was Pearl Primus's drummer, Moses Mianns, a Nigerian who has been credited by several African American drummers (including Chief Bey) with introducing the ashiko drum to the United States and training an entire generation of drummers on this side of the Atlantic. But much of the popularization of hand drumming during the 1940s can be attributed to the Haitian drummer Tiroro, whose solo and ensemble recordings had become quite a sensation, and to an explosion of ethnographic recordings of African music that circulated widely within popular, nonacademic circles.[13]

Some of the earliest such recordings were made by Thurston Knudson and Augie Goupil beginning in 1941. Knudson and Goupil collected percussion instruments from around the world, learned how to play them by observing or studying with master musicians, and recorded what they heard. On the one hand, they were quite precise about the kinds of rhythms they played, where they originated, and the history and functions of the various instruments they used. On the other hand, it is hard to take them too seriously when—in the liner notes to Knudson's album, *Primitive Percussion*—he explains that the bata and ngoma drums they were using come from "the exotic milieu of the world-famous Don the Beachcomber Restaurant in Hollywood."[14]

The ethnographic recording many African American musicians did take seriously was *African and Afro-American Drums,* a two-LP collection assembled by anthropologist Harold Courlander and derived from field recordings made in Rwanda, Nigeria, Congo, South Africa, and Madagascar, as well as Cuba, Haiti, Brazil, Jamaica, Suriname, and New York City.[15] This record circulated widely in the early to mid-1950s, enabling a new generation of musicians to hear a variety of African and Afro-diasporic rhythms and instrumentation. Courlander also documented a growing number of U.S.-born African Americans participating in African or Afro-Caribbean percussion groups. He was surprised to find that "a preponderant number of these newer groups are composed not of Puerto Ricans or other West Indians, but of native Americans, many of whom come from rural areas of the South."[16]

It has become axiomatic to date the appearance of "authentic"

African drums in modern jazz to 1947, when Chano Pozo, the renowned Cuban drummer, composer, and dancer, moved to the United States and joined Dizzy Gillespie's big band. Gillespie and Pozo's collaboration on George Russell's "Cubano Be, Cubano Bop" is generally regarded as a landmark recording, not only for its use of heavy Afro-Cuban percussion but because Pozo injects West African–derived spiritual and cultural practices into his performance. At one point midway into the song, Pozo delivers a Lucumi chant (Lucumi, or Santeria, is the Cuban version of Yoruba religion). Pozo had the credentials to perform such sacred music; he was initiated into the Abakua secret society, whose origins can be traced back to the Calabar region of southern Nigeria.[17] The early fusions of jazz and what was understood to be authentic West African musical practices initially came by way of Cuba, or the African diaspora in Latin America.

Chano Pozo's short-lived experiments (he died a year later from injuries sustained in a bar fight) were soon taken up by Art Blakey. In 1953, Blakey recorded an all-percussion track with Puerto Rican conga player Sabu Martinez titled "Message from Kenya."[18] The title obviously referred to the uprising of the Kikuyu Land and Freedom Army in Kenya, known as the Mau Mau rebellion. The piece has no apparent relationship to Kenya or East Africa generally. Rather, it is based on a story reportedly told to Blakey by Moses Mianns about a hunter "whose cries celebrate the news that he has captured more game than any other hunter in the village, in order to convince the girl he loves of his prowess."[19] Four years later, Blakey recorded another all-percussion piece inspired by African rhythms titled "Ritual," which bore more than a passing resemblance to passages in "Message from Kenya." In his spoken preface he recounts the exact same story, but this time he claims he learned the song directly from the Ijaw people on a visit to Nigeria from 1947 to 1948. He makes no mention of Mianns, who had been in the United States since the early 1940s and who just happened to be Ijaw. The point is that learning the music directly from West Africa gives it greater authenticity, and thus greater cultural cachet.[20]

Introducing Guy Warren

This is what the African music scene in the United States looked like when Guy Warren arrived in Chicago in December 1954 ready to make his mark on the jazz world. As far as Warren was concerned, none of it was authentic or even interesting. He was never impressed with Art Blakey, for example. "Art Blakey bores me to death," he once told an interviewer. "He excites you at first; the first two seconds—and then that's it—he can't go any further than that."[21] Only Warren was capable of infusing jazz with African rhythms, which in his view was tantamount to saving the music. His drive, determination, and musical imagination were matched only by his ego. As he once wrote, "There has never been anybody in the history of Jazz music like me . . . I am to Jazz music what Kwame Nkrumah was to modern African politics."[22]

Warren was born in Accra, in what was then the British colony of the Gold Coast, on May 4, 1923, to Susana Awula Abla Moore, an unmarried teenaged mother, and Richard Mabuo Akwei, a respected educator and headmaster of the Ghana National School. Susana was born in 1905 to Hanna Ahiefor, a native of the Gold Coast, and a British mining engineer known simply as Mr. Moore. As soon as Ahiefor became pregnant with Moore's child, he returned to England before he could meet his daughter or provide her with adequate financial support. When Susana was old enough to begin her studies, she attended Accra Grammar School, where Richard Akwei taught. It is not clear how their relationship evolved, but in 1922 she was carrying his child.[23]

Guy's father named him Kpakpo Warren Gamaliel Akwei, after U.S. president Warren Gamaliel Harding. But besides naming him and financing his education, Richard Akwei barely acknowledged his son. And Guy clearly felt unacknowledged, which is why he refused to take his surname. Not long after Warren left Ghana and relocated to Chicago, Richard Akwei sent him a letter seeking reconciliation, but it was laced with disparaging remarks about his career. "Failure," he advised, "is and must be a stepping stone to success." And as if to rub salt in his wounds, Akwei boasted that his other son, Richard Akwei Jr., had just been appointed to the Gold Coast diplomatic corps.[24] Warren's estrangement from his father would have a profound effect on his music.

Warren attended the Government Elementary Boys' School in Accra, where he led the school band in his last two years (1937–1939) and acted in various local productions.[25] His formative music education, however, came from outside of school: "My house was located next to a bar called the Basshoun. It was a cowboy bar, an imitation of the Western saloon where little bands came to play night after night. They would let me in as a child because I loved to listen to Harry Dodoo, a first class drummer who used to perform tricks and comedy like the American drummer Baby Dodds. I heard the music and learned to sing what they were playing. It was all primarily American music that American seamen brought to Accra, the port."[26]

At fifteen, while attending the Odorgonno Secondary School, he earned a spot as a drummer in the Accra Rhythmic Orchestra, a popular highlife band.[27] Highlife, with its fast tempos and distinctive shuffle beat, was West Africa's most popular urban dance music. It originated in the Fante coast in the late nineteenth century, but by the 1930s and 1940s it had been "modernized," infused with rhythms and styles from other parts of Africa and the diaspora—notably, the cha-cha, tango, calypso, pachanga, marabi music of South Africa, Congo pop music, and Nigerian juju.[28] As was common among highlife bands, the Accra Rhythmic Orchestra peppered its repertoire with a number of jazz pieces, some featuring Warren on drums. In those early days, he mimicked the white swing drummers he had heard on records. As he once explained to Max Roach, "I was in a colonial territory and the history and the music of the Afro-American was exported to me in a different form, in a bastardized form. So I knew about Gene Krupa, and Buddy Rich, and the "Grey" [white] drummers. And I was influenced more or less by the Buddy Rich style, so even though I had a spectrum of drummers to listen to and choose from, I had a partial affinity for the Buddy Rich style."[29]

Warren's musical and dramatic talents earned him a scholarship to the Gold Coast's prestigious Achimota College. He enrolled in the teacher-training program in 1941, but two years later, he lost his beloved mother Susana Moore. She was only thirty-seven years old. Her death and his continued estrangement from his father and his family provoked Warren to look for an escape. With war raging and the presence of American GIs in the Gold Coast growing, Warren considered traveling to the United States. "I was fascinated by [the American GIs]," he explained. "I looked at what the Americans were doing and would go out there and imitate them. How they spoke, their movements, how they walked, how they did everything. I wanted to be like them, you dig?"[30]

Then one evening, while hanging out at a local bar, Warren met Captain Mike Yeltsin, an American military officer who worked for the Office of Strategic Services. Yeltsin immediately detected Warren's exuberance for America and recruited him for the OSS, first as his personal assistant and then as an intelligence agent. Warren dropped out of school and underwent intensive training as a member of the OSS, which, in his words, consisted of learning "how to behave like an American . . . He had de-Africanized and de-Anglicized me and I'd become an American, a GI . . . He wanted me to enter America as an American soldier."[31] Thus, after years of listening to and playing American music, admiring American culture, hearing American seamen tell stories of city life across the Atlantic, Warren suddenly became an American under the aegis of the U.S. military. America ceased to be an imaginary place.

For several months in 1943, Warren's work with the OSS took him to Lima, Peru; Vera Cruz, Mexico; Key West, Florida; and finally

New York City, where he and Captain Yeltsin resided in a small apartment on Bleecker Street in Greenwich Village.[32] He had finally reached his destination—the jazz capital of the world. But his training and work schedule afforded him little time to "play." He did venture into Nick's Tavern in the Village, a club known for Dixieland and Chicago-style jazz, and sat in on drums with trombonist Miff Mole, but he never felt like it was his scene. "I didn't really play at Nick's, just jammed once or twice there. It was an all white rendezvous and I was like a freak there and you know how they love freaks."[33]

Warren was back in Accra before the end of 1943 and began working as a journalist for the *Spectator Daily* while serving as an undercover agent for the OSS. The following year, after he was discharged from the military, he took a position as the jazz disc jockey for the Gold Coast Radio Broadcasting Service and returned to music. In 1947, Warren joined the wildly popular highlife band the Tempos, with E. T. Mensah and Joe Kelly.[34] Their bread-and-butter gigs were mainly at the European Club (later called the Accra Club), playing for white audiences. By 1950 the Convention People's Party, led by Kwame Nkrumah, rose to prominence, organizing strikes and boycotts throughout the country for elections and ultimately independence from Britain. Spaces like the European Club became increasingly fraught with political and racial tensions—tensions that affected Warren profoundly.

One evening in 1949 or 1950, during a break between sets, Warren was speaking with a British army captain. A Canadian patron walked up to the two men and said, "What's an American nigger doing here?" Warren ignored him at first, brushing him off as another drunk patron. But then the man "pushed me and says to me, 'Say sir when you talk to a white man.' So I turn around and give him the belly punch. He doubled up and I let him have it right under his chin and he fell flat. Boom, bam. It was very fast and he was stretched out on the floor. It was pandemonium. For any African to go to a European club and beat up a white man, that was sensational. And everybody panicked. The ladies screamed, the men didn't know what to do. Nobody came close to me."[35]

The incident made Warren something of a local hero, even winning the admiration of Kwame Nkrumah. But it also cost him his gig with the Tempos. He left the Gold Coast soon thereafter and headed to London, where he continued to work as a correspondent for several West African newspapers, hosted a series of jazz programs for the BBC, and played with Kenny Graham, the British tenor saxophonist, and his Afro-Cubists ensemble.[36]

Graham, who was a year younger than Warren, had just left the British military when he formed the Afro-Cubists in 1950. He developed the concept just as a thriving Caribbean jazz scene began to take off in London—fueled, in part, by the influx of Caribbean immigrants who had come after the war to rebuild the city.[37] Warren liked the idea of playing African percussion in an experimental jazz context, but the Cuban emphasis never sat well with him. "We were always clashing on this," Warren later recalled, "that the African conception was what we needed more than the Afro-Cuban." They clashed over other issues as well, namely the perennial problem of song theft. It wasn't uncommon for a bandleader to take composer's credit for tunes written by a sideman, though most musicians found the practice unethical. For Warren, it was unheard of: "I remember I wrote a number called 'The Haitian Ritual' and he copied the number and put his name to it and he gave it to Ted Heath and his band and they recorded it. And he would always steal ideas from me."[38]

He left England and Kenny Graham's Afro-Cubists in 1951, just before the band's debut recording session. But he did not leave empty-handed; he returned to West Africa laden with Cuban percussion instruments (bongos and conga drums) as well as a deeper knowledge of jazz, calypso, rumba, and other diasporic music. Struck by the similarities between West African highlife and Trinidadian calypso, Warren formed his own Afro-Cubist ensemble and traveled throughout the region, performing at the 1953 inauguration of Liberia's president William Tubman. He decided to remain in Monrovia, where he became assistant director and DJ for Liberia's Eternal Love Broadcasting Corporation (ELBC)—the precursor to the National Broadcasting Service of Liberia. For Warren, his stint at ELBC was like earning a postgraduate degree in music. Besides introducing jazz and Caribbean music to West African listeners, Warren recalled fondly, "I played classical music for listeners . . . Duo Bergerac, Rimsky-Korsakov, Berlin, Stravinsky, Mozart, you name it, Handel, Chopin, all of them. I did that for two years or three years. I read their notes, played their music and got to know it."[39]

Warren did not devote all of his time to studying music during his Liberia sojourn. He got to know an attractive African American nurse named Justina Alexander who was working in a Monrovia hospital. By the time she was ready to return to her native city of Chicago, Warren was more than smitten. "I intended to marry her," he explained, "so she arranged for me to go to America. She was in America and arranged for me to get papers to immigrate."[40] In hindsight, Warren believed he loved Alexander, but he confessed that love was secondary to becoming a jazz musician. In fact, once he arrived in Chicago in December of 1954, tensions erupted between them over his aspirations. "She wanted me to do the ordinary 8 to 12, 2 to 5 shifts, and she wouldn't settle with my wanting to be a jazz musician and a jazz musician only. And so she fell out with me."[41] She also fell out with him for other reasons. During her long shifts at the hospital, Warren spent a lot of his free time with his neighbor, a pretty, garrulous young woman named Iris Wilkins. "We'd talk to each other," Warren later confided, "so we started to, you know, coo and caw, and hooh and haah, and lo and behold she became pregnant and she had my first baby in America."[42] Needless to say, Justina Alexander called off the wedding.

Warren's first priority was finding gigs. Within days of his arrival, he headed straight to the *Down Beat* magazine offices in search of places to play. *Down Beat*'s editor, Jack Tracy, introduced Warren to Gene Esposito, who played both trumpet and vibes, and his Jazz Latin group. Esposito liked Warren's playing, both as a drummer and percussionist, and hired him right away, making Warren the first and only black member of a band composed entirely of Italian and Jewish musicians.[43] The money wasn't great (about ten to twelve dollars a week in 1955), but Esposito did not try to rein in Warren's creativity, nor did he succumb to pressure from club owners who refused to hire an integrated band. Esposito lost several local gigs because he had hired a black musician (and the fact that he was African and not "Negro" did not seem to make a difference). But even in the clubs that accepted the band's new percussionist, the audience did not always appreciate Warren's style. They expected to hear Chano Pozo or Sabu Martinez, not West African rhythms. Warren later complained, "in those days, unless you played something Cubanish in your jazz, nothing was happening . . . Anything contrary was Queer, Strange, Bullshit."[44]

Despite these frustrations, he set out to record a groundbreaking LP, one that would fuse African rhythms and jazz but also do much more. He vowed, "I will not only do pure African music but I will do African-American music. I'll do African-European music. I'll do European-American music. I will touch all the areas that I am capable of doing but always with a little African touch. And that's exactly what I did."[45] Within months of his arrival, he was able to secure a recording contract with Decca, thanks to Red Saunders, whom Warren had met through Dan Burley and Herb Nipson at *Ebony*.[46] A veteran Chicago swing and blues drummer, Saunders backed some of the finest musicians at the Club DeLisa, the Band Box, and the Savoy Ballroom, including pianist Albert Ammons and singer Joe Williams.[47] Although Saunders ended up taking half of the album's royalties, *Africa Speaks, America Answers* was hardly a collaboration.

Recorded between April and May 1956 at Universal Studios in Chicago, Warren wrote and arranged all of the compositions and played various percussion as well as the drum kit. Saunders joined him on the drum kit and bamboo drums. Gene Esposito's band supplied the rest. It was arguably the first LP in history that fused jazz and African music—an even more astounding feat from a group whose principal members bear such names as Tony Naponelli, Johnny Frigo, Johnny Lamonica, and Jerry Friedman. (Recall that this was one of the LPs identified by *Time* magazine as an example of "Crow Jim"!) Warren's original compositions did more than fuse traditional African music and jazz—they drew on popular dance rhythms (highlife) and classical music, defying inherited categories.

Several tracks adapt specific sacred rituals from West and Central Africa, while others—like the three highlife songs he composed for the date—are thoroughly modern. "Monkies and Butterflies" stands out among Warren's highlife tunes because it anticipates the style that the Nigerian musician Fela Kuti developed in the late 1960s and 1970s, from the infectious beat to the way he employed female background vocalists. (When Fela worked for the Nigerian Broadcasting Corporation, he was famous for borrowing Warren's records and not returning them.[48]) Warren's weakest take on the genre, simply titled "The High Life," contained banal lyrics palatable to an American audience:

> Try the high life
> You'll enjoy life
> So groove and be happy dancing
> To the high life.

Only on "FR-ED-TO-NE" does Warren try to combine jazz and highlife. Opening with Warren singing in Ga over a fast-paced highlife rhythm, about one-third of the way through the song morphs into a straight-ahead, bebop-style blues. Eddie Baker, a respected Chicago pianist, replaced Lamonica on this track. Certainly the most prominent musician on the date, Baker had backed Miles Davis, Illinois Jacquet, Sonny Stitt, Bill Russo, and Billie Holiday, to name a few. He was also the only other African American at the session besides Red Saunders, and yet Warren never acknowledged his role at the time, despite the fact that the song's title was composed of the names of the musicians on the recording: FR is for bassist Jerry Friedman, ED for pianist Eddie Baker, TO for Tony Naponelli, and NE for "Nero," nickname for Esposito, whose birth name was Genero.[49]

Many of the tunes radically break with tradition and were conceived as modern fusions of jazz and West African music. For example, "J.A.I.S.I. (Jazz as I See It)" opens with Saunders playing the classic swing rhythm, relying heavily on the sock cymbal. Johnny Lamonica comes in playing a dotted sixteenth note figure on piano as Warren sings and plays congas and the rest of the band claps on the first beat of the measure. The music builds underneath a bass pedal point in D, which has a drone-like effect, until the tension is finally released and the entire band swings in D minor. Warren's ambitions to merge classical music with jazz are particularly evident in "My Minuet," a very traditional waltz backed by conga and sock cymbal, but played as if Bach had written it. Similarly, "Ode to a Stream" is a rather experimental piece that seems to be gesturing toward something almost symphonic. Warren's opening invocation ("A silent, restless nomad. Up and down the land, gentle and beautiful. Who cares what you are? We do, my heart and I") is followed by a beautiful violin solo by Johnny Frigo, with Warren playing a melodic line by plucking the piano strings, which in turn is echoed by Gene Esposito on vibes. Saunders creates a watery effect using brushes on the cymbal.

Ironically, what most African American musicians found attractive about Warren's music wasn't his secular, hybrid experiments, but the music's traditional and sacred dimensions. Songs such as "Africa Speaks," "Ode to a Stream," "Eyi Wala Dong" (My Thanks to Him), "Chant," and "Invocation of the Horned Viper" were either based on traditional sacred music or convey spiritual and religious themes. "Invocation of the Horned Viper" recovers a ritual from the Cameroons in which a cock is sacrificed to satisfy "the deadly African horned-viper," a very powerful snake that this particular clan worships. The entire piece consists of Warren's vocals and percussion, most of it supplied by Warren. "Chant" is a narrative piece set in a West African village following the death of the chief. Speaking in Twi,

Warren assumes the role of the royal drummer and calls the warriors to assembly using the bintin obonu (talking drum). That Warren was a "real" African willing to incorporate traditional sacred elements in his music only enhanced his spiritual cachet, not to mention his authenticity. And yet, Warren did not practice any West African religion, nor was he a Muslim or a Christian—despite his frequent use of both Islamic and Christian themes in his music. Warren was a practicing Buddhist![50]

Aflame with the Spirit of Africa

With the release of his first album, Warren set out to promote it and himself. Before the appearance of *Africa Speaks,* he had started to float press releases and articles to various newspapers in Ghana. The *Liberian Age* (May 19, 1955) ran an unsigned piece describing Warren as a big star in the United States who was about to tour with Count Basie. Even Twentieth Century Fox, the article continued, wanted to retain him as a technical consultant for movies dealing with Africa. Likewise, the Accra *Daily Graphic* (December 28, 1956) ran an unsigned article reporting on a concert at DePaul University, where Warren allegedly "out-played and outshined" Candido Camero, the "acclaimed king of the conga and bongo drums from Cuba." "It looks like Guy is now assured a place in America's Jazz Hall of Fame," the piece concluded. "Musicians and fans alike think he is now the greatest and newest drummer to come along since Max Roach, and Kenny Clarke, and Art Blakey, the three kings of the jazz drums." Dan Burley also wrote a short piece on Warren in the February 1956 issue of *Sepia* magazine, calling him "an authentic African prince from a Gold Coast tribe in Accra." And Etta Moten, a Chicago radio personality, reportedly called him "one of the greatest percussionists in the world."[51]

All the praise and press, however, yielded little income. *Africa Speaks, America Answers* did not sell well, and thanks to Saunders's arrangement with Decca, Warren earned only half the proceeds. After nearly two years in Chicago, with about as much money as he had when he first arrived, Warren decided to try his luck in New York. He immediately landed a job playing at the African Room, where calypso and Afro-Cuban music were featured. The fact that two such venues existed—the African Room East on Third Avenue and the African Room West on Seventh Avenue—was further indication of the growing popularity of African and African-based music like calypso. But it also meant the music was highly commercialized and marketed in a manner that played on stereotypes. On his opening night, Warren

> put on my beautiful blue velvet shirt and kofi hat. I was dressed beautifully, very respectably, and proudly, as an African. As I was going on stage the owner of the club, Harold Kanter, stopped me and said, "No no. You gotta change. You gotta put on what they wear there." Shirt with no sleeves, trousers rolled up, torn and tattered, straw hat—plantation stuff! . . . So here I was broke, ready to be thrown out of my hotel. He tells me, "Either wear that or you don't get the gig." I tell him, "I'm not going to go on and do that." Because that is what belittles Africa. In my country we don't do that, dress like that, unless you are a farmer . . . So Harold says, OK. And I played like I was full of fire. I was full of fire. I played like I had never played before and the whole place was aflame with the spirit of Africa.[52]

The audience also felt the spirit, for they screamed with delight and demanded an encore. Kanter was persuaded. He not only relented on his dress code, but he invited Warren to play there indefinitely. "Gradually I got the cast to start putting on African clothing and wearing dignified costumes and the raggedy, tattered impression of the African that you see was thrown overboard. And the place started to have dignity and the audience also came and enjoyed it and everything changed."[53]

During his stay at the African Room, Warren met most of the city's leading percussionists. Few impressed him, though he found one exception whom he believed understood authentic African drumming as opposed to the more popular Latin and Caribbean styles. His name was James Hawthorne Bey, better known as Chief Bey, or as Warren nicknamed him, "General Lefty."[54] At the time, Bey identified himself as a native of Senegal, and Warren believed him. "His attitude and everything about him was so African . . . But later on when I got to know him at close range he said he was from South Carolina. That's why I admired him so much that on his own, without guidance or anything, he had come very close to the African culture."[55] Born James Hawthorne in Yemassee, South Carolina, he grew up in Harlem, across the street from Abyssinian Baptist Church. It was in a church basement that Hawthorne discovered "African culture" in the form of a black woman named Ismay Andrews. A former student of Asadata Dafora and a member of his dance company, Andrews taught African dance classes at the Harlem Mother African Methodist Episcopal Church, where she taught Hawthorne and other interested boys to play drums. He proved a devoted and attentive student. "She was my first mother," Bey recalled. "For four years she wouldn't let me play drums; she only allowed me to play the bell so I could learn to keep time."[56] He took the name "Bey" upon joining the Moorish Science Temple (a black Islamic sect founded by Noble Drew Ali) and continued his drum training under Moses Mianns. Through Mianns, Bey began playing with Katherine Dunham and Pearl Primus, eventually adopting the moniker "Chief." Bey also worked with the Nigerian drummer Michael Babatunde Olatunji in 1956 (who claimed to have given him the honorific of "Chief").[57]

By the time he met Warren, Bey was already an accomplished drummer. They teamed up immediately and performed at the African Room as "Chief Bey and his Household." Warren hired Bey for his next album, this time for RCA-Victor: *The Guy Warren Soundz: Themes for African Drums*, recorded in 1958. Warren had conceived of the music for drums and trombone and wanted to hire Lawrence Brown of Duke Ellington's orchestra (Warren had played with Ellington briefly in Chicago).[58] With Bey and Brown on board, he hired two more drummers, Robert Whitney and Phillip Hepburn, and recorded the LP in Webster Hall, New York City, on May 22 and 23, 1958, three weeks after his thirty-fifth birthday. Once again, Warren composed all of the music, though it was markedly different from *Africa Speaks* in that he was less interested in fusing jazz and West African music than in experimenting with ceremonial music and foregrounding the drums and voice. Warren occasionally plays flute, and he deftly uses Brown's trombone as a largely unaccompanied voice. The song that would eventually become his best-known and most-recorded composition, the strikingly beautiful "Love, the Mystery Of" was written specifically for a dance performed at the African Room. Originally performed by John Lei, a former Dunham dancer, and Jean Neal, Warren said it "portrays a youth and a maid brought together for the first time by that mysterious force of love."[59] It opens with solo trombone by Lawrence Brown, but he quickly fades out, leaving only drums, percussion, and voice. Many of the songs are built around Warren's improvisations on the bintin obonu or bongos, played against the other percussionists. "Blood Brothers," however, is more of a dialogue between Warren and Bey, titled after the two men "performed a secret African ceremony which made us Blood Brothers" on New Year's Day, 1958. They both deliver a virtuosic display on their instruments, but the song is also an acknowledgment, if not a tribute, to Bey's identity as a Muslim. Warren opens the piece with the greeting, "A salaam a lekum," and Bey responds in kind and then launches into his solo. Warren replies with his talking drum and by chanting in Hausa, which he reports "is a form of Arabic used by Mohammedans all through West Africa. The song is a praise to Allah for bringing General Lefty and me together."[60]

Warren does not abandon the drum kit, nor does he give up the jazz fusion idea. He does attempt to push instruments beyond the cultural contexts in which they are best known. On "The Talking Drum Looks Ahead"—the only track on which he employs James Styles, on bass, and Earl Griffiths, on vibes—Warren takes advantage of the talking drum's tonal range in order to play a melodic jazz line over a swinging, twelve-bar blues. Warren dedicated the song to "my idol Thelonious Monk." Warren saw Monk live in Chicago three years earlier and appeared frequently at his New York gigs, but the two men had not met at the time of the recording. As soon as Warren could get his hands on a test pressing, he personally delivered a copy to Thelonious and his wife, Nellie, along with an elegant carving of "Sasabonsam," the Ashanti god of the forest, and a copy of *Africa Speaks, America Answers*. Monk was reluctant to play the disc at first, and even expressed some skepticism for Warren's ideas. But once Monk put the record on, he liked Warren's music so much that he borrowed the melody from "The Talking Drum Looks Ahead" and recorded a slightly altered, slower version as a solo piano piece less than a year later. He titled it "Blue Hawk" as a tribute to his old boss Coleman Hawkins, but it could also be heard as a sly tribute to the Ghanaian drummer.[61]

As with his piece for Monk, most of the compositions on *Themes for African Drums* are meditations on personal relationships, including difficult ones. "My Story" recounts Warren's sad childhood, the loss of his mother, and his father's refusal to recognize him. The lyrics say it all: "My mother is dead; I have not even a father; Nevertheless, I will play my drums and dance always; for such is my solace." "My Story" is a fairly long piece (over ten minutes) consisting primarily of percussion and voice. He employs Brown's trombone as "my inner voice; it comforts me at the beginning and at the end of the song."[62] In the final bars, Warren breaks down emotionally and begins to weep, followed by a sublime melody played unaccompanied by Lawrence Brown. It is a remarkable performance, especially for the late 1950s, when masculinity was considered to be in crisis, and drumming was generally perceived as a hypermasculine activity. This display of vulnerability is startling, especially for a black male jazz musician and especially for Warren, whose whole persona was built on the cool pose.

"The Lady Marie Drum Suite, Parts I and II" is also autobiographical, revealing Warren's emotional vulnerability. It is based on Watusi ceremonial rhythms, which he adapts to the modern drum kit. He plays all the parts usually assigned to an ensemble of hand drummers. He composed it for his patron and lover Marie Wilson Howells, whom he described in the LP's liner notes as "a most gracious lady. I honestly and truly believe she is the reincarnation of my mother, although, unlike my mother who was tiny in build, Marie is tall and majestic like a Watusi." And unlike his mother, Howells was a southern-born white woman, a scion of one of Arkansas's wealthiest plantation families, and married. She was also twenty-nine years his senior—older than his mother.[63] In spite of her marriage, she and Warren sustained their illicit affair for several years, beginning in 1958. "This black attendant would escort me upstairs in the elevator and leave me up there. And then the doors would open and she'd be standing there waiting for me and the doors would lock and the elevator would go down and we would embrace and start doing our stuff. This went on and on . . . She gave me financial security, spiritual security. She gave me security period."[64] She followed Warren to Ghana in 1960, after he decided to return permanently, and tried to persuade him to move to the Caribbean with her. "Gradually Marie wanted to stand between me and my music. She was demanding that I give her more time than I gave to my music."[65] Warren chose music.

Themes for African Drums received very few reviews, despite Warren's enthusiastic promotion. RCA-Victor also actively promoted the album but marketed it by playing on primitive African stereotypes. Rather than use Warren's image on the dust jacket, RCA hired a model whom they believed looked more "authentic." The man is shirtless, crouched on the ground playing wildly with his mouth wide open, as fire blazes in the background. In front of him is another drum, hand carved and lying on its side in what appears to be a tuft of savannah. Warren hated it: "It wasn't my idea at all. My idea was to have me playing the talking drum and they put that on the back side of the album. And they put this guy with his mouth wide open and the fire behind him . . . It's all a white man's idea of selling a product. Now that's what happens if you leave it to them to sell your product, you know . . . You have to do it yourself the way you want it, right? Then you can't blame nobody."[66]

"A Complete Fraud"

The executives at RCA-Victor were unpleasantly surprised by the dismal sales of Warren's album. Interest in African drums had been steadily growing among jazz and popular audiences, especially after Art Blakey recorded *Drum Suite* and *Orgy in Rhythm, vols. I and II,* LPs that employed Cuban and Puerto Rican percussionists alongside additional jazz drummers.[67] But the really big event that ultimately overshadowed Warren's entire output was the appearance of Michael Babatunde Olatunji's *Drums of Passion* on Columbia Records, recorded in the summer and fall of 1959 and released in 1960.

Olatunji is credited often as the first musician to create authentic African drum music in the United States. But as far as Warren was concerned, Olatunji was even more of a hustler than African American musicians creating faux African music. Throughout his memoir, first published in 1962, Warren referred to Olatunji as "a traitor to Africa" and a "complete fraud." And he told one interviewer, "People think that just because you come from Africa you can play drums— that whatever you play is right. No sirree!! I mean, just because you come from America, it doesn't mean to say you can play baseball."[68]

Warren had good reason to be upset. The Nigerian-born Olatunji was not a formally trained drummer. He picked up the drums as a student at Morehouse College in Atlanta. Indeed, in 1950 when he and his cousin, Akinsola Akiwowo, boarded a ship bound for the United States, he planned to study politics at Morehouse, possibly obtain a graduate degree, and return to his homeland to become a diplomat or political leader. Although he did express a passing interest in music, telling one Atlanta journalist upon his arrival that he "wanted to compose operettas in his native tongue and is interested in drama," Olatunji had no intention of becoming a musician.[69] He quickly emerged as a major force in student government (ultimately becoming president of the student body in his senior year) and a dynamic voice in Atlanta's black churches. A fervent Christian, he frequently addressed congregations about Africa, debunking racist myths about Africa and promoting a new type of missionary work that both proselytizes and empowers Africans.[70] But it was the pervasive myths about African "savagery" and "backwardness" that led Olatunji to pick up the drum and intersperse his frequent lectures with the rhythms and songs of his homeland. Dr. Willis James, a professor of music at Spelman College and a renowned expert on folk music in the African diaspora, mentored Olatunji. It was James who first brought Olatunji to the Music Inn in the Berkshires, where he performed with legendary Afro-Cuban percussionist Candido, and James encouraged him to compose music for the glee club at Morehouse. In 1953, Olatunji formed an ensemble made up largely of Atlanta University students, performing a mixture of percussion, song, and dance celebrating what he understood as African folk traditions.[71]

Despite his group's growing popularity, Olatunji did not veer off his career path. In 1954, after graduating from Morehouse, he enrolled in a doctoral program in public administration and international relations at New York University while playing a prominent role in the All-African Students Union of the Americas. He had planned to write a doctoral dissertation on the impact of colonialism on the communal ownership of land in Nigeria.[72] But he also continued to perform, launching the ensemble Drums of Passion. In fact, the move to New York City gave his group greater visibility and provided a deeper pool of talent. By 1956, Drums of Passion consisted of a large group of mainly African American dancers, singers, and three other core drummers—Chief Bey, Thomas Taiwo Duvall, and Montego Joe.[73] The three men hailed from South Carolina, Washington, D.C., and Jamaica, respectively. In 1957 Olatunji contributed to an LP of African lullabies sponsored by UNICEF, and later that year he played at what would prove to be a fateful Christmas party in Greenwich Village. Among the party's guests was the venerable Ralph Hunter, the choral director for Radio City Music Hall. Completely taken with Olatunji's music, Hunter promptly introduced him to Rayburn Wright, Radio City's house arranger, who went about creating an "African drum fantasy" featuring Olatunji and the Radio City Symphony Orchestra. The piece debuted in the fall of 1958 and was warmly received. Olatunji and his Drums of Passion suddenly became an overnight sensation. He appeared on the *Today Show,* the *Ed Sullivan Show,* and the popular game show *To Tell the Truth.* He was featured in *Sepia* magazine and juggled an avalanche of invitations to perform all over the country. Best of all, Columbia Records, the premier label, offered him a record contract.[74]

When Columbia released *Drums of Passion,* Olatunji was already a rising star in the United States. Yet as a drummer, at least, he was virtually unknown among his countrymen. Moreover, musicians familiar with the ensemble understood that, musically, Olatunji was one of the weaker links. His three core drummers, Chief Bey, Montego Joe, and Thomas Taiwo Duvall, not only anchored the recording but by some accounts had helped Olatunji develop musically.[75] The fact that African American drummers served as the main anchor for what got billed as the first authentic African drum record remained a well-kept secret for many years.

Drums of Passion departed sharply from Warren's work, not to mention that of Art Blakey and his contemporaries, in that it was composed entirely of African percussion and voices, much of it considered "traditional." Although Olatunji would quickly become the preferred percussionist among jazz musicians, he ignored jazz in favor of other kinds of Afro-Atlantic musical fusions. One of his original compositions, "Odun De! Odun De! (Happy New Year)," was based on Christian hymns he heard in church, and like everyone at the time, he did incorporate highlife as well as rhythms from Latin America. "Kiyakiya (Why do you run away)" is based on highlife rhythms—it asks why people are in such a hurry. *Drums of Passion* would sell an astounding five million copies.

Needless to say, the sudden success of Olatunji was a source of frustration for Warren. Even before Olatunji's career took off, the rival drummer had become a thorn in Warren's side. In March of 1957, Olatunji—not Warren—was invited to Chicago to perform at an elite ball celebrating Ghana's independence.[76] For Olatunji it was a gig for Africa; for Warren it was a slap in the face, a flagrant act of betrayal. And if this wasn't bad enough, Warren's revered leader, President Kwame Nkrumah, invited Olatunji to address the All-African Peoples Conference in Ghana in December of 1958, and then asked him to serve as a cultural ambassador, offering to have drums shipped to him from Ghana.[77] Warren was beside himself, especially since he was in the throes of trying to persuade some label to pick up his third album. Tentatively called *Voice of Africa*, Warren recorded it on his own in 1959. He had finally gotten the famed producer and impresario John Hammonds interested in it, or so he thought. Warren sent Hammonds the dub and waited patiently. A year later, after he had decided to return to Ghana, he received a cable from Hammonds: "Cannot contemplate recording you now. Have inherited Olutunje [*sic*]. Letter follows."

Warren spent most of 1961 writing nearly a dozen record labels desperately trying to sell his latest recording. He struck out at Savoy, Prestige, Capital, RCA, Atlantic, and Riverside, to name a few. In most cases, he received outright rejections with no explanation, but he did receive one illuminating rejection letter from Esmond Edwards of Prestige (one of the only African Americans in the industry). Edwards said he liked the idea of combining jazz and African music, but thought his record "lacks some of the excitement that is possible to develop with this concept." In other words, Warren's LP just wasn't "African" enough, despite all the singing and chanting in Ga and Twi.[78] Dejected, Warren fired off an angry reply to Edwards: "I thought PRESTIGE WAS THE HIPPEST RECORDING COMPANY IN THE BUSINESS . . . for now I see I am wrong."[79]

Edwards wanted a record that would sell to consumers who desired the wild, hip-gyrating music associated with Africa. Warren sent him a creative, hybrid recording that defied categorization. Although he hired Richard Davis on bass and Ollie Shearer on vibes and marimba, the recording was practically a one-man show, with Warren playing all percussion parts, flute, piano, and vocal. Warren sought new ways to transform the modern drum kit into a modern African instrument and to pursue new musical fusions juxtaposing traditional, ceremonial music with modern rhythms and harmonies. "Hail the Soundz," for example, plays Pygmy rhythms from the Congo on his drum kit, transforming them into a "rolling, almost boogie-woogie rhythm."[80] "My Anthem," featuring Warren playing up-tempo, exuberant rhythms on the drum kit, is his celebration of music as a mode of worship. The song is inspired by Psalm 150 of the Bible, which calls devotees to

Praise him with trumpet sound; praise him with lute and harp!
Praise him with tambourine and dance; praise him with strings and pipe!
Praise him with clanging cymbals; praise him with loud clashing
    cymbals!

Warren seems to explore many dimensions of sacred music, including the Pentecostal (African American) or Holy Roller (Caribbean) shouts, as he shouts "hallelujah" at key moments throughout the song.

None of these songs fit easily into the then-dominant stereotype of exotic, ecstatic, highly sexualized African rhythms and dance. They do not evoke the jungle or savagery, or the ancient pagan ritual. But the composition that most disrupted notions of "African music" in the American and European imaginary was Warren's two-part, sixteen-minute drum suite titled "The Third Phase." Critics have called it pretentious, in part because the opening of the suite's main theme is based on Beethoven's Fifth Symphony (he uses the bass drums to quote the three G's and E♭ in the opening melody). The piece was created as a kind of parable representing the three phases of man—birth, life, and death. It is a sly reference to the riddle of the Sphinx, with the drummer symbolically performing man crawling in his infancy, walking upright, and then walking on three legs (requiring a cane). The closing rhythms draw from Ghanaian funeral ceremonies, but as the liner notes boast, "This rhythmic pattern, which usually takes five to six drummers to play as a team, is here played by Guy alone."

After a frustrating year of begging various record labels to consider his demo, Milt Gabler of Decca agreed to release it in 1962—three years after it was recorded—under the title *African Rhythms: The Exciting Soundz of Guy Warren and His Talking Drums.*[81] By this time Warren was through with the United States. He remained in Ghana and continued to compose and record, but in terms of the American jazz scene he nearly disappeared. Indeed, his next LP, *Emergent Drums: The Voice of Africa Speaks through the Soundz of Guy Warren of Ghana,* was recorded in London in 1963 as a solo project. Warren played all instruments—drums, flute, piano—and sang. Although he would continue to record over the course of the decade, he moved in radically new directions, exploring traditional music across the length and breadth of the African continent as well as collaborating with more experimental musicians on the London jazz scene.[82]

Ironically, he faded from the American scene just as more and more bandleaders scrambled to augment their groups with authentic African drummers. Cannonball Adderley hired Olatunji and percussionist Ray Baretto for what turned out to be his only top-forty hit, "African Waltz," in 1961. And flutist Herbie Mann had become an overnight sensation with his eclectic style of Afro-Latin jazz. Not surprisingly, around 1960 he hired Olatunji and Chief Bey, who was now officially deemed an authentic Senegalese. In his liner notes to *Herbie Mann at the Village Gate,* Willis Conover wrote: "Chief Bey, white-robed and pillbox hatted, who has to tell cabdrivers *not* to take him to the UN, is from Dakar."[83]

Predictably, in the wake of Olatunji's success, Africans from the continent began to replace Latin American percussionists. The trend was signaled quite strongly on Art Blakey's 1962 album, *The African Beat,* in which he replaced his regular stable of Cuban and Puerto

Rican percussionists with either Africans or African Americans—namely, Chief Bey, Montego Joe, Garvin Masseaux, James Ola Folami (from Nigeria), Robert Crowder, and the great percussionist and singer from Nigeria, Solomon Ilori.[84] For Blakey, *The African Beat,* like his earlier outings, synthesized African and African American musical traditions. Blakey was not trying to demonstrate that jazz drumming derived from Africa, or that all of this music was cut from the same cloth, but rather that there is a musical compatibility and dynamism between what African drummers do and what American jazz musicians do. Ilori praised Blakey for being "able to make the fusion succeed, because that fusion already exists in him. He has listened by now to a great many African recordings and has also heard as many African drummers as he could in live performance."[85] Warren is barely mentioned, although they do record one of his tunes under the incorrect title "The Mystery of Love."

Authenticity and Its Discontents

In the end, it seems clear that Warren was one of the pivotal figures behind the "African invasion," or the "African musical renaissance" of the late 1950s. Barring evidence to the contrary, he really did introduce highlife to the United States. But Warren just wasn't African enough to be marketable. Thanks in part to the OSS, Warren spoke with a slight American accent. He dressed mostly like a hipster, always donned a hat and sunglasses, and didn't have an African name. And his mercurial personality did not help him win friends and influence industry people.

His main problem was musical: he was too experimental in a world where African rhythms were associated with wild excitement, hip gyrations, and raw sexuality. He created a fusion that was more than blues riffs over African rhythms, but one in which rhythm, harmony, melody, and instrumentation changed as a result of synthesis. He wanted to play the talking drum like a horn and the drum set like an ngoma, bata, bell, and conga put together. (And eventually he did: by the early 1970s, he had modified the jazz drum set, replacing Western instruments with carved wooden drums of the Akan people of central-western Ghana, which he played with two long, curved wooden sticks that are traditionally used for fontomfrom and atumpan drums.)

On the other hand, he was too African and too black to be taken seriously by those who claimed the mantle of serious music. In a *New York Times* article from November 1, 1959, titled "Shifting Tides in African Music," Robert Shelton quotes a prominent musicologist who bemoans the loss of traditional tribal music in favor of "diluted" popular music "modeled after American jazz, 'jive,' and rock and roll." And yet, Shelton goes on to praise the fusion experiments of white composers. He cited Mieczyslaw Kolinski's *Dahomey Suite for Oboe and Piano,* which, in Kolinski's words, is his attempt to "blend the non-harmonic structure of West African Negro songs with the harmonic, polyphonic language of contemporary Western music." And he was especially impressed with Fred Katz, who had just released *Folk Songs for Far Out Folk* on Warner Bros., which included three "African-derived numbers." Katz wrote in the liner notes: "I think it is time for jazz players and composers to extend their horizons toward other cultures rather than to 'Tin Pan Alley' tune pickers . . . I know this album is a humble beginning, but it is a beginning."[86]

Katz's unchallenged assertion, printed in America's leading daily newspaper, essentially wrote Guy Warren out of modern music history. It struck a quiet yet devastating blow, not only to Warren's original contributions, but also to the efforts of his competitors and colleagues in the "drum wars"—from Olatunji and Art Blakey to Asadata Dafora and Chief Bey. War weary and disgusted with America, Warren returned home for good, continuing to make music and participating in the nation's political life. If he had expected a hero's reception, he was disappointed. He discovered quickly that his own countrymen were about as ready to embrace his musical innovations as the Americans. Although he certainly had his share of die-hard fans on both sides of the Atlantic, local critics panned his debut performance of "The Third Phase" at the first Accra jazz festival in 1960.[87]

Although Warren never completely gave up his dream to revitalize jazz with African rhythms, his interests clearly varied throughout the rest of his life. *Emergent Drums* (1963) was virtually bereft of jazz influences, while *Afro-Jazz* (1969), recorded in London with British musicians, returned to his earlier efforts to fuse highlife and jazz but with an avant-garde sense of harmonic freedom. He deepened his study of traditional music, recording and performing with various indigenous drum troupes, and his own compositions eventually dispensed with the jazz influences so prominent during his U.S. sojourn.[88] His political involvement also deepened. He remained a close friend and confidant of President Kwame Nkrumah and endured significant backlash after Nkrumah was deposed in a U.S.-backed coup in 1966. In fact, it was Nkrumah's overthrow that compelled Warren to spend so much time in London during the late 1960s and 1970s. But Ghana was home. He eventually settled in Achimota, changed his name to Kofi Ghanaba in 1974 as a patriotic gesture, raised a family there, and finally earned the national recognition he craved.

And yet, America kept calling . . . and Ghanaba answered. In Haile Gerima's film *Sankofa*, Ghanaba's character and his music represented the link between Africa's slave past and the African American present. A few years later, he made his last appearance in the United States with none other than Randy Weston's African Rhythms band. Unfortunately, misunderstanding between Ghanaba and Weston's group marred his experience, providing further evidence in his mind of the bankruptcy of American culture and the utter inability of Americans to grasp African rhythms. At least this is what he told me the first night I interviewed him in 2004, just four years before he died. Before the interview ended, however, he had asked me to help arrange his return to New York to debut his all-drum arrangement of Beethoven's Fifth Symphony.

2 | The Sojourns of Randy Weston

I am convinced that there lies a wealth of uncharted musical material in [African folk songs]
which I hope, one day, will evoke the response in
English and American audiences which my Negro
spirituals have done.
—Paul Robeson

Africa at last! About fifty drummers were there to
greet us, and a few in our delegation got down on
their knees and kissed the good earth. Then all of
a sudden amidst this whole scene, a guy comes
running over to me and he says, "Well, you finally
decided to come back home, you been gone four
hundred years, what took you so long!" Man, the
tears were streaming down my face I was so over-
joyed.
—Randy Weston

Just as Guy Warren dreamed of coming to America
and infusing jazz with his unique African rhythms, Randy Weston
dreamed of coming "home" to Africa. But unlike Warren, he had no
grand ambitions to bring jazz to the continent or to launch a musical
revolution. He simply wanted to connect with his ancestors' people,
learn from the master musicians, and draw on the rhythms and
sounds of Africa to enrich his own music. And unlike Warren's
American sojourn, Weston's first pilgrimage to Africa did not end in
frustration and disappointment. On the contrary, he had hit the musical and cultural mother lode. He made new discoveries, witnessed
traditional music whose complexity and sophistication boggled the
mind, and yet found a world that felt eerily familiar—an urban, bustling, diverse, modern cultural scene not unlike his hometown of

Brooklyn. As soon as he set foot in Lagos, Nigeria, Weston quickly realized that he had not only reconnected with his ancestral past but opened a door to a modern, dynamic, uncharted future.

The African Village of Bedford Stuyvesant

Randy Weston needed no political awakening to teach him that Africa was "home." Ever since he could remember, his father, Frank Weston, "used to always stress to me that I was an African born in America. This was a very revolutionary identification to make at the time, but that's how he thought and what he taught me."[1] And that is precisely how he saw himself. A proud descendant of Jamaican Maroons, Frank Weston was born in Balboa, Panama, in the heart of the Canal Zone, on September 25, 1894.[2] His parents were part of a wave of Caribbean migrants recruited to build the Panama Canal. During the First World War, Frank and his brother Armand joined another West Indian migration, first to Cuba and then a few years later to the United States. On July 17, 1924, Frank boarded the SS *Esperanza* in Havana bound for New York, leaving behind an indelible assertion of his identity on the ship's manifest: under the category of "Race or people," he is listed as "African."[3]

Weston may have been the only "African" on board, but in 1924 nearly a million black people around the globe shared his sentiments. He was, after all, a staunch Garveyite in an era when Marcus Garvey's Universal Negro Improvement Association (UNIA) earned the distinction of being the largest black organization in the world. UNIA's paper, the *Negro World*, had the widest circulation of any black newspaper in history. Indeed, it might not be a coincidence that Frank Weston arrived in New York just days before the UNIA's Fourth International Convention of the Negro Peoples.[4] He might have packed into Carnegie Hall to hear Garvey speak on the evening of August 1, and he might have found his way to Harlem to check out UNIA activities in Liberty Hall. But his main objective was to find a home, and his one destination was Brooklyn.[5]

He had not been in the city long when he met Vivian Moore, a petite, brown-skinned woman who was also new to Brooklyn, having trekked from Elizabeth City, Virginia, where she and her mother had been live-in domestic workers. Born in 1898 in Meredithville, a tiny town in eastern Virginia about twenty miles from the North Carolina border, she had briefly married, had a child, and divorced before gathering up her baby daughter Gladys and heading north, presumably in search of a better life.[6] She still had to scrub floors for a living, but she became Mrs. Vivian Weston, and on April 6, 1926, she gave birth to her only son, Randolph Edward Weston. Unfortunately, the marriage lasted only about three years; by 1930 Frank Weston had remarried and Vivian and Gladys had moved out, though they remained in Bedford Stuyvesant.[7] Randy lived with his father, but he remained close to his mother and sister, splitting his time between households. Culturally, Randy enjoyed the best of two worlds: his mother exposed him to the rollicking, soulful music of the black church with its Deep South roots; his father surrounded him with the cultures of the British and Spanish Caribbean. Indeed, his entire Brooklyn neighborhood embodied the multiethnic, multinational diversity he had come to know as the African diaspora.

Although the extraordinarily diverse cultural climate undoubtedly shaped Weston's music, it was his father's political and intellectual influence that would prove decisive. The senior Weston spoke fondly of Marcus Garvey and Africa's glorious past. His shelves were loaded with books by J. A. Rogers, William Leo Hansberry, W. E. B. Du Bois, and others. Randy recalls how his father hung "maps and portraits of African kings on the walls, and was forever talking to me about Africa. He would take me to various meetings of black folks; some things I didn't even understand myself at the time because I was too young to understand. But he was planting the seeds for what I would become as far as developing my consciousness of the plight of Africans all over the world."[8] In an era when Tarzan movies reigned supreme and characters such as Steppin' Fetchit had become the media's dominant image of black manhood, the kind of education

Randy received at home was nothing short of revolutionary. Moreover, Frank Weston's example as an entrepreneur taught Randy the importance of independence and self-sufficiency. In 1940, he opened his own barbershop on Pacific Street and Kingston Avenue, and a couple of years later opened a small restaurant called Trios at 340 Sumner Avenue—a street that later would be renamed Marcus Garvey Boulevard.[9]

Frank and Vivian insisted that their son take piano *and* dance lessons—not an easy feat for a kid who, at age twelve, was already six feet tall and wore a size twelve shoe! "I didn't want to play piano," Weston later recalled. "It was like forced labor."[10] And his piano teacher, the stern Mrs. Lucy Chapman, sometimes seemed like an overseer. Her singular emphasis on European classical music completely turned him off. They both gave up after about three years. Frank Weston would not be defeated, however, so he found another teacher known simply as Professor Atwell.[11] Rather than try to mold him into a concert pianist, Atwell encouraged his student's love of Duke Ellington, Count Basie, Earl Hines, Jimmie Lunceford, Nat Cole, Art Tatum, and Coleman Hawkins—a love nurtured by a community of young, aspiring musicians. (In fact, it was a neighborhood friend, drummer Al Harewood, who taught Randy the first popular song he could play: "The Isle of Capri."[12]) By the time Randy enrolled in Brooklyn's Boys High School, he had begun making a name for himself as a piano player. At sixteen he became the principal pianist for Spencer's Hard Rockers, one of Brooklyn's most popular bands, and a couple of years later gigged with guitarist Huey Long.[13]

Yet Randy Weston's formative musical relationships and education took place outside the dance halls and clubs. He developed a close friendship with his neighbor, bassist Ahmed Abdul-Malik. A Muslim convert just nine months younger than Weston, Abdul-Malik had begun experimenting with the oud (a pear-shaped stringed instrument used in Middle Eastern music and similar to the European lute) and the kanoon (another stringed instrument from the region resembling a zither or dulcimer but played on the lap) when they were both in their late teens. These instruments demanded more elaborate scales that included quarter tones and eighth tones (the Western diatonic and chromatic scales can only accommodate half-tones) essential to music of North Africa and the Middle East. Abdul-Malik, who studied Arabic scales, or *maqām,* could hear these microtones, or "notes between notes," and recognized the unlimited possibilities of improvising on modes consisting of as many as twenty-four divisions within an octave. Abdul-Malik had clear memories of the two of them exploring what he called "Oriental music" and then trying to apply what they heard to jazz.[14] At jam sessions, Abdul-Malik would direct Weston to play scales rather than chords and to lay out during his solo so that he could explore pitches on his bass that fall outside the tempered scale. Weston recalled how he and Abdul-Malik "used to experiment in local bands as kids . . . trying to play the notes between the cracks. Guys just weren't into that at the time and we used to get thrown out of local bands for trying to be different. I was already searching for something different."[15]

Just as Weston was beginning to consider a career in music, Uncle Sam called his number. In 1944 he was drafted into the U.S. Army Signal Corps, sent to Fort Dix, New Jersey, for six weeks of basic training, then stationed just outside New York before being sent west—first to the state of Washington and then on to Okinawa, Japan. Even though he played very little during his stint in the service, mainly because pianos were hard to come by, Weston chose to reenlist after the war ended, serving a total of three years in the military. He rose to the rank of staff sergeant in charge of supplies, and while stationed in Okinawa he did what he could to "share" whatever material and food he had available with the local population ravaged by the conflict.[16]

Upon his discharge in 1947, Weston returned home to Brooklyn and took over Trios while his father opened another restaurant in a brownstone on Lafayette. He also married a neighborhood girl named Mildred Mosley two years later and started a family: together the couple had three children—Pamela, Niles, and Kim.[17] Randy played when he could, but he was not yet convinced that he could make it as a musician. On the other hand, he came back home amid a veritable revolution in the music, and some of its progenitors happened to be his Brooklyn neighbors. Drummer Max Roach, also a graduate of Boys High School, backed the likes of Charlie Parker and Dizzy Gillespie, whose fast tempos, extended harmonies, and complex, irregular melodies were all the rage. These were exciting times: the age of modern music, abstract expressionism, nuclear weapons, anticolonialism, a postfascist future, and a radical revision of the world's map. Under Randy's management, Trios became *the* gathering place in Brooklyn for young black intellectuals to discuss music, politics, and art. He installed a jukebox with music of Thelonious Monk, Bud Powell, Dizzy, and Bird, as well as Stravinsky and Alban Berg, and he transformed the back room into a jazz photo gallery where the regulars would sit for hours and hold forth. Randy recalls, "Everybody would come by and we would discuss everything from communism in China to politics and racism, to whatever various musicians were doing."[18]

He cooked, cleaned, kept the restaurant in order, but the pull of music was too much to ignore. He began working with a variety of R&B performers such as Bull Moose Jackson, Frank Cully, and the Clovers, and he gigged with Art Blakey, George Hall, Eddie "Cleanhead" Vinson, and various Brooklyn musicians—notably trumpeter Kenny Dorham, Max Roach, and saxophonist Cecil Payne.[19] Tragically, Weston, like so many of his friends and fellow musicians, was affected by heroin—a drug that ravaged black urban communities after World War II. By the early 1950s, many of Weston's friends were strung out or had died from an overdose. He, too, eventually succumbed to the drug: at one point, the six-foot seven-inch Weston had deteriorated to a skimpy 180 pounds. Fearing he might wind up on the streets or in the morgue like so many of his friends, he chose to leave the scene altogether. During the summer of 1951, he closed Trios and, upon the suggestion of a friend, hopped a bus to the Berkshire Mountains in search of tranquility, fresh air, decent food, and a space to wean himself off drugs.[20] It proved to be an auspicious move; besides breaking his addiction he discovered a vibrant music and cultural scene—one that would open another path to Africa.

Berkshire Blues

Weston found work right away at the Seven Hills Resort in Lenox, Massachusetts, first as a handyman and then as a breakfast chef. At night, after most guests retired, he would sit at the piano and practice. A few weeks later, he moved on to another job at Windsor Mountain doing much the same thing, except that most of the guests were there to attend concerts at nearby Tanglewood. When word got out that their tall, handsome cook played piano at night, Weston began to draw an audience—an enthusiastic and encouraging audience.[21] A couple of his co-workers told him about the Music Inn nearby in Stockbridge. Founded by Stephanie and Philip Barber, the Music Inn was a kind of jazz and folk alternative to neighboring Tanglewood. They turned the grounds of the once-spectacular Wheatleigh summer cottage into a resort, a club, a fairly large performance space (known as the Music Barn), and later the home of the Lenox School of Jazz. The Barbers bucked convention by establishing a jazz resort in the very heart of the playground of New England's blue-blood elite and for defying what was then standard practice of refusing service to African Americans.[22]

For Weston, the Music Inn was a cultural oasis. He remembers attending his first Jazz Roundtable discussion led by a bespectacled professor named Marshall Stearns. "I walk in, sit down, and heard this guy explain that jazz has West African roots. I never heard anyone say this, let alone a white scholar, but I had been interested in Africa since I was kid, so I said, 'I have to know this guy.'"[23] Stearns was, indeed, a formidable presence. A professor of English at Hunter College and a leading authority on Chaucer, he had earned a law degree from Harvard, a master's degree from Yale, and a stellar reputation as the academy's greatest champion of jazz. The year after Stearns met Weston, 1952, he was hard at work on his book, *The Story of Jazz,* and had just officially turned his Greenwich Village apartment and his massive collection of recordings, sheet music, magazines, posters, and miscellaneous documents into the Institute for Jazz Studies.[24] Weston was equally impressed with Dr. Willis James, an African American folklorist, musicologist, singer, and Spelman College professor whose research linked black field hollers and work songs to African traditions.[25]

Weston approached Stephanie Barber and offered to work there as a dishwasher or cook just so he could be around the music and the intellectual environment. Barber hired him but quickly discovered he was more than an expert dishwasher. "He came out after everyone had gone to bed," she recalled. "I was there checking something in the office, and he played [piano]. And I thought, 'Oh my dear.'"[26] She invited him to perform for their guests and he put together his first trio consisting of fellow Brooklynites Willie Jones (drums) and Sam Gill (bass). Weston promptly retired his dish towel, becoming a resident musician and one of James' and Stearns' most attentive students and interlocutors.

Although the scholars' influence is undeniable, it was the array of artists who participated in the annual Jazz Roundtables that most profoundly shaped Weston's understanding of the jazz/Africa nexus. The regular luminaries included the poet Langston Hughes, dancer and choreographer Geoffrey Holder, and the Great MacBeth, the calypso singer whose quadrilles inspired Weston to compose in waltz time.[27] In the summer of 1953, for example, the roundtable's theme, "From Folk Music to Jazz," featured a group of Haitian singers and dancers, Brownie McGhee and Willis James performing "Negro folk songs," pianist Eubie Blake and vocalist Jimmy Rushing, along with Pete Seeger and dancer Al Minns—all to demonstrate how folk music of the African diaspora constituted the roots of blues and jazz. One of the highlights of the two-week roundtable was a performance by Randy Weston's trio augmented by Candido, the great Cuban percussionist.[28] Weston's collaboration with Candido marked a critical step in his journey to Africa. He had wanted to incorporate African and Afro-Cuban rhythms in his music at least since the late 1940s, after hearing Chano Pozo with Dizzy Gillespie's band. The Jazz Roundtables proved to be an ideal location to deepen his knowledge of, and connection to, African rhythms. It was there, in the quiet solitude of the Berkshires, that Weston met Nigerian drummer Babatunde Olatunji and witnessed long discussions between Olatunji and Candido about Yoruba culture and the spiritual imperatives of music. And it was there that he met the renowned dancer, choreographer, and drummer Asadata Dafora.[29]

At summer's end, Weston returned to Brooklyn, which was in the throes of its own African cultural renaissance. Indeed, by the mid-1950s, Brooklyn had become a veritable center of African music. Bilal Abdurahman, a fellow Bedford Stuyvesant musician who came up with Weston and Abdul-Malik, invited Prince Efrom Odok, the renowned Nigerian dancer and drummer from the Calabar region, to hold drum workshops and rehearsals at Junior High School 258 on Macon Street. Any Brooklynite with a passing knowledge of the local African music scene would have been familiar with Odok, a New York resident for over three decades whose Africa House on West 140th Street in Harlem had become a center for lectures, workshops, and musical performance.[30] Abdurahman first saw Odok perform with Asadata Dafora at the Manhattan Center and was mesmerized by his talent and elegance. And he was equally impressed with his willingness to come to Brooklyn and teach music at the community level. According to Abdurahman, Odok was "one of the first African elders interested in helping people understand more about Africa." Drummers who participated in Odok's workshops gathered at Fulton Park on Sunday afternoons with their djembes, congas, chekeres, bells, dunduns (bass drums), and a variety of other instruments. The drums were so prevalent that Fulton Park was nicknamed Brooklyn's Congo Square.[31] Indeed, the neighborhood seemed to be turning into an African nationalist village: the headquarters for the United Sons and Daughters of Africa, founded by David Kenyatta in 1953, was just a stone's throw away on Fulton Street, and Brooklyn's first African restaurant opened right across from the park.[32]

Weston was undoubtedly aware of the growing presence of African music and anticolonial politics in the community, but even after three or four summers at the Berkshires, incorporating African rhythms had not yet become his main priority. In a questionnaire he filled out for jazz critic Leonard Feather in 1954, Weston wrote that his primary goal was to "organize a jazz trio . . . and play a lot of new material in a variety of moods, definitely modern but yet not too far from the public."[33] His adoration of Duke Ellington, Count Basie, and Nat Cole never waned, but he had also been listening to a wide range of music, including the twelve-tone compositions of Alban Berg. He had first been introduced to Berg's music at Max Roach's house. "It was Berg's way of writing—like the use of whole tones—that fascinated me."[34] Weston had also fallen in love with the music of another pianist and composer who made frequent use of whole-tone scales, Thelonious Monk. To Weston's ears his dissonant harmonies and angular lines epitomized a new modernism. He first met Monk while he was still in the service, and after he was discharged the two men developed a very close relationship.[35] Although Weston's sound contained echoes of Monk, it was unmistakably original and "definitely modern." "I had my own musical concept in mind," Weston recalled. "It started off with the waltzes I wrote. When I was up in the Berkshires and I started to compose, people said to me, 'What you're doing is different than what everybody else is doing.' The power of Duke Ellington and Thelonious Monk, who were both composers who more or less played only their own material, was a heavy influence on me. I admired that kind of self-sufficiency and wanted to emulate them. Even in the early days I was considered a composer first and a pianist second."[36]

When Bill Grauer, co-founder of Riverside Records, first heard Weston at the Music Inn during the summer of 1953, he was so impressed that he immediately offered him a recording contract. For Grauer, signing Weston marked a significant departure from the label's original agenda. He and Orrin Keepnews, critic and producer, had just launched the fledgling label a couple of years earlier with reissues of early jazz and blues recordings by Jelly Roll Morton, Louis Armstrong, James P. Johnson, Bix Beiderbecke, Albert Ammons, Blind Lemon Jefferson, and Ma Rainey, and studio recordings of contemporary Dixieland and Chicago-style jazz bands.[37] Weston represented Riverside's first foray into "modern jazz." And while producer Orrin Keepnews appreciated Weston's music, they clashed over how best to present it, though the limits imposed on Weston had more to do with financial considerations than art. Keepnews budgeted for a solo piano LP; Weston wanted to record his trio. The label compromised by allowing Weston to include bassist Sam Gill. Weston wanted to record his own compositions along with folk songs he had grown up with or learned from the folklorists and artists he met in the Berkshires. Keepnews believed that the best way to sell a new artist was to record a disc of familiar tunes by a popular composer. So on April 27, 1954, Weston and Gill laid down eight iconoclastic tracks of Cole Porter songs, released several months later as *Cole Porter in a Modern Mood*.[38]

The disc received much critical acclaim and was immediately followed up with another session in January of 1955, this time in a trio setting with Art Blakey on drums. Weston also included two of his own originals, namely "Pam's Waltz," written for his daughter and inspired by calypsonian quadrilles, and "Zulu," his earliest African-inspired composition. Weston wrote "Zulu" after an anthropologist told him he looked like a member of the Zulu nation in South Africa. Interestingly, the song does not incorporate African rhythms or South African idioms but instead draws its harmonic and melodic language from Ellington and Monk, though the introduction bears a slight resemblance to Dizzy Gillespie and Chano Pozo's Afro-Cuban classic, "Manteca." Based on an unusual AABBCC twenty-four-bar structure, the song's harmonic structure and chord voicings have "Monkish" characteristics, though rhythmically it is much closer to Caribbean music.[39]

In other words, Weston's first recordings in the mid-1950s demonstrate his stated intentions to play original music that is "definitely modern but yet not too far from the public." But for him, connecting with the public did not necessarily mean jazzing up pop tunes. As he explained to writer Paulette Girard in 1956, "What I want to do is apply folk music to jazz. You can retain the folk rhythm and improvise against it. You can do calypso, waltzes, anything!"[40] And as his stature as an artist grew, he was in a better position to realize his musical intentions. He received a huge boost in 1955 when Riverside released his trio LP to rave reviews, and *Down Beat's* international critics poll voted him "New Star Pianist."[41] Keepnews had him back in the studio at the end of August to record a second trio LP, with Gill and drummer Wilbert Hogan. And again, Weston mixed folk music with old standards, recording the Russian classic "Dark Eyes," and what Keepnews described as "a lightly Afro-Cubanized treatment" of the calypso "Fire Down There."[42]

Weston had become a serious student of folk music and traditional African music. On several discs he recorded between 1956 and 1957, he continued to include the occasional Caribbean folk songs like "Hold 'Em Joe," and "Run Joe," and he recorded a soulful solo piano rendition of the old spiritual, "Nobody Knows the Trouble I've Seen."[43] He listened to ethnographic recordings when he could, caught live performances of African and Afro-Caribbean drummers, dancers, and singers at venues like the African Room on Seventh Avenue and at the Music Inn, and continued to hang out with Ahmed Abdul-Malik. In fact, in 1956 Abdul-Malik replaced Sam Gill as Weston's regular bassist, and his influence is readily apparent. In March of that year, with Abdul-Malik, drummer Wilbert Hogan, and baritone saxophonist Cecil Payne, Weston recorded the North African–inspired "Little Niles." Written for his five-year-old son, "Little Niles" would go on to become one of Weston's best-known and most unusual compositions. A sixty-four-bar waltz, the A and B sections are built on what appears to be a B♭ melodic minor scale but in reality is much closer to an Arabic scale (*maqām*) of the Hijaz family.[44]

Abdul-Malik knew the scale and may have introduced it to Weston. Whatever the case, Africa now became his musical reservoir.

A New Dawning Breaks . . . Africa!

In 1956, the French colonies of Morocco and Tunisia and the British colony of Sudan were granted independence. The following year, Ghana became independent of Britain after a long, protracted struggle, and in 1958 the Republic of Guinea was born when the people of the former West African colony voted for complete autonomy rather than join the French Union. Two years later, seventeen other African countries gained their independence, setting in motion a process that would ultimately result in the decolonization of the continent. Like so many other black people around the globe, Randy Weston was moved by the seemingly rapid and occasionally bloody birth of independent African nations. With the black freedom movement heating up on American soil, these anticolonial victories seemed particularly poignant. So in 1958, Weston began composing a serious musical work as "a symbolic gesture . . . to show our pride that some of the countries in Africa were getting their freedom."[45] He ambitiously set out to pay homage to the continent's past and future by creating "a large-scale suite to illustrate that the African people are a global people and that what we do and who we are comes from our collective experience, from our African cultural memory . . . I wanted this suite to be performed by African people not only from different parts of the world but also from different areas of music. This idea had been in my head for years, and finally in the late '50s it started coming together."[46]

Indeed, in just the two years between Weston's initial sketches of the suite and its historic recording, many things "started coming together" that profoundly shaped the final product and deepened his political and cultural ties to Africa. First, he met his muse and future collaborator—trombonist, arranger, and composer Melba Liston. She was a member of Dizzy Gillespie's band, which had just completed a State Department–sponsored tour of South America, when Weston spied her on the bandstand at Birdland. Born in Kansas City and raised in Los Angeles, Liston cut her teeth on West Coast swing and bebop bands but had been largely overlooked and underappreciated because of her gender.[47] In Liston, Weston found not only a brilliant arranger who understood his vision of combining jazz, blues, and folk idioms, but one who shared his passion for music of Africa and the diaspora. Weston recalled how they would get together and listen to tapes of Congolese traditional music that, to their ears, sounded like "hillbilly music, the blues, modern music" combined.[48] They first collaborated on Weston's LP *Little Niles,* recorded in October 1958 and released on the United Artists label the following year. It was an important recording for several reasons. For one thing, it was Weston's first LP composed entirely of his own compositions, and Liston had arranged each one (and played trombone).[49]

Second, Weston's budding friendship with Langston Hughes became a fruitful collaboration. Hughes wrote the liner notes for *Little Niles,* and in 1959 he began reading poetry with Weston's trio in clubs and galleries throughout New York.[50] From the moment he conceived of the suite, Weston wanted Langston Hughes to write an invocation—a "freedom poem" proclaiming a new era of African independence. Hughes delivered:

> Africa, where the great Congo flows!
> Africa, where the whole jungle knows
> A new dawning breaks, Africa!
> A young nation awakes! Africa!
>
> The Freedom wind blows
> Out of yesterday's night
> Freedom![51]

Weston was pleased, to say the least: "Langston's poem set an absolutely wonderful tone for that recording session. Remember, the

whole point of [the suite] was to talk about the freedom of a continent; a continent that has been invaded and had its children taken
away, the continent of the creation of humanity. And Langston felt
that, he *knew* it deep down in his soul."[52]

Third, as Weston was working on the suite, his involvement in
political and cultural activism rose exponentially. Besides becoming
a frequent participant in benefits in support of Civil Rights,[53] he and
Marshall Stearns launched a program in 1958 to teach the history of
jazz in New York public schools. Stearns—and sometimes Weston
himself—would give short lectures, beginning with the music's African origins, and Weston's group—Cecil Payne, Ahmed Abdul-Malik,
and drummer Scoby Strohman, would demonstrate. Later they added
dancers Al Minns and Leon James.[54] A good deal of Weston's ener-
gies, however, went into improving the conditions of fellow musicians. "We were going through a lot of changes as far as racism,"
Weston recalled, "and a lot of crazy things were going on for black
musicians."[55] With support from Melba Liston, Gigi Gryce, Ray Bryant, Nadi Qamar, Sadik Hakim, John Handy, and others, Weston
founded the Afro-American Musicians Society to address problems
ranging from low pay, the poor conditions of jazz clubs, royalties,
publishing and recording contracts, the absence of black music at
new venues such as Lincoln Center, and the overall concern that "the
music [was] disappearing from the black neighborhoods." The AAMS
built strong ties to notable black activist-intellectuals, ranging from
the labor leader A. Philip Randolph, to the left-wing attorney Loften
Mitchell, to one of Harlem's leading black nationalist intellectuals,
John Henrik Clarke. Although the group fell apart after a year, it did
succeed in getting an antidiscrimination clause added to all contracts.[56]

While Weston was ratcheting up his political work in the United
States, his main inspiration remained the African independence
movement. More than any other organization, the United Nations
Jazz Society served as his conduit to the political ferment on the continent. The UN Jazz Society was founded in March 1959 by two Afri-

can American musicians who happened to be UN staff—trumpeter and composer Bill Dixon, and a former alto player named Richard Jennings. They initially set out to form a UN jazz ensemble but settled for something akin to a UN jazz forum at which jazz musicians, critics, and scholars could come face-to-face with world diplomats. Jennings and Dixon looked to jazz as a vehicle for progressive diplomacy, especially in support of African and other Third World nations, as a parallel initiative to the State Department tours abroad. Randy Weston not only performed frequently for the society, he also attended many of the Friday lunchtime lectures and workshops. In December 1959, a month after his own inaugural concert for the society, Weston listened to Donald Hanson, a UN Housing official assigned to West Africa, give a talk, "Percussion and Jazz in Africa."[57] More important, the United Nations became a fount of ideas and inspiration for his suite dedicated to African freedom. Richard Jennings introduced Weston to Africa's most notable ambassadors and dignitaries, who in turn shared crucial insights into their respective national histories, cultures, and languages. He was particularly taken with a young Tanganyikan professor and UN petitioner named Tuntemeke Sanga. Sanga, who devoted much of his time arguing for his country's independence, also promoted ki-Swahili (an East African and Indian Ocean language) as a possible lingua franca for the entire continent. So impressed was Weston that he not only recruited Sanga to translate Hughes's freedom poem into ki-Swahili, but asked him to recite it on the recording.[58] Thus the suite's title was born: *Uhuru Afrika,* meaning "Freedom Africa."

Weston completed *Uhuru Afrika* in the spring of 1959, and he and Liston worked feverishly arranging and orchestrating the four-part suite for big band. He expected United Artists to record it since the label had just released *Little Niles* to glowing reviews, but they balked at first, citing the cost of big-band sessions. In truth, they feared that the material was politically explosive. But rather than reject the project outright, the executives at United Artists offered a deal: they would make *Uhuru Afrika* if, in the interim, Weston rec-

orded a jazz treatment of a Broadway musical. In the wake of Shelly
Manne's best-selling LP *My Fair Lady* released in 1956, jazz record
labels scrambled to put out jazz versions of entire Broadway scores.[59]
Weston reluctantly agreed and picked the very latest musical to hit
Broadway. *Destry Rides Again,* a musical comedy based on the 1939
film of the same title, had just opened at the Imperial Theater in February 1959 to rave reviews. Weston and Liston took on the task of
turning ten tunes from Harold Rome's book into modern jazz pieces.
Given the material he had to work with, the results are stunning. But
as far as Weston was concerned, *Destry Rides Again* fell short of the
artistic standard he set for himself. And as if to compound his disappointment, United Artists reneged on their agreement to record *Uhuru Afrika.*[60]

Fortunately, Morris Levy's Roulette Records embraced the project without hesitation. A small label with big ambitions, Roulette was
famous for recording Count Basie, Tony Bennett, Pearl Bailey, and
rock and roll and pop singers such as Frankie Lymon and Jimmie
Rodgers. It was also famous for not paying artists on time—if at
all—and its alleged mob connections were legendary.[61] In fact, tensions erupted when Weston refused to give Roulette publishing rights
to the music.[62] But any dirt associated with Roulette was quickly
washed away when Randy Weston and Melba Liston led twenty-four
musicians, two vocalists, and one radical African scholar and activist
(Tuntemeke Sanga) into the recording studio on November 17 and
18, 1960. Weston had hired some of New York's finest musicians,
and the band represented a significant cross-section of the African
diaspora as well as Africa. Clark Terry, Freddie Hubbard, Benny Bailey, and Richard Williams made up the trumpet section; Jimmy
Cleveland, Slide Hampton, and Quentin Jackson played trombones;
and French horn player Julius Watkins filled out the brass section.
The reed section consisted of Sahib Shihab (alto and baritone), Gigi
Gryce (alto and flute), Yusef Lateef (tenor, flute, and oboe), Budd
Johnson (tenor and clarinet), Jerome Richardson (baritone and pic-
colo), and Cecil Payne (baritone). The "strings" were composed of

guitarists Kenny Burrell and Les Spann (who also doubled on flute), and bassists George Duvivier and Ron Carter. But the heart, the soul, the pulse of the band was the drum section. Weston recruited Babatunde Olatunji; Cuban congueros Candido Camero and Armando Peraza; and drummers Charlie Persip, Max Roach, and Wilbert G. T. Hogan.

The band came to the session prepared. They had had two rehearsals, both at 9:00 AM, an ungodly hour for musicians who typically work until the wee hours. But as Weston boasts, no one was late, partly because the musicians were moved by the session's symbolic and historical importance.[63] When Charlie Persip heard Hughes's poem and the suite in its entirety, "I began to get kind of inwardly emotional about it, because we were just starting to become aware of our African heritage and starting to really get our pride together as black people. Once I did the album, when I heard the music it kind of got to me, it really helped to get me more involved emotionally with my African heritage."[64]

The first movement, "Uhuru Kwanza," opens with Professor Sanga reading Hughes's invocation—first in English and then in ki-Swahili—over Candido's drums and someone else striking and scraping a "jawbone of an ass," or what Afro-Peruvian musicians call a *quijada*. The entire band responds in unison to Sanga's "call" with shouts of "Africa" and "freedom," culminating in a collective joyous holler. The second part of the first movement, more than any other part of the suite, is propelled by West African rhythms. The rhythm is in $^{12}/_8$ time, giving it that essential two-over-three feel common in much West African music. Weston enters with a rhythmically precise, six-note rolling whole tone scale, blending his piano into the percussion section. The horns enter behind Weston and the band quickly segues into the song's main theme—a three-note motive to which the word "Uhuru" could be sung. Solos are limited to percussionists and Duvivier's and Carter's softly bowed basses. Melba Liston's orchestrations as well as her conducting reveal a keen attention to dynamics, which she employs for dramatic effect. The horns quite literally shout "uhuru," taking on a more militant, defiant tone through the course of the piece. It musically enunciates the message Weston hoped "Uhuru Kwanza" would convey, "that African people have a right to determine their own destiny."[65] As Langston Hughes beautifully described in his liner notes to the LP, "The french-horn of Julius Watkins and the deep trombones of Jimmy Cleveland and Slide Hampton combine in persistent fanfare as the call of freedom mounts, and Olatunji puts his heart into the beat of his drum. Then only the basses are left whispering freedom, Uhuru—Uhuru . . ."[66]

Surprisingly, much of the suite does not attempt to foreground African rhythms or create a fusion of jazz and African music. Rather, Weston wrote in a style evocative of Duke Ellington and Billy Strayhorn, whose own long-form suites were characterized by lush harmonies, shifting tempos, lyricism, and modern sophistication. All of these elements are evident in the suite's second movement, a lovely ballad titled "African Lady," which was written as a paean to his mother, Vivian, "and all those strong sisters like her who had to toil and scrub folks' floors to make that measly $15 a week, and they would never complain, never beg." Weston wanted to convey musically "such dignity I can't even begin to describe."[67] To sing the lyrics Hughes penned, Weston selected Martha Flowers, a classically trained soprano better known in the concert world than in jazz circles, and Brock Peters, an actor and folk singer whose rich baritone voice elicited echoes of Paul Robeson.[68] Over verdant harmonies, Flowers sings of hope and bright futures ahead for the continent—here gendered as woman—as Yusef Lateef and Les Spann employ flutes to paint an image of birds singing and Benny Bailey uses his muted trumpet to great effect to evoke the sun rising on a new Africa.

> Sunrise at dawn
> Night is gone—
> I hear your song,
> African lady
> The dark fades away,

> Now it's day,
> A new morning breaks.
> The birds in the sky all sing
> For Africa awakes
> Bright light floods the land
> And tomorrow's in your hands
> African lady

As Flowers's voice fades the band builds to a crescendo and doubles the tempo, propelling Cecil Payne's brief but swinging baritone sax solo. The band returns to its original tempo and subtle accompaniment by the time Peters takes the mic. The second chorus continues to proclaim Africa's sunrise, but the lyrics are closer to a sonnet than an ode to a new nation.

> Goddess of sun
> And of sea
> My lovely one,
> African lady,
> Your eyes softly bright
> Like the light
> Of stars above.
> Smile and the whole world sings
> A happy song of love
> Dark Queen! In my dreams
> You're my Queen!
> My Queen of Dreams,
> African lady!

Most Weston fans probably had heard the suite's third movement, "Bantu." He debuted it two years earlier at the Newport Jazz Festival as "Excerpt from Bantu Suite." The introduction and melody changed very little, but it sounded radically different in a big band context compared to the original trio setting.[69] "Bantu" opens with a slow, plaintive melody played first by trombone and accompanying brass, and then taken over by Weston on piano. The influence of Ellington and Monk is apparent here, both in its lush harmonies and angular melody. Once Weston wanders down to the keyboard's lower register to close out the introduction, the band explodes into what Hughes describes as "jubilation." The band returns to the head-nodding 12/8 time that drove the first movement, but this time the drums are even more prominent. A collective percussion solo takes up nearly one-third of the eight-and-a-half minute piece, with Weston himself joining in on the quijada and Sahib Shihab improvising on soda bottle and top opener.[70] For Weston, the collective music generated by African rhythms was the perfect metaphor for "Bantu," which in his words "signified all of us coming together in unity."[71]

The fourth and final movement, "Kucheza Blues" (which roughly translates as "playing the blues"), anticipates "the glorious moment when Africa would gain its full independence and black people all over the world would have a tremendous global party to celebrate."[72] Fittingly, it is a joyous, up-tempo, playful blues in 3/4 time that consciously bridges the gap between the traditional twelve-bar blues form and its African origins. Langston Hughes remarked famously in the liner notes that had he been charged with naming the suite, "I would have called the final movement 'The Birmingham-Bamako Blues,' for in this section there are overtones of both Alabama and Africa, Dixie and the Negro Motherland."[73]

Uhuru Afrika was not just another jazz record. It was a manifesto, a declaration of independence for Africa and mutual interdependence between the continent and its descendants. The entire project, from the music to the program notes, celebrates the bonds between Africans and the African diaspora—past, present, and future. Hughes makes a case not only for the African roots of jazz, but for the African American influence on emerging modern jazz in Africa. He even suggests that the manner in which the band improvised followed patterns common in traditional African music:

In African tribal music there are a variety of free forms traditional in overall pattern, but which allow for spontaneous improvisation within the form itself . . . At the two recording sessions of the American salute to an emerging continent, there was at times so much going on, musically speaking, that nobody in the studio could follow a bar-tight score. But at such moments, no one needed to do so. Out of the rhythmic fervor engendered, waves of spontaneous creativity rose on the pulse of a common musical emotion to break against the microphones in sprays of exciting sounds—and all this within the basic pattern of an overall conception.[74]

The response to *Uhuru Afrika* was mixed. On the one hand, music critics found the work innovative and praiseworthy. *Billboard,* for example, gave it four stars, describing it as an "Afro-American salute to New Africa" and praising its "exciting score" and "stirring lyrics," which together "produce a strong emotional experience."[75] At the same time, the album was released amid a highly charged political atmosphere. In January of 1961, protests erupted around the world after Patrice Lumumba, the popular thirty-five-year-old prime minister of the newly independent Belgian Congo, had been executed by forces headed by Colonel Joseph Mobutu. Five months earlier, Mobutu, who enjoyed support from the Belgian government and the U.S. Central Intelligence Agency (CIA), overthrew the elected government in a military coup and placed Lumumba under house arrest. The United States, Belgium, and other Western democracies perceived Lumumba as a threat when he turned to the Soviet Union for help in dealing with a secession movement in the mineral-rich Katanga region of the Congo. Lumumba eventually escaped and attempted to form an army to take back control of the Congo, but he was captured in December.[76] Word of his death drew hundreds of protesters to the United Nations, including dozens of jazz musicians, and precipitated alarmist articles in the press predicting a proliferation of "Negro extremist groups."[77] White liberals who supported integration and nonviolence condemned growing militancy and "separatism," and appealed to African Americans for more patience and less anger.

In the jazz world, in particular, *Uhuru Afrika*'s appearance coincided with Candid Records' release of *We Insist! Max Roach's Freedom Now Suite*. Recorded two months before *Uhuru Afrika*, the *Freedom Now Suite* was originally conceived as a joint project with the singer and songwriter Oscar Brown, Jr., but creative differences led Brown to withdraw. The LP consisted of five movements documenting the black freedom movement in the United States as well as the struggle for self-determination in Africa. "All Africa," featuring Olatunji, is dedicated to the anticolonial movement, while "Tears for Johannesburg" pays homage to the men and women killed in the Sharpeville massacre.[78] Max Roach and his wife, Abbey Lincoln, not only performed the *Freedom Now Suite,* they practiced what they preached. They participated in protests and pickets and sought to draw the jazz world's attention to persistent racism and inequality. In a sense, their activism was not much different from Weston's short-lived Afro-American Musicians Society. However, the activism and the strident politics embedded in the music generated a backlash from many white liberals in the jazz world.[79]

In spite of *Uhuru Afrika*'s celebratory, upbeat tone, Weston felt a definite chill in the jazz world. As he explained to Art Taylor back in 1968, "At the time it was a bit unpopular, especially with white people—even white people who were friendly to me. They would hear it once and they wouldn't want to hear it anymore. Especially the first part, where you have the poem." To compound matters, Weston's refusal to hand over his publishing rights to Roulette had unforeseen consequences. "They wanted to make some sort of deal where I would be giving them power over my music. They promised to do a big promotion on me, but I have learned one lesson: Never sell a song. Never give the rights of a song. I don't care how sad you think it is. Never sell a tune! I refused, and therefore the album got buried. There was no publicity put behind it."[80] Ironically, *Uhuru Afrika* and *Freedom Now Suite* received a great deal of publicity in South Africa:

the government banned both LPs. The South African Board of Censors minced no words—they vowed to censor all records by African American artists, "particularly any that use 'Freedom' in the title."[81]

Flying Home

Several months after the release of *Uhuru Afrika,* Weston finally fulfilled his lifelong dream to visit Africa. In November of 1961, John A. Davis, director of the American Society for African Culture (AMSAC), offered Weston a last-minute invitation to join a delegation of African American artists and educators to participate in a celebration launching AMSAC's inaugural Africa center in Lagos, Nigeria. The two-day "cultural exchange" was conceived as a series of panel discussions, exhibitions, and performances showcasing black art and culture on both sides of the Atlantic. But unbeknownst to Weston, the invitation was hard-won. Given Weston's knowledge of Africa and his growing reputation as the jazz world's most vocal champion of African music and culture, Davis's initial reluctance to include Weston seems surprising.[82] Yet, when we examine AMSAC's origins, Davis's ideological concerns, and Weston's experience with the society, we learn not only that both men had sharply divergent agendas, but that genuine cultural exchange between Africa and the diaspora was difficult. And Cold War liberalism, not to mention prevailing assumptions of Western superiority, turned a difficult situation into one fraught with tension.

The idea for AMSAC originated in September 1956 at the First International Conference of Negro Writers and Artists in Paris. Called by Alioune Diop, editor of *Présence africaine,* the gathering of distinguished intellectuals agreed that African freedom and the preservation of the continent's history, art, and culture ought to be their top priority. Thus the Société africaine de culture (SAC) was born, followed by its U.S. affiliate, AMSAC, in December of 1956. AMSAC's original founders included distinguished scholars like Horace Mann Bond and Mercer Cook, the eminent attorney Thurgood Marshall, and the incomparable Duke Ellington. Its founding executive director, John A. Davis, was a veteran Civil Rights activist as well as a noted political scientist who held a doctorate from Columbia University and a bachelor's degree from Williams College. He served on the faculty at Lincoln University for several years, where he met and taught future African nationalist leaders, including Ghana's Kwame Nkrumah and Nigeria's Nnamdi Azikiwe. Davis eventually joined the political science department at City College in New York and ran the Council on Race and Caste in World Affairs (CORAC), which received much of its funding from the CIA. In fact, in 1958 CORAC and AMSAC merged, making the society a direct beneficiary of CIA funding.[83]

Davis and other leaders embraced Cold War liberalism and promoted a noncommunist path for African independence. Not surprisingly, AMSAC's strident anticommunism kept W. E. B. Du Bois and Paul Robeson, two veterans of the anticolonial movement, from supporting the organization. Through the Council on African Affairs, both men had worked tirelessly in support of decolonization, but their left-wing affiliations made them prey to anticommunist witch-hunts and anathema to U.S. foreign policy interests.[84] Indeed, the CIA financially backed AMSAC largely because the intelligence agency regarded it as a foil for the Council on African Affairs.

To call AMSAC a "CIA front," however, would be an overstatement. Its members represented a fairly wide cross-section of opinion, and there is little evidence that dissent was suppressed. Nevertheless, AMSAC was an exclusive membership organization and to join one needed to be nominated and then approved. In June 1961, A. C. Thompson, the UN observer for the American Committee on Africa and Weston's friend, recommended him for AMSAC membership. Thompson made a compelling case, drawing attention to his collaborations with Langston Hughes and the release of *Uhuru Afrika,* but Davis ignored the request.[85] Three months later Thompson tried again, indicating that Weston "wishes to become a member of the Society." His enthusiastic endorsement reminded Davis of his "African suite" and pointed to his recent performances at the United Nations.[86] This time Davis at least replied, but only to ask for Weston's résumé. Weston's desire to be a part of AMSAC was palpable; within days he dispatched a copy of his résumé along with a cover letter making a case for membership. "I have a deep and sincere interest in African music," he wrote, "and I am anxious to connect myself as closely as possible with the artistic history and development of that continent. I feel that by learning more about African music I will further my own development as a composer."[87]

Davis still wasn't convinced. In a long letter outlining his vision for the Lagos festival, the musicians he had in mind were Ray Charles, Nina Simone, and Olatunji, whom he believed "can demonstrate the blending of African and American Negro music."[88] As he and his staff, Yvonne O. Walker and Calvin Ralluerson, director of the new AMSAC Africa Center in Lagos, worked on finalizing the program, Davis always meant to include jazz, but he insisted on a diversity of genres that would grant concert music, folk songs, and blues equal time. Pianist Billy Taylor, Lionel Hampton, and vocalists Billy Eckstine, Sarah Vaughan, and Carmen McRae were just a few of the names bandied about.[89] Hampton agreed to go with a smaller band, but he still needed a pianist. When Billy Taylor could not make the trip, Yvonne Walker reached out to Randy Weston.

Weston was brought on board in mid-November, leaving him just a month to put together a band and obtain his passport, visa, and inoculations.[90] He recruited the usual suspects—his old friend Ahmed Abdul-Malik on bass, drummer Clarence "Scoby" Strohman, dancers Al Minns and Leon James, and the talented tenor saxophonist Booker Ervin, best known for his work with the bassist and bandleader Charles Mingus. Initially, Weston and his group were hired to back Lionel Hampton, who had been asked to close the festivities with a "big Afro-American jam" that would include the African musicians. But as the program evolved over the final weeks, Weston was given space to perform his own music.[91]

All told, thirty-three delegates were selected to participate in the two-day symposium on culture, scheduled for December 18 and 19. The U.S. delegation comprised some of the leading names in visual, literary, and performing arts: Langston Hughes; choreographer Geoffrey Holder; singers Nina Simone, Odetta, and Brother John Sellers; painters Hale Woodruff, Charles White, Hughie Lee-Smith, and Ernest Critchlow; concert pianist Natalie Hinderas; and the distinguished educator and AMSAC founder Horace Mann Bond. For Weston, the trip wasn't just a homecoming but a reunion of sorts. Besides Langston Hughes and members of his trio, *Uhuru Afrika* singers Martha Flowers and Brock Peters were included, as well as Weston's mentor from the Music Inn, Willis James.[92]

The two-day festival opened the morning of December 18, with sparsely attended panel discussions on the arts and scholarship in West Africa and black America—primarily the United States with some scattered references to the Caribbean and Latin America.[93] Each panel was to include Nigerians and Americans, with scholars and artists paired up to discuss music, visual art, theater, dance, and so on. Weston served as a panelist along with Langston Hughes, Willis James, Geoffrey Holder, and Hale Woodruff. Also participating were Nigerian musicians Femi Bucknor, Bobby Benson, and Zeal Onyia; poet and singer Francesca Yétúndé, a Nigerian daughter of Brazilian repatriates; and a young playwright named Wole Soyinka.[94]

The evening musical performances were well attended. Olatunji and Scoby Strohman opened the first night with a drum "Prelude," evidently establishing the night's theme of the African roots of black music. Traditional drumming ensembles, blues and folk singers, along with demonstrations of early jazz dominated the evening. The featured artists included Nina Simone (backed by Ahmed Abdul-Malik, Scoby Strohman, and Simone's regular guitarist Al Schackman), Brock Peters, and Randy Weston's ensemble. Al Minns and Leon James joined Weston for a couple of numbers, providing a capsule demonstration of the history of black vernacular dance. Olatunji also joined Weston, leading a small ensemble of "talking drummers." The following night featured classical music, dance, and modern jazz. Concert pianists Femi Bucknor of Nigeria and Natalie Hinderas of the United States opened the proceedings, followed by classical vocal performances by Christopher Oyeshiku and Martha Flowers. Tiv women dancers performed opposite Geoffrey Holder, whose choreography fused Caribbean folk forms and modern dance. Singer Francesca Yétúndé took the stage as well, followed by another performance by Nina Simone.[95]

Lionel Hampton's band closed the festival with his much-touted, highly anticipated "Afro-American jam session." Besides Weston and Olatunji, Hamp employed his regular band members: trumpeters Virgil Jones and Dave Gonzales, Ed Pazant on reeds, bassist Lawrence Burgan, and drummer Oliver Jackson. They closed with a rousing and exceedingly long rendition of Hamp's signature jump tune, "Flying Home," supplemented by an ensemble of some of Nigeria's finest jazz musicians: saxophonist Bobby Benson, and trumpeters Zeal Onyia, Mike Falana, and Chief Bill Friday. The jam-session atmosphere Hamp tried to recreate fell flat, as did the entire performance. Weston was at the piano, stunned and a little embarrassed, especially as the band left the stage and wended its way through the audience. He knew the Africans were underwhelmed. In preparation for the concert, Weston recalled, they "rehearsed a lot of good music, but once the show started [Hampton] went into his 'show biz' routine, with a lot of clowning around. I guess the Africans felt like he was insulting them. They didn't know he does that stuff all the time! Things went downhill after that."[96]

Hampton's disappointing performance was just the tip of the iceberg. During their week-long stay, some of the delegates came off as patronizing and arrogant, and AMSAC officials tended to privilege American artists over Africans, resulting in performances or talks by West African artists being cut short.[97] And the Nigerian critics were simply not impressed with the experiment in cultural exchange. The local press panned the festival, calling it "badly organized," a "downright insult," and an "unqualified flop."[98] Ironically, the critic for the *Lagos Daily Express* reserved his harshest criticisms for his countryman, Babatunde Olatunji, confirming what Guy Warren had been arguing all along. "It was a sad spectacle," he wrote, "to see Olatunji trying to play the talking drums before a Nigerian audience." The writer also dismissed Lionel Hampton as "a cheap entertainer clowning about the stage with an idiotic expression on his face, his tongue sticking out and inarticulate sounds uttering from his mouth."[99]

The American delegates, on the contrary, left Nigeria enlightened, overwhelmed with emotion, and anxious to return. For Willis James, the festival merely confirmed his belief that "Africa, is indeed, our 'Promised Land.' We have merely 'viewed' it. The difficult battle to reclaim it should be engaged by ourselves as well as by those very admirable people there. Anything less would be most ungrateful." Oliver Jackson appreciated the kindness shown him by local Nigerians, despite the poverty and deprivation resulting from colonial rule. "It makes me realize," he reflected upon his return home, "how cruel the British were during all the time they had control of Nigeria." If there was one general complaint, it had to do with what Al Minns called the "barrier between the people and the Americans." The delegates stayed at the exclusive Federal Palace, attended too many official state dinners and receptions, and were largely cordoned off from ordinary Lagos residents.[100]

The only significant point of contention among the Americans centered on the inclusion of classical music in the festival, and the controversy involved but a small minority of delegates. Still, the debate is important for what it reveals about Davis's and AMSAC's cultural agenda. In his follow-up questionnaire, Langston Hughes questioned the value of including classical music in the program "to show that African or American artists can perform European or 'white' material. This has already been proven. The cultural exchange should be on an *Afro*-American—*African* basis." Davis disagreed, scribbling an emphatic "No" in the margins next to Hughes's comment.[101] On the other hand, Natalie Hinderas took the opposite view. She felt the classical music portion of the program was poorly presented. She would have preferred a smaller venue and an audience made up of "selected groups of cultured Nigerians" to a large out-door stadium playing opposite a jazz ensemble. "Classics and jazz are difficult to present together," she explained. "Keener insight and plan-ning could utilize classical artists to far better advantage. Also, as an added suggestion, accord the same amount of enthusiasm toward classical musicians as to the jazz artists in publicity and exposure."[102] Davis took note of these suggestions.

For Weston, the Nigerian trip was never about the performance or the panels or the official festival proceedings. It was an opportu-nity to study the music, discover his ancestral homeland, and con-nect with the people. And it changed his life. In a letter to Davis re-flecting on the impact the trip had on him, Weston mused, "there is nothing like actual travel in Africa to deepen one's understanding. Although I had long been interested in Africa's music and had heard many tapes and recordings of it, there was nothing quite like hearing it in person and talking to those who made the music or were very close to it. I heard such fantastically complex and subtle rhythms and lovely melodies—and so many!—that they will influence my music for the rest of my life."[103] Although he deliberately sought out tradi-tional music, most of the "fantastically complex and subtle rhythms" he heard he had found in popular urban music—highlife, so-called "African jive," even jazz. Their brief stay limited Weston's investi-gation of local music to the nightclubs and the streets of Lagos, but what he heard both reinforced and deepened his own under-standing of the profound musical and cultural connections across the diaspora. As he put it, "I became more aware of African culture, West Indian culture, even more aware of the culture of the American Negro—the very basic blues."[104]

He was also aware that jazz had taken root in Nigeria decades before the AMSAC delegation arrived—a fact that clearly escaped bandleader Wilbur de Paris, who believed his 1957 visit marked the first moment in history that Nigerians had ever heard jazz.[105] Thanks to radio broadcasts of Louis Armstrong, American films featuring jazz performances, and the proliferation of records introduced by

African and American sailors, jazz began to take off in the early 1940s. Glenn Miller's "In the Mood" spun on nearly every gramophone in Calabar, and at least one U.S. merchant marine—an African American named Jack O'Dell—fondly remembered disembarking from his ship in Lagos in 1944 and hearing Duke Ellington's "Main Stem" competing with the din of street traffic.[106]

Nigerians who served in the armed forces during the Second World War were key players in the spread of swing and modern jazz, though none more important than Bobby Benson. A veteran of the navy, he had studied saxophone, bass, drums, piano, and guitar with musicians in Europe, Latin America, and the United States during his tour of duty, participating in various military bands along the way. A mechanical failure left his ship inoperable and adrift at sea for over a month. When he and his crew were finally rescued and taken to London, Benson eventually fled the Merchant Navy for a life in show business. In 1946, he made his debut with Les Ballets Nègres, a largely Afro-Caribbean troupe in London, and he subsequently met his wife Cassandra, a dancer of Scottish and Caribbean parentage.[107]

Upon returning to Nigeria in 1947, the cosmopolitan multi-instrumentalist was poised to turn Lagos into the center of West Africa's popular music scene. He and his wife launched the Bobby and Cassandra Theatrical Party, a variety show combining theater and music performed largely by the Jam Session Orchestra—a band of talented local musicians Benson formed in 1948. Orchestra members included saxophonists Magnus Iworare and Audu Kano, trumpeter Chief Bill Friday, Jubril Isa on clarinet, and Benson at the piano. Although the band lasted only two years, it was known for its jazz, improvisational style, and ability to excel in both swing and highlife. The Theatrical Party led Benson to open the Caban Bamboo Night Club and to found a jazz ensemble called the Nigerian Jazz Club in 1953. The small combo, consisting of the phenomenal trumpeter Zeal Onyia, saxophonist Paul Isamade, drummer Bayo Martins, and Benson on piano limited their repertoire almost entirely to modern jazz. The British-trained Steve Rhodes followed suit the next year, forming "the Modernaires," and in 1955, saxophonist Chris Ajilo formed the Agil Jazz Club. Unfortunately, none of these groups developed much of a following, and both Benson's and Ajilo's bands folded almost immediately. Few Nigerians in the 1950s were into jazz, especially its modern bebop and hard bop variety. The folks who patronized the Lagos club scene preferred highlife and other dance music to jazz.[108] As Zeal Onyia lamented, "The Nigerian public is a dancing one, always going for the boisterous and emotional element of music. Only very few Nigerians can allow music [to] make an intellectual impression on them."[109] Onyia had even suggested that the Nigerian Broadcasting Corporation contributed to the situation by promoting local, traditional music over modern jazz.

Whereas African American jazz musicians found in highlife a stimulus for enriching and transforming jazz, in Nigeria—at least for some modernists—highlife had become an obstacle. The limited market for popular music positioned highlife and jazz in competition, in spite of the fact that many jazz musicians were just as comfortable playing highlife and other forms of dance music. It wasn't a matter of embracing or rejecting one or the other; rather, highlife came to be seen as choking the life out of modern jazz.

The highlife versus jazz debate came to a head after Louis Armstrong toured Nigeria and Ghana in 1960. *Drum*, a magazine based in West and South Africa, decided to organize a forum for African musicians to weigh in on the meaning of Armstrong's visit, and the responses ultimately centered on what kind of music Nigeria, Ghana, and other West African countries should embrace as their national popular music. Nigerian trumpeter Victor Olaiya, known in both jazz and highlife circles, felt strongly that "indigenous Nigerian highlife must remain predominant in the field of Nigerian music." And Nigerians themselves demonstrated his argument. "When Louis played a calypso for example, the people gave him a greater applause than when he played a jazz number." Bobby Benson merely echoed Olaiya's sentiments. "Louis is great! But for the present, the reigning thing in Nigeria—as in Ghana—is highlife and calypso." Likewise,

Roy Chicago, leader of the Rhythm Dandies, loved Armstrong's performance and then added, "But jazz is not the music of West Africans."[110] Ivan Annan, a Ghanaian DJ and music critic, came to a similar conclusion, but it had less to do with national pride than with what he perceived as a lack of sophistication among West Africans. Like Onyia, he lamented the lack of support for jazz and the fact that jazz musicians in Ghana "are ridiculously few for a country with such a rich musical tradition."[111] The Nigerian journalist Nelson Ottah was even less sanguine than Annan. For him, West Africans disliked jazz because "we haven't got the concentration." It is not the music but the people who are to blame: "real jazz places such heavy demands upon the minds of our people, that, rather than make the effort necessary to understand it, they reject it outright." Highlife, he argues, is simple music, based on a repeated four-bar phrase that makes no serious demands on the listener. This explains why "lower forms of imported music such as Rock 'n Roll and some of the more sickly types of Western pop songs are not only understood but enthusiastically accepted by the same audiences here."[112] His solution? Bring more modern jazz artists to Nigeria.

Even the most frustrated exponents of modern jazz knew that highlife could be challenging when played well. The same can be said about the blues. But Ottah's screed does point to an important truth: while the roots of jazz may be traced to Africa, music never stays still. It is dynamic and shifting all the time. Highlife grew up on African soil; jazz did not. For Nigerian audiences to embrace the music, greater exposure was required. And an occasional performance by Louis Armstrong or Wilbur de Paris, Herbie Mann or Lionel Hampton, was not enough to convince the majority of Lagosians to sit down and listen to Zeal Onyia improvise dissonant riffs over substitute chords in ¼ time. What the Nigerian jazz scene needed was a bridge—someone steeped in modern jazz but attuned to highlife and other local genres. Randy Weston became that bridge.

Weston befriended Bobby Benson immediately. He spent practically every free night at the Caban Bamboo nursing a glass of whiskey and checking out the music. He not only absorbed local jazz and highlife bands, but on weekends heard traditional musicians Benson brought in from the countryside. One night he heard a family of balafon players; the women turned bolts of cloth into percussion instruments. He had never seen anything like it. "The music was so inspiring," he recalled,

> that at one point I jumped up and got the spirit, I just had to go sit with these people. So I sat down with the group, just like I belonged with these people. The music started getting more and more intense and the next thing I knew I could feel myself leaving the earth. This music was so powerful I was literally levitating, or so I felt. I actually began to feel that if I didn't get away from these people I might still be going up and up in the universe somewhere! That was my first experience with the power of traditional African music. I panicked and jumped down off the stage, with everybody busting out laughing. I slinked back to my table, but fast. That music was too deep for me.[113]

But he could not wait to return. Eight days was just enough to initiate friendships and connections and to fuel his desire for a longer visit. He and Benson remained fast friends. Just days after Weston returned to the States, he penned a beautiful letter to his new friend praising his music and promising to work with AMSAC to bring Benson's group to the United States. Weston had already begun to learn Benson's tune, "Niger Mambo," and sketch out a new composition in his honor, titled "Caban Bamboo High Life."[114]

Weston took seriously his mission to build deeper links between African American and African musicians, and redoubled his earlier efforts to put black jazz artists more generally on a stronger economic foundation. He lectured on African music at the United Nations, Harlem's Afro-Arts Cultural Center, and other venues in and around New York. He co-founded Ndugu Ngoma (ki-Swahili for "brothers of the drum"), a group of musicians who had split from the Afro-American Musicians Society. They organized workshops and benefit concerts to support struggling musicians, and tried to raise the level of knowledge regarding events in Africa. He also served on the board of the African Jazz-Art Society, an organization committed to promoting jazz education and combating "juvenile delinquency."[115] And he continued to organize and present his "History of Jazz" program, touring public schools and colleges across the state.[116]

Although these were all worthwhile efforts, Weston saw in AMSAC a possible pathway to accomplish both of his objectives—to deepen trans-Atlantic cultural exchange and to generate opportunities for black musicians. As soon as his application was finally approved in May 1962, he wasted no time. In July, at the invitation of Willis James, he headed to Washington, D.C., where he and his band participated in an AMSAC-sponsored lecture and demonstration, "Afro-American Music and Its Relationship to African Music." James spoke on the African roots of field hollers and spirituals while Weston, along with Olatunji, drummer Scoby Strohman, and saxophonist Booker Ervin, provided musical demonstrations.[117] The following month, Weston sent John Davis a brief letter pledging to do more with the society on behalf of black musicians: "Without such organizations working for the betterment of Afro-American jazz our struggle would be considerably more difficult."[118] Davis encouraged Weston to come up with some concrete suggestions. And he did.

One year later, Weston submitted a detailed, four-page report outlining his vision for how AMSAC might support black jazz musicians, who in his view faced one of the worst crises in the music's history. He warned of a growing number of talented musicians who could not find work or recognition, and "whose morale is at a desperately low level." Consequently, alcohol and drug use continued to rise, but he also noted that in "subtle and less immediately horrifying ways, many more musicians are dying as artists every day, either giving up altogether and leaving music . . . or spending endless, grueling, killing, wasted days, months, years trying to find *some* way to play their music and express themselves without having to sacrifice their integrity."[119] Weston believed AMSAC could help reverse the trend by elevating jazz musicians to the status of "scholars, writers, and artists," sponsoring lecture demonstrations by musicians that could incorporate more cultural exchange between Africans and African Americans, and simply acknowledging jazz as black music with deep roots in Africa. Weston worried that the latest tendency to call jazz "American music" played down black contributions and indirectly contributed to the marginalization of black musicians. Only by returning the music to the black community and restoring the bonds between black people and jazz, he stated, would we be able to reverse the cycle. Weston was unequivocal: "Jazz must be brought back to the people, where it belongs, and not be found only in the gangster- and huckster-ridden show-biz world." He called for a shift in venue from the jazz clubs to public schools, hospitals, rest homes, parks, playgrounds, churches, rallies, "gatherings and social functions in all walks of the Afro-American's life."[120]

It was a tall order, to be sure, but Weston delivered a set of concrete recommendations supporting AMSAC's agenda to develop cultural exchange with Africa. He suggested running articles on jazz history and jazz-related events in the AMSAC newsletter; adding works on jazz and African music (print and recordings) to the society's library holdings; expanding their existing recorded radio series to include the "story of the struggle of the Negro jazz musician to attain first-class status in the artist world"; and employing jazz musicians for benefits to aid African students. The latter was important to Weston, not simply because it generated work for musicians but because it put young Africans directly in contact with musicians. His objective was to promote cultural exchange. He called for more African tours (as well as more American tours by African artists) and implored Davis to include jazz musicians in these exchanges. "[I]t is time," Weston wrote, "for the two musics to meet, explore and understand each other on a much more extensive basis, for the interest in each other's music is growing steadily."[121]

Davis's response was sympathetic but terse and noncommittal. He did promise to add jazz-related material to the newsletter and to the library, and said he would consider starting a New York–based lecture series on jazz and finding ways to integrate the music into its arts and literary programs, but made no firm commitments. As to the rest of the proposal, Davis was silent.[122]

Weston found Davis's response disappointing. He had poured his heart and soul into the report, itself a distillation of thoughts and experiences accumulated over the past year. The year 1963 proved particularly productive and enriching for Weston. In April, he recorded a second big-band LP dedicated to African independence. Released that summer as *Music from the New African Nations Featuring the Highlife,* the disc reflected an even deeper grounding in African music than *Uhuru Afrika,* drawing on folk forms, popular urban dance music, and works by modern African composers. Although the band was slightly smaller than the *Uhuru* sessions, the music—arranged masterfully by Melba Liston—was no less ambitious.[123] Nearly half of the tracks are based on Nigerian highlife rhythms, most notably "Caban Bamboo Highlife," his tribute to Bobby Benson's influential Lagos nightclub, and one of his favorite Benson compositions, "Niger Mambo." "Congolese Children" is Weston's adaptation of a Bashai folk song he had heard some Congolese boys sing during his first visit to Africa, which he transformed into an up-tempo highlife tune over Monk-style dissonant chords. Weston takes his homage to Thelonious even further, dropping a quote from Monk's "Jackie-ing" at the end of his solo. Weston also pays tribute to the enigmatic Guy Warren by including a rendition of his "Love, the Mystery Of." Weston found the tune so compelling that he began using it as his regular "sign-off" piece at the end of each set or concert. And he revisits his earlier composition, "Zulu," quickening the pace and propelling the melody with exotic shuffle rhythms and a slight Afro-Cuban tinge. "In Memory Of" and "Blues to Africa" do not conform to the theme of highlife but are characteristic of Weston's compositions. The former is a haunting, bluesy funeral dirge for the great musicians who are no longer with us, while the latter is one of Weston's signature blues in ¾ time.

Although the historical importance of *Uhuru Afrika* is undeniable, I want to suggest that *Music from the New African Nations* was equally significant because it grew directly out of Weston's visit to Africa, confirming his argument that there is no substitution for travel, experience, and interpersonal cultural exchange. His quest for authentic African music took him not to the "bush" but to the night-clubs of Lagos, to the propulsive urban rhythms of highlife whose roots are as much diasporic and global as they are local. Weston him-self described highlife as "something like the calypso." Most impor-tant, he came to realize that merely borrowing or transferring rhythms or melodies from Africa wasn't enough. "African music is extremely complex," he explained soon after the release of *Music from the New African Nations*. "You have to know everything about African life and culture in order to play the music. African drum-mers, for instance, have to know poetry."[124]

In May, soon after recording *Music from the New African Na-tions*, Weston returned to Nigeria under the auspices of AMSAC. Traveling with the artist and author Elton C. Fax, Weston spent a week roaming the country, lecturing at universities, holding work-shops, collecting and studying local music, and performing. He had more opportunities to play on this trip than he had during the 1961 festival, performing with five traditional drummers, appearing with Bobby Benson's band on Lagos television, and again at Benson's Ca-ban Bamboo Nightclub—where he shared the stage with a modern jazz quintet led by a hip young trumpeter named Fela Ransome-Kuti.[125] The Nigerian press lauded Randy's every move. Commenting on his Caban Bamboo appearance, the critic for the *Lagos Sunday Post* wrote, "It was delightful watching him on the piano. Such ease, such mastery!"[126] Barbara Wilson, executive secretary of AMSAC in Lagos, featured Weston on her radio show and debuted *Music from the New African Nations* before it had been released in the United States. And in Ibadan, he played with Nigeria's jazz royalty—bassist and composer Steve Rhodes, drummer Bayo Martins, and pianist Wole Bucknor, founder of the legendary Afro-Jazz Group.[127] He also recognized the value Nigerians placed on cultural preservation during his visit to the Mbari Cultural Center in Ibadan, the inspiration for his composition "A Night in Mbari." In fact, it was in Ibadan, during another radio interview, that Weston articulated what would be a linchpin of his plans for AMSAC: the creation of a huge, trans-Atlantic music archive. As he put it,

> Many of the African musicians didn't realize the effect indigenous African music has had on jazz . . . and now that we have talked about it, we're going to set up our own private exchange program of information and tapes. I came away with many tapes of indigenous music which I know will be helpful to me in my work and to other jazz musicians and I look forward to receiving more of them. I've just begun to realize what a rich variety of music there is in Africa. I'd like to go back there for at least a year and just listen and tape it and then bring it home and translate it into the jazz idiom.[128]

Indeed, as he told Ira Gitler a few months following his return from Nigeria, he planned to apply for a grant to undertake a thorough study of West African music.[129]

Weston soon discovered, however, that many of the Nigerian jazz musicians were just as anxious to come to the United States, though the lofty aims of cultural exchange hardly figured in their decision. They needed to make a living. Despite the growth of jazz in West Africa, gigs were few and far between, and financial security had eluded most Nigerian jazz musicians. Two years after his last visit, Weston received a few desperate letters from drummer Bayo Martins, announcing plans to bring his brand of jazz/African music fusion to America and practically begging Randy "to be my business manager and agent in America." He expected to record with Weston's ensemble and prepared to sign a contract. "Randy," he implored, "you really have to get things started for me to enable me to get a visa to America."[130] After explaining that he was not a business manager, and that "jazz is at a very low point these days in the United States," Weston referred the matter to Yvonne Walker, the AMSAC administrator, but nothing came of it.[131] Realizing that AMSAC possessed neither the power nor the will to work effectively on behalf of jazz musicians on both sides of the Atlantic, Weston stopped asking for the society's support. He continued to keep the staff informed about his activities until some time in 1966, at which time he quietly withdrew from the organization. Three years later, AMSAC ceased to exist.

African Cookbook

Meanwhile, Weston set out to implement his ideas independently. Upon his return from Africa, he gave concerts featuring *Music from the New African Nations,* but sustaining an eleven-piece band was simply not financially viable.[132] He pared down to a sextet consisting of tenor saxophonist Frank Haynes, Ray Copeland (trumpet), Ahmed Abdul-Malik (bass), Lenny McBrowne (drums), and Big Black (Daniel Ray) on percussion. Weston employed his new ensemble to resurrect the "History of Jazz" program he had developed with Marshall Stearns and Langston Hughes. This was his way of returning the music to black communities and elucidating the connections between Africa and jazz. His objective was clear. As he explained in his preliminary funding proposal, the purpose of the program was to "help the Negro community, especially, to understand and welcome its only indigenous art form, and through the music to have more pride in itself and what it has achieved." Rejecting a "huge, star-studded concert," he needed a level of financial support that would enable him to take "our music to the people themselves"—to the public schools, churches, libraries, community centers, youth groups, hospitals, as well as "political, social, civil rights and cultural organizations." Fortunately, he secured funding from the Musician's Trust Fund, administered by the American Federation of Musicians Local 802, as well as a grant from the Pepsi-Cola Company.[133]

Weston also revamped the "History of Jazz" program to reflect recent developments in music as well as his own evolving perspectives on African culture. The revised version, co-written with pianists

Louis Brown, Ray Bryant, and Nadi Qamar, now opened and closed with Africa and included more of the African diaspora. Big Black began the program by demonstrating African rhythms on congas, and then the band would slip into the calypso tune "Sly Mongoose" before moving to spirituals and work songs. The birth of jazz is signaled by "When the Saints Go Marching In," New Orleans–style, and from there Weston's sextet played examples of the blues, swing (via Count Basie's "Jumpin' at the Woodside" and Ellington's "C Jam Blues"), and bebop. But even their bebop example took on a diasporic cast, emphasizing the Afro-Cuban contribution by featuring Big Black on Dizzy Gillespie's "Woody N' You." The program continued with Thelonious Monk's "Well, You Needn't," a taste of rock 'n roll, and a demonstration of avant-garde jazz, finally concluding with a rousing performance of Weston's composition "African Cookbook," which represented the "Renewal of African Influence."[134] A powerful vamp in 6/8 time, the melody evokes North Africa, the rhythm is derived from south of the Sahara, and the impact on audiences is electric. Its modal harmonic form makes it an ideal vehicle for soloists, who are free to improvise along a single mode (scale) rather than cyclical chord progressions. "African Cookbook" was a hit with schoolkids, and it would prove to be one of Weston's most popular and most requested songs.

Weston was no fan of rock 'n roll or the jazz avant-garde, but he included these genres to prove a point: all of this music could be traced back to Africa. "I've listened to African music," he explained to drummer and author Arthur Taylor three years later, "and I've heard everything from old-time blues to avant-garde. Africa is the creative source. It is the whole power of the music in the countries that have been influenced by African culture, such as Brazil, Cuba, and the United States. Wherever African people have settled, they have created a new music which is based on African rhythms. There is a great West African influence in Brazil, also very much in Cuba and in Puerto Rico. Gospel music, spirituals—they're all African."[135] Weston and his sextet took this message to schools and churches all over

Brooklyn, Manhattan, Queens, and the Bronx, and with every successful performance or lecture came more requests. They could hardly keep up with the demand. Dick Read, a journalist who attended the first two "History of Jazz" programs, was struck by the audience's attentiveness as well as the capacity of Weston to topple stereotypes in a matter of minutes. "Suddenly I thought of the miles of film footage these young people must have been exposed to, showing savages with bones thrust through their noses, flailing at logs or kettles. I saw with new clarity what Randy and the other groups were doing through this series of concerts. Listening, I watched the faces of this bright and eager audience as they were taken through slavery with song."[136]

Weston had expected to return to Africa in the spring of 1966 as a delegate to the First World Festival of Negro Arts held in Dakar, Senegal. Dwarfing AMSAC's 1961 festival in Nigeria, this historic event backed by the U.S. State Department brought together hundreds of dancers, visual artists, writers, and musicians from throughout Africa and the African diaspora. A veritable who's who of black culture, a few of the American notables included Katherine Dunham, the Alvin Ailey Dance Company, James Baldwin, and the U.S. contingent's official leader, Langston Hughes.[137] Oddly, the American committee for the festival never seriously considered Weston because its chairperson, white New York socialite Virginia Inness-Brown, knew close to nothing about jazz. They chose Duke Ellington's orchestra— a wonderful choice, both for the festival and for Duke, affording him his first opportunity to perform in Africa. Ellington, who shared Weston's interpretation of jazz's roots, exclaimed, "After writing African music for thirty-five years, here I am at last in Africa!"[138] But critics and participants alike complained of too much European concert music and too little jazz. As African American writer Hoyt W. Fuller observed, "There is nothing particularly 'Negro' about a pianist playing Bach preludes and a soprano singing Verdi arias."[139]

Weston did not have the luxury of wallowing in disappointment. Sudden changes in personnel left his band on the verge of collapse.

Near the end of 1965, Weston hired tenor saxophonist Booker Ervin after Frank Haynes succumbed to cancer at the age of thirty-three.[140] A couple of months later, Ahmed Abdul-Malik left the band in order to return to school, and in his place Weston hired Bill "Vishnu" Wood. But with jobs increasingly scarce, the group finally disbanded in the fall of 1966—just before Weston received another invitation to tour Africa. This time the offer came from the U.S. State Department, and it consisted of a three-month tour through West and North Africa with a stop in Beirut, Lebanon.[141] In spite of his misgivings about the State Department and its motives, Weston considered this a dream come true. He had seen only one country in Africa, Nigeria, and never stayed more than eight days. Now he was poised to visit thirteen African countries—Senegal, Mali, Upper Volta (today Burkina Faso), Niger, Ghana, Cameroon, Gabon, Liberia, Sierra Leone, Ivory Coast, Egypt, Algeria, and Morocco—as well as Lebanon. He hoped to immerse himself in local cultures, collect music from a wider circle of nationalities and ethnic groups, and experience a far more diverse landscape than what he had come to know in Lagos and Ibadan. Moreover, he would see firsthand how the young nations whose freedom he championed several years earlier now fared.

The romance of independence and African unity had faded considerably by the time Weston and his band began the tour in January 1967. Political instability, economic crises, and a general erosion of democracy plagued virtually every nation on the State Department's itinerary. Algeria's nationalist hero and first president, Ahmed Ben Bella, had been deposed by the military in 1965.[142] A year later, President Kwame Nkrumah of Ghana, once the hope of Africa, was overthrown by a CIA-backed coup d'état. Nkrumah had moved too far to the left for American comfort and had become too authoritarian for many of his own citizens. In Sierra Leone in March of 1967, the military seized power after the All People's Congress (APC) defeated the ruling Sierra Leone People's Party (SLPP). For a year, the military regime blocked the APC from taking office until another faction of the military opposed to the SLPP launched a "counter coup" enabling

APC officials to take power. The creation of the Mali Federation in 1959, merging Senegal and what was then called the French Sudan (Mali), began as an exemplar of regional development and African unity. A year later it collapsed. President Modibo Keita then turned Mali into a one-party socialist state with strong ties to the Eastern Bloc and China. Weston recalled his stay at Bamako's Grand Hotel "was like something out of a spy novel, with Vietnamese on one floor, Chinese on another, and East Germans on another; it seemed to be a hotel of tremendous intrigue."[143] Despite efforts to redistribute wealth through extensive nationalization, Mali's economy virtually collapsed in the face of a currency crisis, Western isolation, unfair global trade terms, mismanagement, and an increasingly undemocratic regime. A year after Weston's visit, Keita was overthrown in a military coup. Senegal's first attempted coup came much earlier. In 1962, Prime Minister Mamadou Dia led a failed military coup against President Leopold Senghor. Not only did he weather the insurrection, but he and his party rewrote the constitution to consolidate his power. The threat of Gabon becoming a one-party state prompted the military to depose President Léon M'Ba in February of 1964, until French troops re-established civilian rule the very next day. Still, the die was cast; by March of 1967, the ruling Bloc Démocratique Gabonais (BDG) won all forty-seven seats in the National Assembly. M'Ba died later that year and Vice-President Omar Bongo succeeded him. One of Bongo's first acts as president was to dissolve the BDG and establish the Parti Démocratique Gabonais (PDG) as the nation's only legal political party. In Upper Volta, the military overthrew President Maurice Yaméogo following mass protests and strikes by students, labor unions, and civil servants calling for his ouster. Immediately after his election in 1960, Yaméogo had banned all political parties besides his own Voltaic Democratic Union. In 1966, a committee of army officers deposed Yaméogo, dissolved the National Assembly, and suspended the constitution. And while General Abdel Gamal Nasser had clearly consolidated his rule in Egypt, just months after Weston's visit the nation would suffer a devastating loss at the hands of Israel in the Six-Day War.

These were rough times for Africa. A century of colonialism, two decades of the Cold War, and a global economy that saddled Third World countries with mounting debt left the "new African nations" in a constant state of instability. Under such conditions, democracy gave way to dictatorship and military regimes, the suppression of civil society, and violence. Weston had no illusions. He knew fully well that postcolonial Africa was a long way from "Uhuru," and he had no interest in pushing U.S. foreign policy or becoming a Trojan horse for American investments. His role as "cultural ambassador," in his mind at least, meant serving as a bridge between Africa and some 22 million black people in the United States, and his music was intended to strengthen those bonds and bring momentary peace and beauty to societies racked with crisis. State Department briefings took a backseat to his more immediate task: putting together a band.

Of his original 1966 group, trumpeter Ray Copeland and bassist Bill Vishnu Wood remained with Weston for the tour. Tenor saxophonist Clifford Jordan replaced Booker Ervin, Ed Blackwell—known for his brilliant work with Ornette Coleman's quartet—took over the drum chair from Lenny McBrowne, and Chief Bey filled the gaping hole left by Big Black. Weston also invited his implacable secretary, tour manager, and dear friend, Georgia Griggs. The only female and the only white person (besides State Department officials) in Weston's entourage, she documented the trip and persistently criticized American officials, whom she felt betrayed a colonial mentality. Weston also brought along his sixteen-year-old son Niles (later Azzedin) as an informal "band boy," although his main motive was to introduce his son to Africa. Niles had become a gifted percussionist in his own right, and his dad figured that three months on the continent was worth three years of private lessons.[144]

The group played an array of Weston originals, from "Hi Fly" and "Gospel Monk" to the Nigerian-influenced "A Night in Mbari." They usually devoted the second set to the "History of Jazz," culminating in a lively rendition of "African Cookbook." In every country they visited, "African Cookbook" roused audiences to a near frenzy. The people were so engaged, clapping, dancing, rocking to the music, that they would not let the band stop. Few performances of "Cookbook" lasted less than half an hour. Weston recalled one concert in Cairo, Egypt, when the people "got into it and simply took the rhythm away from us with their vigorous handclaps. They were actually throwing our rhythms back at us, as if to tell us, 'We know that rhythm, that's our rhythm,' which it was, of course. Chief Bey was tired, but he simply could not stop playing the drums; they wouldn't let him stop."[145] The Egyptian response so alarmed the U.S. embassy that the American ambassador asked Weston to cut "African Cookbook" from his repertoire because he thought the music was inciting the crowd. Weston refused.[146]

Weston did not have to work very hard to establish a link between African music and jazz. The combination of Weston's creative employment of African rhythms and scales and the global reach of Black Power's influence primed critics and audiences to recognize—and embrace—the jazz-African nexus immediately. The response was a far cry from the stone-faced Nigerians who had endured Lionel Hampton six years earlier. During a concert at Freetown University in Sierra Leone, Chief Bey's drum solo on "Congolese Children" set the auditorium on fire. As one reporter put it, "The crowd went wild at the unbelievable, almost ritualistic performance of Bey on conga. Truly, Bey was remarkable."[147] In a story promoting Weston's Algiers concert, the Algerian paper, *El Moudjahid*, enthused: "This is the proof that jazz is most popular in Africa, its cradle . . . Without 'transplanted' Africans, jazz would never have existed."[148] During a concert in Gabon, a local musician emerged from the audience playing an *mvet*—a cross between a zither and a harp, associated with the Fang people of Gabon—and spontaneously jammed with the group. Weston was amazed: "He improvised, played group passages with the band and even joined us quietly during the piano and bass solos. He had no trouble at all playing with a jazz group."[149] In another instance, Weston invited a group of master balafon players in Bitam, Gabon, to bring their xylophone-like instruments and perform with the band.[150]

Interactions with local musicians and learning indigenous traditions had the most profound impact on Weston, and most of these encounters occurred offstage. He rarely parted with his tape recorder and set out to document everything, from formal music and dance performances at the University of Ghana, master drummers in Liberia, to the sounds of wind, insects, and birds in the forests of Gabon. Sometimes Weston and members of his band would drive around just listening for music. As soon as they heard something, they parked the car and walked toward the sound, then were often greeted by friendly locals who brought food and drink.[151]

Enriching as these encounters were, the tour was not without problems. Faced with the sheer distance of the tour, they could not travel with a full-sized acoustic piano, so Weston had to settle for an inadequate portable electric piano. He could barely squeeze a sound out of the instrument since few venues possessed adequate sound systems. But Weston's biggest headache was his official State Department escort, Harry Hirsch, and some of the American ambassadors he encountered. Hirsch and other officials unsuccessfully tried to persuade Weston to play more rhythm and blues and less modern jazz, arguing that Africans were simply not that sophisticated. Hirsch also complained to his superiors that band members were wearing dashikis and other African garb on their off time, making it difficult to distinguish them from the locals. For the State Department, the point of their cultural ambassadorship was not to demonstrate camaraderie and solidarity with the Africans but to represent American culture and an American point of view.[152] Weston disagreed, and he said so in his final report to the State Department, co-written with Georgia Griggs. For Weston and Griggs, the whole point of the tour was "to establish rapport with the African people in order to share our cultures and to encourage understanding between the peoples of their countries and ours." Hirsch, in particular, was singled out for undermining the group's morale. The report found it "demoralizing to be subjected to unnecessary criticism and tension as it tended to distract us from our main purpose and caused us all to waste time and energy on matters that could have been handled easily and tactfully . . . It is a shame that the United States ever sends people with what we (and many Africans) consider to be 'colonial' mentalities any place overseas, for they make a very bad impression on nearly everyone who meets them."[153]

Nevertheless, Weston returned from the trip more committed than ever to engaging and studying African culture. Political and economic instability did not dampen his belief that Africa was the future, rich with cultural resources, human capital, and spiritual reserves. Indeed, he no longer believed tours and programmatic cultural exchange were enough. In his final report he suggested that artists consider long-term residence on the continent: "U.S. artists actually living among the people and working with them could have an impact no group passing through for a few days could ever hope to have. After talking to many Africans in every country we visited about this I feel that such a program would be enthusiastically accepted everywhere, even in those countries supposedly unfriendly toward the United States. There are, really, unlimited possibilities in such a program."[154]

Flying Home . . . Again

Weston practiced what he preached. Back in the United States, all he thought about was living in Africa. He gave a talk at the Duke Ellington Society in New York not long after his return in which he announced plans to go back, study African languages, folklore, and music, and create opportunities for African musicians in the United States.[155] The music scene in the States also fueled his desire to leave the country. Jazz musicians had become either so avant-garde or so commercial that, in Weston's view, they had lost touch with the people, the culture, the very heart of the music—the blues.[156]

He first considered moving to Nigeria. It seemed like the natural choice: he had extensive contacts there, had appeared in the national media, and the Nigerians spoke English. But civil war had just broken out in July 1967, after the predominantly Igbo states in the Southeast attempted to secede from the nation.[157] Before he had a chance to weigh other options, Morocco sought *him* out. Weston's group was so popular that local radio DJs were inundated with requests to rebroadcast the band's recent performance in Marrakech, which had aired on Radio Maroc. The American Embassy begged Weston to return in June to participate in the "1967 Festival du Jazz" in Rabat.[158] He agreed, fell in love with the place and the people, and realized his search was over. Seven months later, he packed a few essentials, gathered two of his children—Niles and Pamela—and fled a bitterly cold New York for the warmth of the Moroccan sun. He would not return for five years.

Randy Weston, a Garveyite son whose father insisted they were Africans, whose mother impressed upon him the value of the sacred, walked away from commercial opportunities in order to study with masters of traditional music, develop a dialogue with African artists of all genres, and continue what had evolved into a spiritual quest. After a short stay in Rabat, he relocated to Tangier where he opened the African Rhythms Cultural Center—a combination performance space, club, and arts center. It became a hub for the kind of cultural exchange Weston had longed to establish between African and African American musicians and artists. But his most profound cultural engagements occurred at a more local level when he came in contact with a group of dark-skinned musicians known as the Gnawa (or Gnaoua). He learned that they were the descendants of slaves taken from Sub-Saharan West Africa—Mali, Ghana, Mauritania—and were renowned for their sacred healing songs. Over time they became part of the Sufi order in Morocco. Utilizing instruments such as *karkaba* (huge metal castanets) and the *hag'houge* (a three-stringed lute with a resonant middle-register bass tone), Gnawa M'Alem (master healers) play complex rhythms with shifting time signatures and tempos and scales far more elaborate than the Western twelve-tone scale. They believe that everyone has a color and a note to which he or she vibrates, and when the M'Alem play the people respond to the colors they hear.[159]

Weston became a student all over again, studying with the Gnawa M'Alem, learning the culture, rediscovering music, and finding his own color. He would eventually develop a collaborative relationship with these master musicians that has lasted to this very day, synthesizing North African music and African American blues while retaining the spiritual core central to both.[160] His recordings with the Gnawa M'Alem reveal not only a keen knowledge of the music but a willingness to subordinate his own voice to maintain the integrity of the traditional form. On *The Splendid Master Gnawa Musicians of Morocco*, for example, a recording he made with nine M'Alem in 1994, Weston appears only on one song, "Chalabati," in which his sparse phrases blend subtly into the overall sound.

Weston's lifelong engagement with African cultures set him on a path from which he has never strayed. Weston succeeded in creating "new spirituals," sacred music grown from the soil of ancient traditions from Benin to Brooklyn, transformed by his own spirit and imagination. Listening to albums such as *The Spirits of Our Ancestors* (1991), *Saga* (1995), *Earth Birth* (1995), *Khepera* (1998), *Spirit! The Power of Music* (2000), *Ancient Future* (2002), and most recently, *The Storyteller* (2010) makes one want to dance and pray all at once. His insistence that "jazz" is essentially African music, African music is at its core sacred, and African culture has shaped world history has not won many friends among the mainstream critical establishment. But none of this mattered to Weston because his objective was never fame, fortune, and good reviews. Like his hero Paul Robeson, Weston recognized a power in music much greater than all of us.

Guy Warren trio performing at the Africa Room, 1958. Ollie Shearer on vibes; Ray McKinney on bass; and Guy Warren at the drums.
Courtesy of the Kofi Ghanaba Estate.

Guy Warren at his home after he returns to Ghana, about 1966.
Courtesy of the Kofi Ghanaba Estate.

Kofi Ghanaba (Guy Warren) at home playing his modified drum kit of carved wooden drums of the Akan people of western Ghana. The two large fontomfrom drums on the floor in front of him function as bass drums, the apentemma drum directly facing him serves as a kind of snare drum, and the two standing fontomfrom and two atumpan to his right and left are used as tom toms.

Photograph by the author.

Randy Weston, Ahmed Abdul-Malik, and other members of the AMSAC festival entourage preparing to depart for Lagos, Nigeria, December 1961. *Left to right:* Dr. Horace Mann Bond, Natalie Hinderas, Randy Weston, Nina Simone, Martha Flowers, and Ahmed Abdul-Malik.

Courtesy of the Moorland-Spingarn Research Center, Howard University.

Babatunde Olatunji, holding a talking drum, and Randy Weston exchange ideas during a rehearsal for a two-day symposium on culture in Lagos, Nigeria, sponsored by the American Society for African Culture (December 1961). Scoby Strohman is seated at the drum kit, and standing near the piano wearing a cap is noted Nigerian musician and composer Bobby Benson.

Courtesy of the Moorland-Spingarn Research Center, Howard University.

Randy Weston and Melba Liston work on a score during a recording session for *Music of the New African Nations, Featuring the Highlife* (April 1963). Looking on from behind is saxophonist Budd Johnson.

Photograph by Chuck Stewart; © Chuck Stewart. All rights reserved.

Ahmed Abdul-Malik and his trio, ca. 1960. *Left to right:* Calo Scott (cello), Ahmed Abdul-Malik (oud), Bilal Abdurahman (percussion).
Courtesy of Rahkiah Abdurahman Eason.

Sathima Bea Benjamin and the Dollar Brand Trio at the Antibes Jazz Festival, Juan Les Pins, July 1963. *Left to right:* Sathima Bea Benjamin (vocals), Abdullah Ibrahim (Dollar Brand) (piano), Johnny Gertze (bass), Makaya Ntshoko (drums).
© *Jan Perssons/*CTSIMAGES.

A year and a half after fleeing South Africa, Sathima Bea Benjamin and Abdullah Ibrahim find work in Europe. They are pictured here arriving at Copenhagen Main Railway Station in 1963. *Left to right:* Danish jazz promoter Jens Ehlers, Makaya Ntshoko, Abdullah Ibrahim, Sathima Bea Benjamin, and Johnny Gertze.

© *Jan Perssons/*CTSIMAGES.

3 | Ahmed Abdul-Malik's Islamic Experimentalism

> People think I am too far out with religion . . .
> How can you play beauty without knowing what
> beauty is, what it *really* is? Understanding the Cre-
> ator leads to understanding the creations, and bet-
> ter understanding of what you play comes from
> this.
> —Ahmed Abdul-Malik, *Down Beat,* 1963

In Randy Weston's search for African roots, he discovered new branches that pulled him in surprising directions. He
sought out the ancients and found modern highlife in West Africa;
he carried his tape recorder to the "bush" but in the bustling cities of
Lagos, Ibadan, and Bamako, he met a new generation of Nigerian
and Malian *jazz* musicians anxious to blow; and in the sands of the
Sahara he discovered in the Gnawa another tradition, rooted in slavery, that brought healing music to the northern reaches of the continent—Morocco and Tunisia. Weston had not set out to develop such
a strong musical and cultural connection to Morocco. His heart was
in sub-Saharan Africa, the land of his ancestors. But he was well ac-
quainted with the North and its connection to the Red Sea, the Levant, the Arab world, and the Mediterranean. His childhood friend,
bassist Ahmed Abdul-Malik, never let him forget.

Abdul-Malik had had his sights on North Africa and the Middle
East since childhood. He was always partial to the music of Egypt,
Syria, Lebanon, Sudan, Turkey, as well as musical traditions from the
Indian sub-continent. His objective, as early as the late 1940s, was to
revitalize jazz by composing pieces based on "Eastern" modes or
scales that extend beyond the Western diatonic and chromatic scales.
As he told an interviewer in 1963, he felt jazz had become a kind of
"surface music," a manifestation of what he recognized in the West as

"artificial living." The musician's failure to seek "ultimate truth" had led jazz down a path of "sterility." For Abdul-Malik, however, the infusion of North African and Middle Eastern music wasn't merely a matter of artistic experimentation; his primary goal was to create sacred, devotional music, the music of Islam. Thus, like Weston and Guy Warren, the connection to Africa was more than musical—it was spiritual. And it was personal. His father told him he was an African. But for Abdul-Malik, the claim of heritage was more direct: "My father came from Sudan and migrated here to the United States," he explained to jazz critic Leonard Feather in a 1959 questionnaire. "He used to sing and play songs of the Orient, therefore, it was easy for me to understand the music."[1]

Virtually every one of his critics and fans has come to accept this story of his origins, which is repeated on practically every website or in every encyclopedia entry that mentions his name. But Ahmed Abdul-Malik was born Jonathan Tim Jr., (sometimes spelled "Timm") on January 30, 1927, to Matilda and Jonathan Tim Sr.—both of whom had immigrated from St. Vincent in the British West Indies three years earlier. They also had a daughter, Caroline, born a little more than a year after Jonathan Jr. Jonathan Tim Sr.'s death certificate not only confirms his birth in St. Vincent, it indicates that his father—Abdul-Malik's grandfather—James Tim, and his mother, Mary Daniels, were both from the Caribbean. City directories for Brooklyn, as well as the American Federation of Musicians Union Local 802 directory, confirm the bassist's birth name as Jonathan Tim Jr.[2]

Abdul-Malik's steadfast assertion of his Sudanese heritage tells us a great deal about the power and importance of Africa in the black imagination during the 1930s, 1940s, and 1950s, not to mention the startling ethnic and cultural diversity that existed in Brooklyn's black communities. Ahmed Abdul-Malik cannot be dismissed as a fabrication; he was a product of a time and place, a manifestation of a Bedford Stuyvesant renaissance where a transplanted African culture thrived, Islam took root, and the international movement for Afro-Arab solidarity found its American champions.

Becoming Ahmed Abdul-Malik

The Tim family initially lived at 545 Hopkinson Avenue, just southeast of the heart of Bedford Stuyvesant. Before young Jonathan started school, however, the family moved to 1984 Atlantic Avenue, not far from the street corners where Brooklyn's Arab musicians performed.[3] Even before he was old enough to roam the streets in search of music, Jonathan Jr. began taking violin lessons from his dad, who was never a professional musician. He worked mainly in the skilled trades as a plasterer and took jobs as a general laborer when he had to. Jonathan Jr. proved quite adept on the instrument, so at age seven he enrolled in the Vardi School of Music and Art to continue his violin training, and over time took up piano, cello, bass, and tuba.[4] Joseph Vardi, a concert violinist who co-founded the school with his pianist wife, Anna, always stressed the importance of acquiring a diverse musical knowledge. Years later, Abdul-Malik praised Vardi for insisting, "I acquaint myself with as many different kinds of music as possible. When you learn to understand the feelings of other peoples, you will then understand how these feelings express themselves in their music."[5]

At some point in the late 1930s Jonathan Jr.'s parents divorced, and his father remarried and moved four blocks away to 2117 Dean Street. He continued to live with his father and his new wife, Olive, while his mother moved to Queens. The breakup of his parents was followed by another, more devastating blow: on February 9, 1941, just ten days after young Jonathan's fourteenth birthday, his father died of a bleeding gastric ulcer. He was forty years old.[6]

The sudden loss of his father steeled his determination to pursue a life of music. He took a few lessons from bassist Franklin Skeete, a Brooklyn institution who would go on to record with both jazz and R&B artists from Max Roach and Wynton Kelly to Bull Moose Jackson and Wild Bill Moore. About a year later, he was admitted to the prestigious High School of Music and Art in Manhattan, where his skills on violin and viola earned him a spot in the All-City Orchestra.

To make ends meet, he took paying gigs in high school performing at Syrian, Greek, and "Gypsy" weddings, where he not only played music of the Mediterranean and Middle East, but found his way into a network of Arab musicians around New York. In 1944, during his senior year of high school, he launched his professional jazz career as a bassist with Fess Williams's band.[7]

It is possible that Jonathan Jr. converted to Islam in high school and began using the name Ahmed Hussein Abdul-Malik. Randy Weston, who was only about nine months older than Abdul-Malik, remembered that he was already speaking Arabic and experimenting with the oud and the kanoon during the 1940s.[8] Weston recalled how "Malik would take me down to the Arab neighborhood around Atlantic Avenue in downtown Brooklyn to hear North African musicians. He spoke fluent Arabic so we had no trouble communicating."[9]

Abdul-Malik's competence in Arabic was probably a consequence of his conversion to Islam. Like most jazz musicians in the mid- to late 1940s, he joined not Elijah Muhammad's Nation of Islam but a group calling itself the Muslim Brotherhood (not to be confused with the Egyptian group of that name). The Muslim Brotherhood identified with the Ahmadiyya movement, a strain of Islam founded in 1889 by an Indian Muslim, Hazrat Mirza Ghulam Ahmad (1835–1908), who claimed to be the Mahdi and "redeemer" of the Islamic faith—if not all faiths (such as the Christian "Messiah" and the final incarnation of Krishna). The mere acceptance of another prophet after Muhammad was enough to declare the Ahmadiyya heretics in the eyes of most of the world's Muslims. But they rebelled in other ways as well. Ahmadis translated the Holy Qur'an into different languages, redefined *jihad* as peaceful missionary work, and recognized the founders, saints, and prophets of all major world religions—including Zoroaster, Abraham, Moses, Buddha, Jesus, Confucius, and Lao Tzu, among others—insisting that their teachings converged under true Islam. In the words of Kambiz GhaneaBassiri, "the Ahmadiyya mission represents a Muslim response to modernity" that "turned the table on exclusive Anglo-Protestant claims of rationalism, universalism, and progress by claiming these qualities for Islam."[10]

Mufti Muhammad Sadiq established the first Ahmadiyya missions in black communities of Detroit, Chicago, and Harlem during the early 1920s. The Ahmadiyya was not the first Islamic sect to gain a foothold among urban African Americans. In 1913, Timothy Drew, later known as Prophet Noble Drew Ali, established the Moorish Science Temple and taught that black people were the descendants of the Moors of North Africa and their true religion was Islam. And in 1930, Wallace Fard Muhammad founded the Nation of Islam in Detroit. By World War II, Harlem was home to several competing Islamic or "proto-Islamic" groups, although the Ahmadiyya mission, in particular, had become a magnet for young musicians politicized by racism, the proliferation of black nationalist movements, and the growing interest in Eastern spirituality.[11] Black musicians found the Muslim Brotherhood attractive because it redefined so-called Negroes from a national minority to a world majority, embracing both Africa and Asia as part of a "colored" world. It bestowed upon black American culture a sense of dignity and nobility that appealed to the creators of a new variant of modern jazz the press labeled "bebop." Many black musicians turned to Islam not only as a rejection of the "white man's religion" but also as a means to bring a moral structure to a world suffused with drugs, alcohol, and sex.[12]

It is not clear when or how Abdul-Malik became a member of the Muslim Brotherhood. The first official sighting of his Arabic name, "Ahmad H. Abdul-Malik," appears in the 1949 edition of the Local 802 American Federation of Musicians directory. (The previous year's directory lists him as "Jonathan Timm.")[13] With respect to *how* he joined, we do know that a core group of musicians had been members of Dizzy Gillespie's big band, most having been recruited in 1946 by a trumpet player named Talib Ahmad Dawud (birth name Alfonso Nelson Rainey, stage name Al Barrymore) who had emigrated from Antigua at age eighteen. Among those converted was a talented young drummer out of Pittsburgh named Art Blakey. To-gether, Dawud and Blakey (who changed his name to Abdullah Ibn Buhaina) founded a Muslim Mission that initially met at Blakey's Manhattan apartment but spread across the bridge to Brooklyn. By 1953, close to 200 jazz musicians were said to have joined the Muslim Brotherhood and to have taken on Arabic names. Among them were saxophonists Sahib Shihab (Edmond Gregory) and Yusef Lateef (Bill Evans); trumpeters Idris Sulieman (Leonard Graham) and Kenny Dorham (Abdul Hamid); pianists Ahmad Jamal (Frederick Jones) and Sadik Hakim (Argonne Thornton); and drummer Kenneth Clarke, who later took the name Liaqat Ali Salaam.[14] Blakey, Idris Sulieman, and fifteen other musicians had also recently formed a re-hearsal band, calling themselves the Seventeen Messengers, or just the Messengers. The band was not entirely Muslim, but it did attract several Ahmadiyya followers. The group's name had religious conno-tations—a "messenger" was a Messenger of Allah.[15]

Abdul-Malik was familiar with Blakey and had even worked with him in 1945, though he never joined the Messengers. Despite their strong identification with Islam, the Messengers (later the Jazz Mes-sengers) never explored the possibility of incorporating music from the Middle East. Indeed, during the early 1950s, the jazz world wit-nessed a proliferation of devout Muslim musicians as well as all-Muslim bands, such as Shafi Hadi (Curtis Porter) and the Arab Jazzmen. Yet virtually all of these artists and groups settled for stan-dard jazz fare—swing, bebop, and so on. For most of these artists, conversion was primarily about worship, self-discipline, and about changing one's identity, escaping the degradation of being "Negro" in order to become human and, for better or worse, *exotic*. When Lynn Hope (Al Hajji Abdullah Rasheed Ahmed), a tenor player based in Philadelphia and a member of the Universal Arabic Association, trav-eled south with his all-Muslim orchestra, he would reply thus to at-tempts to Jim Crow his band: "We are not Negroes but members of the Moslem faith. Our customs are Eastern. We claim the nationality of our Arabic ancestors as well as their culture." In almost every case, they were served.[16]

Exoticism also sold. Hope billed himself as "The Amazing Man with the Turban" and thrilled audiences by playing a mix of jazz and R&B and "walking the bar" as he blew his tenor saxophone.[17] Born in Birmingham but raised mainly in Cincinnati, Hope started out with King Kolax's band playing dance music in the late 1940s until he formed his own band, consisting of his sister Mary Hope on piano (also known as Myriam), brother Billy (Unis Ali) on drums, and brother Khalil A. Malik on trumpet and trombone. All the male members of the band wore red fezs while Hope sported a jeweled turban. Their repertoire consisted entirely of blues, standards, and ballads ("Tenderly," "She's Funny That Way," "September Song," "Summertime"). One of the few originals he played that even referenced the Islamic world was "Morocco," and it was little more than a jump blues in $B_\flat$.[18]

Abdul-Malik, on the other hand, had been dreaming about fusing jazz and Arab music since he was a teenager. Besides Randy Weston, the only other artist who shared Abdul-Malik's vision was his neighbor, Bilal Abdurahman. Just eighteen months younger than Abdul-Malik, Abdurahman was a talented multi-instrumentalist, visual artist, and a devout Ahmadiyya Muslim who was as passionate about Africa and the Third World as Weston and Abdul-Malik. Indeed, he was responsible for bringing Prince Efrom Odok to Brooklyn. Born and raised in Bedford Stuyvesant, Abdurhaman fell in love with the music of Basie, Ellington, Louis Jordan, and Nat King Cole, and as a teenager he started out on a set of trap drums. He took formal lessons on the C Melody saxophone and in time became the lead alto player in Ray Abrams's sixteen-piece band. But like Weston and Abdul-Malik, he was drawn to music and musical instruments outside the West. The regulars in Brooklyn's "Congo Square" knew him as an outstanding conga and djembe drummer, who was always introducing new instruments into the mix. After completing a year-

long stint in Korea (1951–1952) for the U.S. Army, he returned to
Brooklyn toting an odd-looking reed instrument he called a "Peri"—
a gift to him from a Korean farmer he had befriended during the
war.[19]

In Abdurahman, Abdul-Malik found a sympathetic ear and a
thoughtful musician with whom to exchange ideas. Everywhere else
he went, however, his ideas were met with hostility or indifference. "I
couldn't find no place to work so I can try these things out," Abdul-
Malik later recalled. "Believe me, they thought I was out of my mind
. . . they thought I should be in the hospital."[20] He had to make a living, so he continued to work with a range of musical groups—from
swing and Dixieland to bop, R&B, and calypso. Over the course of a
decade, he had built an impressive résumé, having worked with Art
Blakey, Don Byas, Freddie Washington, Sam Taylor, Zoot Sims, Coleman Hawkins, and the Great MacBeth.[21] But jobs were few and far
between. During this period he only played one record date, recording two tunes with Freddie Washington's Dixiecrats in 1951—a
session that apparently was never released.[22] In his spare time he
studied oud and composed tunes he believed were akin to the idioms
of Arab music. He took a few lessons from master musicians from
Egypt who had studied at the Arab Music Institute in Cairo, including "an old professor who has a great knowledge and understanding
of Oriental Music and Instruments. They gave me a thorough understanding of the scales and instruments."[23]

The Arab in American Culture

Then, beginning around 1956, the cultural and political ground began to shift, rendering the Arab world a focal point for Americans—
including African Americans, but not always for the same reasons.
Just as Africa became "the thing" in the early 1960s, to use Guy Warren's apt expression, the Middle East became the latest source of
fascination, fear, and curiosity. Consider the larger international political context. Israel's founding and the ensuing displacement of

Palestinian Arabs fanned the flames of rising Arab nationalism. The Egyptian Revolution that brought Colonel Gamal Abdel Nasser to power in a bloodless coup in 1952 radically changed the political landscape, especially as Nasser positioned himself as the world's most visible exponent of pan-Arab solidarity and Third World unity. Egypt took a leading role in the meeting of the Non-Aligned Nations in Bandung, Indonesia, in 1955, and Nasser followed up that gathering with his own Afro-Asian People's Solidarity Conference in Cairo, which drew support from prominent African American leaders. But the event that made Nasser a hero in the Third World and a villain among Western capitalist democracies was his decision in 1956 to nationalize the French- and British-owned Suez Canal Company after Britain and the United States withdrew financial assistance to build the Aswan High Dam. In retaliation, Britain, France, and Israel militarily invaded Egypt until pressure from the United States and the Soviet Union forced them to withdraw. Nasser's ability to weather the Suez Canal crisis of 1956–57 transformed him into an anti-imperialist icon for the Third World and for African Americans, while also rendering him a threat to U.S. hegemony in the region. Indeed, Nasser's efforts to both build pan-Arab unity and obtain arms from the Soviet-bloc countries ultimately led the United States to support questionable regimes in the Middle East opposed to Nasser. Consequently, the United States invaded Lebanon in 1958 when the Chamoun regime was on the verge of being overthrown.[24]

Back in the United States, members of both the Ahmadiyya and the Nation of Islam—while hostile to each other—sought to establish ties with Egypt. Malcolm X had begun praising Nasser and calling for Arab-African unity even before the Bandung meeting. He reached out to Arab and African leaders at the United Nations, and a year after the Suez crisis, Malcolm arranged a meeting on colonialism that brought together representatives from Egypt, Sudan, Ghana, Iraq, and Morocco.[25] Likewise, in 1957 Talib Dawud, along with writer and historian J. A. Rogers, teamed up with an Egyptian named Mahmoud Alwan to found the Islamic and African Institute in Philadelphia. Dawud had also made strident public statements criticizing the U.S. invasion of Lebanon and its overall failure to support self-determination of Muslim nations.[26]

In the realm of American popular culture, however, representations of the "Arab" during the mid-1950s seemed to have very little in common with contemporary political realities. As the national media warned of pan-Arabism and black Muslim "extremism," the United States witnessed a kind of Middle Eastern music fad, fueled by Orientalist depictions of the Arab world. In short, popular media and the record industry succeeded in decoupling Arab music from politics *and* Islam. The central figure behind the growing popularity of Middle Eastern music was a celebrated Lebanese singer, actor, and oudist named Mohammed El-Bakkar. A bona-fide star in Egypt, Saudi Arabia, Syria, and Lebanon, he had acted in, produced, and directed some thirty-two movies before moving to the United States in 1952. In 1954, he made his debut on Broadway, where he enjoyed critical acclaim as the rug seller in *Fanny.* Before his premature death in 1959 (at age forty-six), El-Bakkar also made several popular recordings of Arab music marketed primarily for American audiences.[27] Around 1957, Audio Fidelity hired him to arrange, conduct, and perform on a series of discs called "Music of the Middle East." As a result, Mohammed El-Bakkar and His Oriental Ensemble released seven LPs: *Port Said; Sultan of Bagdad; Music of the African Arab; The Dances of Port Said; The Magic Carpet; Exotic Music of the Belly Dancer; An Arabic Party with Mohammed El-Bakkar.*[28]

How these LPs were packaged and marketed tells us a great deal about representations of Arab music during the period. The music was linked directly to belly dancing, which in turn was associated with exotic female sexuality, not a dynamic art form. Indeed, the common American parlance for this music was "hoochie coochie"— a phrase derived from the French *couche* ("to lie down") that has become a catch-all for practically all exotic and erotic dance, from striptease to lap dance, burlesque to *danse du ventre.* The term was Orientalized in the late nineteenth century after a Syrian belly dancer billed as "Little Egypt" caused a sensation at the 1893 World's Fair in Chicago. Her movements were incorporated into striptease, spawning a generation of "Little Egypt" imposters in night clubs, cabarets, and circus sideshows across the country.[29] El-Bakkar's music covers a range of tempos and moods, revealing some virtuosic performances by the ensemble, and the lyrics (sung entirely in Arabic) are intentionally light and humorous. The kitschy album covers depict scantily clad or semi-nude women. On some, single women strike dance poses; on others, El-Bakkar himself, oud in hand, is surrounded by what is supposed to be his harem. A particularly disturbing image is from *Music of the African Arab,* in which a bare-breasted black woman decked out in harem garb jovially stands on an auction block as men bid for her. If the meaning of the image is not clear, the liner notes leave little to the imagination:

> Visions of voluptuous dancing girls whose lithe bodies twist and turn like writhing serpents about to strike . . . Gruff, unshaven men hungry for the touch of a woman after lonely weeks spent in the desert under a maddening sun . . . Secluded harems where the air is heavy with the aromas of perfume and incense and where luscious fruits are constant reminders of fertility . . . High, arched gateways framing bullet-pocked courtyards where beautiful virgins were once sold into slavery . . .
>
> These are visions of Arabian Africa. And no one today is able to capture these visions through sound with as much authenticity and excitement as Mohammed El-Bakkar . . .

Midway through these extensive notes, however, the tone shifts to a highly technical description of Middle Eastern music, describing instrumentation, polyphony, and structure, even comparing it to Indian raga. But by the end, the author reverts to essentialist assertions while trying to salvage some legitimacy, insisting that these recordings "cannot be described in so vulgar a fashion as 'hoochie-koochie' music (as so many Americans are apt to describe Middle Eastern music which they hear in movies), only because movies and other mass media of entertainment for most people have associated sin with the 'hoochie-koochie' concept. The Arab does not look upon evil and good the way people of the western world do."

On the one hand, the growing demand for Middle Eastern music meant more job opportunities for musicians, including Abdul-Malik, who had cultivated a relationship with the Arab music community in New York. In fact, by 1956 a number of prominent artists hired Abdul-Malik for concerts and recording sessions, including Mohammed El-Bakkar and another Lebanese oud player and vocalist, Djamal Aslan.[30] On the other hand, Abdul-Malik, like most of his fellow Muslims, was not happy with what he saw as the vulgarization, secularization, and sexualization of Arab music. He wasn't alone. In 1955, the Egyptian government passed a law requiring dancers to cover themselves from shoulders to ankles.[31] And within the Ahmadiyya movement, a sharp debate emerged over what was conceived as western sexual laxity and the exposure of women's bodies. Talib Dawud had given an impassioned speech at a 1958 convention where he proclaimed the "disease of the western world is sex" and criticized Muslim women who chose not to fully cover themselves.[32] Given the context, it is not unreasonable to suggest that Abdul-Malik's personal and creative struggle to restore dignity, purpose, and spirituality to music became ever more urgent.

Fortunately, the stars began to align in his favor. In 1956, the same year he began recording with Arab musicians, his jazz gigs increased significantly. Randy Weston's career took off and he hired his old friend for a couple of recording sessions and several club dates. The German piano phenomenon Jutta Hipp also used Abdul-Malik for what turned out to be her last recording session.[33] Then in the spring of 1957 he began working fairly regularly at the Five Spot Café, a small East Village establishment that was quickly becoming the center of New York's jazz universe. With greater visibility came greater opportunities—notably a five-month engagement with the celebrated Thelonious Monk quartet during the second half of 1957.[34] It proved to be an ideal situation, not only because it brought recognition and put him in contact with a true master of the music, but because it created occasions to pursue his own musical ambitions. For one thing, the group's saxophonist, John Coltrane, was sympathetic to Abdul-Malik's desire to apply Arab musical practices and scales (*maqāmāt*) to jazz improvisation. Indeed, it was Coltrane who encouraged Abdul-Malik to continue his formal studies of the oud. "If you really want to know what's going on," Coltrane chided, "you need to study the instrument."[35] They often spoke of possibly collaborating, and Coltrane's constant support over the next few years helped sustain Abdul-Malik, especially when critics dismissed him and gigs were hard to come by.

With encouragement from both Monk and Coltrane, Abdul-Malik formed his first Arab-jazz fusion group in the fall of 1957, consisting of the veteran Syrian-American violinist Naim Karakand, master kanoon player Jack Ghanaim (also spelled Ghanaem), and Mike Hemway (also spelled Hamway or Hamwa) on darbuka—a goblet-shaped hand drum with a thin, tightly stretched drum head. Rounding out the group was Abdul-Malik's Brooklyn buddy, Bilal Abdurahman, who alternated between the duf (a large tambourine without cymbals) and a variety of reed instruments. Abdul-Malik doubled on bass and oud. The group performed wherever they could, mainly cultural venues that did not serve alcohol. In October they played at an opening for artist Hideo Date at the Nonagon Art Gallery in the East Village, followed by gigs at Hassan's Coffee House, the New School for Social Research, and the Labor Temple on 14th Street. Their biggest coup was a guest appearance in April 1958 on the *Today Show* with Dave Garroway.[36]

With so few venues willing to hire the band, Abdurahman, his wife, Rahkiah, and Wali Mansur opened a small restaurant in Brooklyn, providing the group with a regular performance space. Launched officially on July 18, 1958, the African Quarter was situated on Fulton Street near Schenectady Avenue, just across the street from Fulton Park—Brooklyn's "Congo Square." Designated Brooklyn's first African restaurant, it served eclectic but tasty fare and a variety of nonalcoholic drinks. "The décor was North African," recalled Abdurahman. "We constructed low tables and seats, complete with a replica of a huge palm tree."[37] Patrons included African dignitaries, and Malcolm X dined there at least once. But most people crowded into the tiny African Quarter for the music. Abdul-Malik's group played there frequently throughout 1958, but never consistently because just prior to opening the African Quarter, he began another long engagement with Thelonious Monk at the Five Spot Café.

Abdul-Malik's second run with Monk generated even more opportunities. Monk and Randy Weston, both of whom had recorded with Riverside Records, helped persuade Riverside's owners and producers, Orrin Keepnews and Bill Grauer, to give Abdul-Malik a record date so he could finally put his ideas on vinyl. Keepnews had also gotten to know Abdul-Malik while producing live recording sessions of Monk's quartet at the Five Spot in July and August of 1958. It was during this same summer that Monk met and befriended Guy Warren, who introduced him to the possibilities of fusing jazz and West African rhythms. It is conceivable that Warren's influence may have made Monk a little more sympathetic to Abdul-Malik's experiments.

Jazz Sahara

Whatever the case, on an unknown date in October, Abdul-Malik's group—Naim Karakand (violin), Jack Ghanaim (kanoon), Mike Hemway (darbuka), and Bilal Abdurahman (duf)—filed into the lavish Reeves Studios in midtown Manhattan to make what would ultimately be the first Arab-jazz fusion LP, *Jazz Sahara*. He augmented the group with the jazz drummer Al Harewood and tenor saxophonist Johnny Griffin—his bandmate in Monk's quartet.[38] For the session, Abdul-Malik wrote four original compositions: "Ya Annas (Oh People)"; "Isma'a (Listen)"; "El Haris (Anxious)"; and "Farah' Alaiyna (Joy Upon Us)." All songs have a similar structure—a melody line played in unison by all instruments followed by individual improvisation over an ostinato figure that establishes the tonic and the rhythm. Each piece implies a relationship to a specific maqām or Arab mode, but the association is loose and the art of improvisation—what is known as *taqsim*—does not apply here. A maqām is a set of notes made up of two (or more) defined clusters of notes called *ajnas* (in the singular, *jins*) with rules that define its general melodic development. Although any analogies to Western music are inadequate, a maqām might be thought of as a modal system based on octave scales consisting of seventeen, nineteen, or twenty-four notes, but the rules determine where a song begins, when it modulates, and where it ends.[39] Typically, the soloist is bound by a particular melodic progression, beginning at the tonic in the lower end of the scale. Once the maqām is introduced, the soloist can go anywhere within it and even modulate to other maqāmāt, so long as there is always a return to the original.

Rhythmically, Mike Hemway and Bilal Abdurahman play fairly simple yet traditional folk patterns, such as the Egyptian *falaahii* rhythms and *wahda mukallafa*. In the Arab context, rhythmic patterns are called *iqa'at,* and each is fairly precise. Abdul-Malik probably decided to stick with simple, symmetrical patterns in ²⁄₄ time because they allow for easier transition to ⁴⁄₄ swing rhythms. But he and his sidemen steeped in Middle Eastern music knew that there were literally dozens of *iqa'at* with complex time signatures ranging from ⁹⁄₄, ¹³⁄₈, ²¹⁄₈, and ⁴⁸⁄₄. Time in the Arab context tends to be broken down into smaller subdivisions strung together. But Abdul-Malik's reluctance to incorporate more complex rhythms can be explained by the fact that he was not interested in strictly reproducing Arab music. Rather, he wanted to create a musical environment where jazz improvisation could coexist with Middle Eastern forms. Although he demanded precision in the articulation of the melody, he also encouraged the band to feel free to improvise however they wished. When I spoke to Johnny Griffin about the session, he insisted that

Abdul-Malik never gave instructions or even introduced the mode upon which he based his songs. "He never told me what to do. I just got up there and did what I felt belonged."[40]

On "Ya Annas (Oh People)," for example, the melody is built on a G Phrygian scale over a G minor chord, so it should be no surprise that Griffin is completely at ease with the song's harmonic foundations. In fact, for nearly the entire eleven-minute duration of the song, the group never strays from the mode, alternating between notes G and C. Following Jack Ghanaim's lively improvisation and the band's restatement of the melody, Griffin enters by quoting the popular blues riff "Night Train," followed by jazz licks that shift between a harmonic minor scale (the scale popularly identified with "Oriental" music), blues scale, and the Phrygian mode. About two-thirds into the song, the rhythm suddenly shifts from a traditional ¾ rhythm to 4/4 swing, with Harewood overtaking the other percussion with a hard-driving ride cymbal. Here Griffin takes a second solo, in the course of which he quotes Dizzy Gillespie's "Salt Peanuts." For his part, Abdul-Malik takes a brilliant solo on bass, plucking lines that feel more spoken than sung—much like a prayer.

"Isma'a (Listen)" bears a close resemblance to "Ya Annas," both in rhythm and melody. But this time Abdul-Malik plays oud rather than bass—the first evidence we have of him on the instrument. For someone largely self-taught, he shows an astounding competence on the oud, but it is clear that he is not fully comfortable with the instrument. He does, however, make a concerted effort to stay within the maqām and to play the quarter-tones. Again, Griffin hilariously quotes "Salt Peanuts" at the beginning of his solo. However, this time he does not fall back into too many familiar jazz licks and blue notes but tries to explore the mode he hears. He also uses intonation in an effort to reproduce quarter-tones Abdul-Malik and Karakand play on the oud and violin respectively. But on "El Haris (Anxious)" he makes no such effort to play within an Arab idiom, which may be the song's strength. In many respects, it provides a genuine example of fusion. Griffin takes the first solo, opening with a quote from "Surrey with a Fringe on Top" followed by a flurry of rapid bebop licks, all played over a plodding yet steady rhythm and single chord (again, the group simply plays a two-note phrase—G to C—underneath the soloist). Then about one-third of the way into the song, Abdul-Malik shifts to double-time and begins to play a walking bass line in a modern jazz style. The music now swings hard and fast, the way Griffin prefers to play. Perhaps this is why the tune is called "Anxious."

Overall, Abdul-Malik's first outing as a leader turned out well. Although the close similarity in structure, organization, tempo, and in some cases harmony makes the LP seem monotonous at times, Abdul-Malik made a fine debut as an oud player and a composer. More important, in an era when most jazz artists only turned to their imagination to infuse their music with shades of Africa or Asia, Abdul-Malik revealed more than a rudimentary knowledge of Arab music practices. But he also knew he still had a long way to go. His producer, Orrin Keepnews, considered the LP as a significant accomplishment, less for its attempt to fuse jazz and Middle Eastern music than for its pioneering employment of modal music. "In this chord-free music," Keepnews observed, "where a tune does not necessarily follow any rigid conventional pattern of construction in terms of a set number of bars or measures, there can be endless and limitless opportunity for advanced melodic improvisation. There can be room for vast newness within the unhampered framework of this 'old' music."[41] Keepnews perfectly captured Abdul-Malik's intentions: to liberate musicians from the constrictions of chord progressions, allowing more freedom for open-ended improvisation.[42] Several reviewers completely missed the album's advances and instead treated it as an exotic experiment well outside of the jazz idiom. *Billboard*'s reviewer implied that the cultural gap between "East" and "West" was so great as to hinder appreciation from jazz fans. "It 'swings' but the music is rather unappealing to Western ears."[43]

The release of *Jazz Sahara* and Abdul-Malik's nearly seven-month stay with Monk at the Five Spot helped him secure a few more gigs for his group, including a couple of one-night stands at the

Village Gate.[44] It also generated enough notoriety to convince RCA Victor, a bigger and more established label than Riverside, to record his next LP. Consequently, in March 1959, Abdul-Malik was back in the studio, this time with an expanded group made up of his original ensemble (with Ahmed Yetman replacing Ghanaim on kanoon), augmented by trumpeter Lee Morgan, tenor saxophonist Benny Golson, trombonist Curtis Fuller, and Jerome Richardson on flute. In other words, along with Johnny Griffin, Abdul-Malik put together an all-star horn section deeply immersed in the swinging styles of hard bop. This quite deliberate meeting of styles was aptly titled *East Meets West: The Musique of Ahmed Abdul-Malik*.[45] Abdul-Malik composed every tune, each bearing a phonetic approximation of the Arabic: "La Ibky (Don't Cry)"; "E-Lail (The Night)"; "Rooh (the Soul)"; "Mahawara (the Fugue)"; as well as a vocal number titled "Takseem," featuring the gorgeous voice of Jakarawan Nasseur.[46] He also revisited "Isma'a," delivering a shorter, up-tempo version with a more prominent jazz rhythm. Whereas drummer Al Harewood was absent on the *Jazz Sahara* version of "Isma'a," on *East Meets West*, his ride cymbal dominates the second half of the song, driving the dynamic solos by Benny Golson and Lee Morgan. Golson explores fairly abstract, angular lines while making a conscious effort to respect the maqām while Morgan brings his distinctive, soulful imprint, restating the song's theme and then slipping into quotes of "When the Saints Go Marching In." Perhaps inspired by the swifter tempos or the sound density created by the larger band, Abdul-Malik plays bass with more vigor than usual, like a man possessed.

"E-Lail (the Night)" is perhaps the band's most successful effort at fusing hard bop and Arab music. As with "Isma'a," Abdul-Malik incorporated the maqām Shadd Araban, writing an ostinato figure built on a G pedal point with D in the melody (a perfect fifth). Morgan essentially ignores the maqām, choosing to play a blues scale in G minor, which works beautifully with his distinctive phrasing. However, Abdul-Malik did not write every song with fusion in mind. He conceived "East Meets West" as an opportunity to introduce jazz audiences to Arab music, and listeners of Middle Eastern music to jazz. The introspective "Rooh (the Soul)" and head-nodding "Mahawara (the Fugue)" stay clearly within the conventions of Arab music. Abdul-Malik excluded the horns on these pieces and doubled on oud. "Searchin,'" on the other hand, is strictly modern jazz, providing a vehicle for the horns and flutist Jerome Richardson to stretch out comfortably in a jam session environment. The outlier on the LP is a song titled "El Ghada (the Jungle)," composed almost entirely of percussion—darabeka and drum kit. Here "East Meets West" came to symbolize a meeting of West African and "Eastern" rhythms— perhaps a nod to the increasing use of African drums in jazz spurred on by Warren, Blakey, and Olatunji.

East Meets West received very little notice, despite the jazz world's growing fascination with non-Western music—especially North African, Middle Eastern, and South Asian music. Abdul-Malik found few venues open to his brand of Islamic experimentalism, leaving him little choice but to take whatever gigs were available.[47] He spent a good part of 1960 working with Dixieland bands led by Leroy Parkins and Bob Wilber, backing old chestnuts such as "Wolverine Blues," "Careless Love," and "Struttin' With Some Barbeque."[48] Among musicians, especially innovative and curious jazz musicians, Abdul-Malik's knowledge of Middle Eastern music was renowned. John Coltrane, for example, asked him to sit in on oud, particularly on the song "India," during Coltrane's engagement at the Village Vanguard in November 1961.[49] And Abdul-Malik continued to work with Randy Weston, exploring African music and testing the limits of his instrument.

Indeed, his next LP, *The Music of Ahmed Abdul-Malik*, recorded for the New Jazz label (an outgrowth of Prestige) in May 1961, reveals Abdul-Malik pushing in new directions. While Middle Eastern music is still at the core of his work, he explores other dimensions of African and Afro-diasporic forms, and drifts in directions that are arguably on the fringes of "free jazz." For one thing, he chose to eliminate Arab musicians and instrumentation, employing instead Tommy

Turrentine on trumpet, tenor saxophonist Eric Dixon, Andrew Cyrille on drums, and cellist Calo Scott. Bilal Abdurahman was the only band member retained from his last recording session. Consequently, with the elimination of the kanoon, violin, and the additional Arab percussion, Abdul-Malik plays a lot more oud—displaying greater confidence as well as greater mastery over the instrument. One can hear a marked improvement on "La Ibky (Don't Cry)," the only song on the album that had been previously recorded. Abdul-Malik not only picks up the tempo considerably, but alters the rhythm. Andrew Cyrille is playing drums in ⁷⁄₄, Abdurahman plays darbuka in ⁴⁄₄ time, while the soloists alternate between ¾ and ⁴⁄₄.

The remaining compositions, however, do not attempt to fuse Arab music and jazz. "The Hustlers" and "Hannibal's Carnivals" represent Abdul-Malik's forays into fusing calypso and highlife music. "Hannibal's Carnivals," in particular, is unique in that it is built on a forty-bar AABCA structure rather than the standard thirty-two-bar AABA format. In many ways, it is a tribute to his old boss, Thelonious Monk, because the additional eight-bar section of the bridge (C or the second bridge, if you will) is taken directly from Monk's tune "Well, You Needn't." He also included the rather humorous "Oud Blues." Although critic Joe Goldberg describes the song in the liner notes as a "straight Western twelve-bar blues," it is much more than that. Abdul-Malik used the song as a vehicle to demonstrate just what the instrument can do by playing lots of semitones and trills, producing a timbral effect that can be startling to traditional jazz fans.

The star of the session, however, was "Nights on Saturn." Perhaps inspired by Sun Ra, the enigmatic bandleader who claimed the ringed planet as his birthplace, Abdul-Malik suggested to Joe Goldberg that the title and the concept for the song grew out of his "thoughts on the space age, and his ideas of how Orientals might think about outer space."[50] Musically, "Nights on Saturn" is remarkable for the ways in which it emancipated the soloists from harmonic and rhythmic constrictions, anticipating developments associated with the jazz avant-garde. And yet, neither the song nor the music of Abdul-Malik has found a place in narratives about the rise of "free jazz." It opens with Andrew Cyrille alone, setting the tempo in ⅝ time. He is joined by Abdul-Malik, who is playing a bass figure in ⁴⁄₄ time, in lieu of a traditional melody. A few bars later, we hear Abdurahman improvising brilliantly on his Korean peri. He sounds as if he is playing a ghaita—a high-pitched double reed instrument from Morocco—in that he deliberately bends notes and exploits the instrument's ability to create semitones. More important, he is not concerned with staying within a particular scale or tonal center; he is completely free to explore any pitch or scale. And Calo Scott, Tommy Turrentine, and Abdul-Malik follow suit, displaying a startling freedom from form and conventional harmony.

Touring the World

Before his latest LP was released, Abdul-Malik had caught the ear of another Brooklyn-born musician who not only shared his fondness for musics of the "East" but offered him an extraordinary opportunity to tour Latin America and Brazil with his band under the auspices of the U.S. State Department. His parents called him Herbert Solomon, but in the entertainment world the young Jewish kid reinvented himself as the talented saxophonist and flute player Herbie Mann.

Mann, who was four years younger than Abdul-Malik, had fallen in love with the rhythms of the African diaspora. Having worked with Machito and other pioneers of Latin jazz, as well as Art Blakey, he gravitated toward Afro-Cuban music, calypso, and neo-African rhythms.[51] In 1959, he formed the "Afro-Cuban Sextet," which quickly became an overnight sensation and one of the few modern jazz groups to cross over into the realm of popular music. Mann's approach to what he called "ethnic jazz" also caught the ear of the State Department, which selected his band to represent the United States on a fourteen-country tour of Africa in the early part of 1960.[52] Being only the third jazz artist to visit Africa sponsored by the State Department (Wilbur de Paris and Louis Armstrong preceded him), he must have sensed some resentment from black musicians who had been experimenting with African music and had a stake in making the trans-Atlantic voyage. And he surely came off as arrogant, portraying himself as a savior of traditional music in the face of modern African indifference. Before he set foot on the continent, he told the *New York Times* critic John S. Wilson, "I've heard that a professor at an African college has said that the youth of Africa want to forget about their culture, that the new music of Africa is jazz . . . So maybe they'll resent my music. On the other hand, I might be able to show them that their music is not something to be ashamed of."[53] Even a public affairs officer who accompanied Mann and his Afro-Cuban Sextet on the trip sensed his "cavalier, condescending attitude." Ironically, he reserved most of his condescension for the Sudanese, whom he described as "uncultured" and unsophisticated, preferring Dixieland to modern jazz.[54]

As one might expect, it was Mann who returned from Africa enlightened—not the other way around. He had become more cognizant of Africa's musical diversity and attempted to draw more directly from the conventions, styles, and practices he witnessed during his travels. He coupled his band more directly to Africa, changing the name from the "Afro-Cuban Sextet" to the "Afro-Jazz Sextet" very soon after his return.[55] And like everyone else on the jazz scene seeking to "Africanize" their music, he added at least one highlife song to his repertoire. He also hired Babatunde Olatunji as a regular member of the band. When they performed at the Newport Jazz Festival on July 2, 1960, Mann introduced a movement from his "African Suite" titled "Bedouin," a North African–influenced tune in 6/4 time featuring marimba, flute, and percussion. He also performed "Uhuru," a lively, percussion-heavy vamp in 12/8 time featuring the drumming and vocals of Olatunji, who sang about the imperative for freedom in ki-Swahili. In his introduction, Mann described the song as the "last movement of our 'Evolution of Jazz Suite'" and soberly noted that "Uhuru" is "what we heard shouted all over Africa. It means freedom."[56] Later in the year, he released *The Common Ground* for Atlantic Records, featuring Olatunji. Intended as a musical statement of his African experiences, the jacket photo shows Mann sitting under a thatched-roof dwelling teaching an African boy to play flute as his mother (or what appears to be his mother) stands in the foreground, with her back to the music but listening intently. The band recorded "Uhuru" (augmented by Maya Angelou and Dolores Parker on vocals), "Sawsa Sawsa De" (translates roughly as "OK, OK" in ki-Swahili), which sounds as if it was composed by Olatunji, and "High Life" alongside the title track, a vehicle for the percussion section. He also pays tribute to the Middle East with "Baghdad, Asia Minor," but after the first few bars the song shifts into a fairly standard Latin jazz tune.[57]

By the time Abdul-Malik received the invitation to join Mann's Latin American tour during the summer of 1961, *The Common Ground* had been released to critical praise, former Guy Warren sideman Chief Bey had been added to the ensemble, and Mann was being billed as "America's leading purveyor of African rhythmic elements in jazz."[58] Mann hired Abdul-Malik to play oud, not bass (although he did end up playing bass behind Coleman Hawkins and Roy Eldridge, who were also tapped for the tour). He wanted to include a stronger, more authentic North African and Middle Eastern element in his music. Mann had even incorporated "Isma'a" into his repertoire, featuring Abdul-Malik on oud. And fortunately, some of the band members—notably Curtis Fuller and Kenny Dorham—knew Abdul-Malik well or at least had played with him.[59] For Abdul-Malik, traveling and discovering other musical cultures had a far greater impact than performing. Despite the State Department's efforts to discourage interaction with local people, Abdul-Malik met a group of Muslim musicians in São Paulo, Brazil, who happened to be fluent in Arabic. He jammed with them and also found time to play with a modern samba group. He recalled fondly how the people were willing to share music, instruments, and records, essentially giving him a crash course in Afro-Brazilian music.[60]

He had barely settled back into Brooklyn before taking off again—this time to Africa. In mid-December, 1961, he accompanied his old friend Randy Weston on an eight-day trip to Nigeria sponsored by AMSAC. The visit to Nigeria proved even more influential than his travels to Brazil. Like Weston, he came back from his incredibly short stay in Lagos full of ideas and anxious to put them down on vinyl. The opportunity came in late August, 1962, when he recorded his second LP for New Jazz, *Sounds of Africa*.[61] With the possible exception of "Nadusilma," the compositions included here suggest that Abdul-Malik had moved even further away from his objective of creating a new Islamic music.

He hired a slightly larger and essentially different band for the date—the only holdovers being Calo Scott and Bilal Abdurahman. He hired Richard Williams on trumpet, Edwin Steede on alto, tenor saxophonist Taft Chandler, and Rupert Allyne on flute. He also expanded his rhythm section, replacing Andrew Cyrille with Rudy Collins and adding two Olatunji sidemen, Chief Bey and Montego Joe. African percussion became the ensemble's anchor, as is evident in the group's rendition of "Wakida Hena." Another highlife-meets-calypso, the song features Chandler and Steede—both of whom grew up with Abdul-Malik and had played in calypso bands before—and a brilliant "talking drum" solo by Chief Bey.

In some respects, the presence of Chief Bey and Montego Joe really distinguished *Sounds of Africa* from all of Abdul-Malik's previous recordings. On two songs in particular, "Communication" and "Suffering," the percussion is foregrounded. And while these examples may seem like vehicles for Bey and Joe to explore more traditional West African drumming, upon close inspection, we discover startling moments of innovation and experimentation. On "Communication," for example, we hear the fairly common two over three (or four over six) rhythms, as Richard Williams improvises over an ostinato pattern in C minor. But once we shift our attention to Abdul-Malik, we hear him exploring several different patterns in ⁶⁄₄ time, shifting occasionally into phrases that might be described as ²⁄₄, ⁴⁄₄, and ⁵⁄₄. Rather than create tension between Abdul-Malik and the percussionists, the shifting patterns and close listening between the men generate an uncanny connection, a deeper level of communication.

Abdul-Malik also tried his hand at creating a "pop" hit, perhaps with the urging of his record label. With Cannonball Adderley's 1961 release "Africa Waltz" getting radio play and slipping into the top 40 charts, the label wanted something catchy and danceable. They got it in the form of "African Bossa Nova," a jaunty little twelve-bar blues that not only worked as dance music but exploited the burgeoning bossa nova fad.

Despite the creative success of these last two albums, Ahmed Abdul-Malik, inspired by his travels to Brazil and Nigeria, still believed he had much to learn about "Eastern" music. He continued to advance on the oud and, upon the suggestion of John Coltrane, took up formal study of Indian music with Dr. Wasantha W. Singh, a renowned musician and music scholar. The music of India, Somalia, and Sudan became his primary preoccupation. He was especially attracted to these musical forms because they contain, in his words, "Japanese-like effects and something like the blues." He had grown critical of jazz musicians for being too close-minded about other music, warning that they would "cut themselves off from development by sticking to only chords or simple scales."[62] His warnings were prescient, if not a bit ironic. After all, at the very moment when the "free jazz" movement had taken off and a new jazz avant-garde was born, Abdul-Malik was encouraging fellow musicians to look to the ancient sounds of Africa, Asia, and the Middle East for the road to even greater freedom.

Sadly, his own path to greater freedom proved unsustainable. In 1963 and 1964, Abdul-Malik would make his last two albums as a leader. The first, titled *The Eastern Moods of Ahmed Abdul-Malik,* turned out to be his most experimental recording to date, and his most revelatory. Mainly out of economic necessity, he had pared down his regular group to a trio consisting of Bilal Abdurahman doing multiple duty on clarinet, alto saxophone, flute, peri, and percussion, and bassist William Henry Allen doubling on percussion. His explanation for the group's size also suggests that he had begun to grow weary of the jazz world and the music industry generally. As he explained in the liner notes, he chose Abdurahman and Allen because "they had open minds and were interested in what I was trying to do. Most musicians don't try to help one another."[63] Unlike his last two outings, he returns to his Middle Eastern and North African roots but seems less interested in his original fusion experiments. Of the five songs recorded that day, only two possess even a semblance of jazz or blues idioms—an animated, "Eastern"-influenced version of Gershwin's "Summertime," with Abdurahman soloing on every instrument at his disposal, and "Ancient Scene," an up-tempo, modal piece in 6/4 time. The remaining three compositions are influenced by North Africa, Indian ragas, and music from Somalia. "Shoof Habebe" was based on Somali sacred music, whereas "Magrebi" is a throwback to *Jazz Sahara*. It shares a similar pulse, the strong melodic statement at the beginning, and the use of the maqām as the basis for improvisation. But unlike his style in earlier recordings, Abdul-Malik's oud-playing on *The Eastern Moods of Ahmed Abdul-Malik* is far more inventive, displaying a greater range and control of the instrument. On "Sa-Ra-Ga' Ya-Hindi," a powerful piece inspired by Indian raga, Abdul-Malik uses the oud to evoke the sound of a sitar and sarod. As he explains in the LP's liner notes, he was never wedded to playing the oud in a traditional fashion. The oud, he states, "is a beautiful instrument. It doesn't have to sound like it does in Egyptian music, but like I feel it should sound in the musical contexts in which I'm using it."

Eastern Moods did not sell very well (and if Prestige had not picked it up, it might not have been released at all). Abdul-Malik was already showing signs of resignation and frustration with interpretations of his work. He had grown weary of critics and musicologists who did not think his music passed the litmus test of authenticity. "These people," he explained in the liner notes, "would say that I was playing things out of place, and that I couldn't discipline myself." He pushed back. "In playing my oriental things, I feel it is my job to know as much as I can about the feeling, language, customs and characteristics of the people, and then to interpret these musically, adding my own things—but always in such a way that I don't leave the other musicians hanging. I don't try to play the music before I know what I'm doing."[64]

Perhaps it is telling that for his next and final recording session as a leader he chose to limit the repertoire to jazz only. The resulting LP, *Spellbound,* would be Abdul-Malik's first completely jazz re-cording under his name. He selected some of the most respected art-ists in the business—violinist Ray Nance, saxophonist Seldon Powell, drummer Walter Perkins, pianist Paul Neves. But then he did some-thing extraordinary: he hired Sudanese oud master Hamza El Din, whom he met through Randy Weston. Rather than force jazz musi-cians to play the music of North Africa and the Middle East, or a variation of it, Abdul-Malik wanted to hear what would happen if a master musician from the Arab world were thrown into an entirely jazz context. They recorded three classic standards, "Body and Soul," "Never on Sunday," and "Song of Delilah," explored an original bal-lad ("Spellbound"), and jammed together on "Cinema Blues." For the most part, Hamza El Din is barely audible, and the band chose to play over him rather than with him. Indeed, when he takes a solo on "Song of Delilah," everyone drops out and he plays unaccompanied.[65] Still, it is a beautiful meeting of minds, and while the result is hardly revolutionary, it proved Abdul-Malik's point that the oud—or any world instrument, for that matter—can be adapted to the jazz con-text. He believed the inverse ought to be true, as well: that the instru-ments of jazz should be flexible enough to adapt to the world. But that would require a change of attitude, a greater openness and flexibility. He did not believe most jazz musicians had arrived at this point, and it broke his heart. It is perhaps telling that, years later, he would identify *Spellbound* as his favorite of all the sessions he led.[66]

A Joyful Noise for God

Ahmed Abdul-Malik certainly did not quit music. He continued to work when he could, playing occasional dates with Earl Fatha Hines, Lee Konitz, and Randy Weston, but gigs and recording sessions began to dry up from the mid-1960s through the 1970s. Instead, Abdul-Malik devoted himself to the pursuit of knowledge, community service, and spiritual uplift. He served as musical director of the Bedford-Stuyvesant Youth in Action, which served about five hundred poor, predominantly black kids. During his spare time, he took classes at New York University, earning his bachelor's degree in music education in 1969, followed by a master's degree eight years later.[67] He began teaching at NYU in 1970, and he served as an adjunct professor at Brooklyn College, but he never gave up playing. Indeed, he and Bilal Abdurahman continued to collaborate well into the early 1990s, even though Abdul-Malik had survived two strokes and suffered from diabetes. The performances were infrequent and largely limited to community centers, churches, universities, and cafes in Brooklyn or the Village.[68]

Abdul-Malik had not given up his studies of Arab music or the oud. He resumed his formal study of the oud with Simon Shaheen, perhaps the greatest living oud player in the world and one of the leading exponents of Arab music.[69] Shaheen recalled Abdul-Malik approaching him about lessons in 1986. He found Abdul-Malik's knowledge of Arab music rudimentary, at best. "We had to begin with the basics. He did not know the maqām system so I had to teach him." Abdul-Malik did share a copy of *East Meets West* with Shaheen, who saw it as yet another unremarkable example of an American musician interested in "Eastern" music for its spiritual qualities. He did not believe that any major jazz musician who incorporated this music had ever seriously studied it, including Abdul-Malik. It is likely that Abdul-Malik's stroke had adversely affected his memory by the time he met Shaheen, and given Shaheen's immense knowledge and expertise, his minimal expectations were quite high. Still, considering Abdul-Malik's lifelong study of this music, Shaheen's appraisal is surprising. However, Shaheen's recollections confirm Abdul-Malik as a deeply spiritual man, serious about the study of music. In spite of poor health, he made tremendous progress and began playing "seriously in the traditional context. He understood the maqām system and I even taught him specific repertoire. He was making progress until he had his [second] stroke." He persevered, returning to Shaheen's tutelage during the early part of 1993. Shaheen had even suggested he focus on the bass and explore playing it in an Arab context, and he invited Abdul-Malik to perform with him. But Abdul-Malik never fully recovered. Shaheen vividly recalled their last lesson together. "He did not look well. His eyes would wander as if he were asleep. He needed insulin, so I called the hospital and they sent an ambulance."[70] He died days later, on October 2, 1993.

Until his last moment of consciousness, Abdul-Malik tirelessly pursued his dream of understanding the music of his ancestors—real or imagined—and continuing their tradition of making a joyful noise for God. In the process he made astonishingly modern music using ancient materials, ushering in a new world on the wings of very old and established beliefs.

4 | The Making of Sathima Bea Benjamin

Jazz . . . is what liberates you. It is the most liberating music on the planet.
—Sathima Bea Benjamin, interview, *Jazz Weekly*

In the era of decolonization, when much of the black world saw Africa as the beacon of hope for the future of humanity, honoring and embracing African cultures underscored the continent's arrival on the world stage. For African Americans, especially, identification with Africa and the Third World transformed a minority struggling for basic civil rights to a world majority demanding human rights for all formerly colonized and oppressed people. The journeys of Guy Warren, Randy Weston, and Ahmed Abdul-Malik reveal that the elements of indigenous culture they celebrated were not always ancient and traditional but new and modern—highlife being perhaps the best example.

But as most of the continent celebrated political independence, in South Africa the white minority–ruled racial state tightened its grip. In 1948, the predominantly Afrikaner National Party came to power and immediately implemented legislation intended to weaken multiracial struggles for social democracy, labor rights, and racial equality. The apartheid laws, as they came to be known, further codified racial segregation and severely limited rights of nonwhites in South Africa. The laws prohibited marriage and sexual relations across the color line; classified the entire population by four "racial" categories of Bantu (Native), Asian, Coloured, and White; divided residential rural and urban areas strictly by race; segregated public accommodations; barred black workers from striking; and essentially outlawed every liberal antiracist organization under the guise of anticommunism. The Bantu Education Act (1953), passed a year before the U.S. Supreme Court declared "separate but equal" education unconstitutional, created a draconian, state-run education system based on the principle of separate and unequal. The apartheid state imposed a national curriculum for Africans allegedly suited to their status as a permanent cheap labor force. All these restrictions were enacted under the guise of preserving "traditional" cultures. Science and anything but the most remedial math were prohibited, and the social science curriculum promoted white supremacy and nonwhite inferiority. The act was just one example of the apartheid regime's twisted deployment of "traditional culture" as a weapon to subjugate Africans. There was no room for "Natives" in modern South Africa, except as maids, cooks, and laborers. In this severely segregated context, something modern and international, like jazz, was considered anathema by the apartheid state. To South Africa's black and "Coloured" population, however, modern jazz potentially embodied an inherent critique of apartheid's racial illogic. As mass opposition to the regime grew during the 1950s, jazz served as one of the prevailing soundtracks of struggle.

This social and political cauldron produced some of South Africa's greatest musical figures, notably Miriam Makeba, Hugh Masekela, Chris McGregor, Letta Mbulu, and Abdullah Ibrahim. And it was that same turmoil that caused them to flee their country. Whereas African American artists like Randy Weston sought freedom by traveling *to* Africa, generations of South African musicians sought freedom in escape, in exile. It often meant finding their distinctive voice in diaspora, one among the many dispersed communities of black folks whose very art (blues, jazz, calypso, and so on) had profoundly influenced the musical cultures of South Africa.

One of those exiles, singer and composer Sathima Bea Benjamin, is rarely mentioned in the pantheon of South African artists, despite a half-century in the music business and praise from none other than Duke Ellington. Nor has she earned full acceptance and recognition in the American jazz world. Some might glance at her career and chalk it up to bad luck. In 1959, Benjamin recorded what should have been the first LP in the history of South African jazz, but it was never

released. Four years later, Duke Ellington produced a historic recording session with her for Reprise Records, but the label decided she
wasn't commercial enough and shelved the record. It was finally released in 1997 as *A Morning in Paris.* The few critics who have paid
attention to Benjamin regard her as one of the great musical story-
tellers. She is known for delivering lyrics with the kind of patience
and emotion that leaves audiences hanging onto every word. As Jon
Pareles, a critic for the *New York Times,* wrote in 1983, "in song after
song, Miss Benjamin could make a word cry out with just a flicker of
vibrato."[1] And yet, from the time she left South Africa in 1962 until
quite recently, Benjamin has always had to scuffle for work.

Much like Guy Warren, Benjamin was not "African" enough to
be marketable, and too "African" or exotic to be taken seriously as a
great jazz vocalist. Once she complained, "People write books and
things about jazz singing and they don't include me. So what is the
reason? Sometimes I think it's because I don't come from Georgia."[2]
On the other hand, as a Coloured South African whose repertoire
excludes township music or traditional Xhosa songs, Benjamin has
been considered less authentic than, say, Miriam Makeba. Although
late in her career she began to sing standards over Cape Town's
unique shuffle rhythms, she fashioned herself as a jazz vocalist and
has remained squarely in the idiom. And yet, Benjamin is as much a
product of apartheid and the struggle to overthrow it as Makeba, and
she, too, has composed liberation songs, paeans to her homeland,
and worked tirelessly in support of the African National Congress (ANC). Benjamin and Makeba both became professional singers during apartheid's formative years, when jazz was hailed as a
music of freedom. Jazz in South Africa was an expression of the nation's defiant present and liberatory future—thoroughly modern, urban, sophisticated, and nonracial. Jazz stood in stark contrast to the
retrograde, segregationist ideology of the regime. But whereas many
of Benjamin's contemporaries and compatriots, including Makeba,
abandoned jazz for township music or indigenous folk songs, or attempted to fuse the genres in an effort to root their music in South

African soil, Benjamin never strayed from her devotion to modern jazz as "the most liberating music on the planet." Her singular commitment to jazz made her South Africa's leading jazz vocalist and one of the central figures linking U.S. and South African musical culture. Ironically, that same commitment ensured her marginalization, as beautiful romantic ballads and torch songs lost their relevance in a highly nationalistic era of urban militancy. And as a Coloured South African woman working in a genre too often construed as black-and-white, male, and essentially American, Sathima Bea Benjamin had to struggle just to be heard.

Nations in Me

Benjamin's world had always been cosmopolitan. Her family's roots extend across three oceans. She was born Beatrice Bertha ("Beattie") Benjamin in Johannesburg on October 17, 1936, and her father, Edward Benjamin, descended from the island of Saint Helena off the coast of South West Africa. His mother, Eva Thwaites, immigrated to Cape Town as a young girl and married Alfred Chambers Benjamin, another Saint Helenian who made the trek to South Africa to seek his fortune. The tiny island had been a crossroads linking Europe, Africa, and the Americas ever since the Portuguese landed there in 1502, embodying the extremes of freedom and unfreedom that have defined the Atlantic World. Saint Helena was a depot for slaves, a possession of the East India Company, a British Crown colony, and a destination for "Liberated Africans" after the British abolished the slave trade and sent its fleet out to enforce its decree. Saint Helena became the home for Chinese "coolie" labor, Afrikaner prisoners of the Boer War, and Napoleon Bonaparte, who lived his final years there as a British prisoner.[3]

Benjamin's mother, Evelyn Henry, traced her roots to the island of Mauritius, situated off the east coast of Africa in the Indian Ocean. Like Saint Helena, Mauritius was a British possession occupied by a cross-section of the world. The people spoke Mauritian Creole,

French, English, Rodriguan Creole, Swahili, and some Arabic. An island of immigrants hailing from Africa, India, China, the South Pacific, and Europe, together they created a distinctive Mauritian identity and culture. Evelyn Henry's mother, a Filipina native named Francesca de la Cruz, was one of those immigrants.[4]

Benjamin's parents grew up in Cape Town, but after they married and Evelyn was expecting, Edward relocated to Johannesburg to find work. Evelyn followed, enduring the long train ride to Johannesburg alone and seven months pregnant with Beattie. About a year later, Evelyn bore another daughter, Joan, but her marriage had already begun to unravel. Evelyn and Edward soon divorced, and the two girls lived for a while with their father and his new wife. When family members learned that Edward's wife beat the children severely, they were promptly sent to Cape Town to live with their paternal grandmother, Eva "Ma" Benjamin. Beattie was about five at the time. A strict disciplinarian and devout Anglican, Ma Benjamin was devoted to her two grandchildren. She was also devoted to her native land. Remembered as "very British in her ways, although she was quite African-looking," her strong identification as a Saint Helenian and British subject left an indelible impression on young Beattie.[5]

For Beattie, apartheid did not signal a dramatic shift from past policies. Even in Cape Town, renowned for its long tradition of liberalism, race-mixing, and cosmopolitanism, segregation was a way of life. "The English had apartheid you know," she explained. "In my mind, they put it already into practice. There weren't any signs. They weren't seen, but you knew your place . . . I only went to colored schools, only had colored friends. Everything was just with your own ethnic group. You couldn't really go over to visit even the Africans in their township. You couldn't do that. And you never went to the white side."[6] The racial realities, relative poverty, and deep sense of familial displacement left Beattie feeling isolated and a bit melancholy. "I was a lonely child, and along with my daydreaming, which I indulged in constantly, music was my only solace." Benjamin grew up listening to her grandmother hum some of the old British popular songs from operettas and early Tin Pan Alley musical theater. She told critic Francis Davis, "I was very attracted to the music of Victor Herbert, songs like 'Indian Summer' and 'Ah! Sweet Mystery of Life,' which I still perform. Musicians ask me, 'How do you know those songs? You weren't around in the 1920s.' And I tell them, 'No, but my grandmother was.'"[7]

Through her grandmother's old radio-phonograph she discovered Nat King Cole, Doris Day, Frank Sinatra, Sarah Vaughan, Ella Fitzgerald, and other American jazz and pop singers who influenced her early singing style.[8] Their impact proved decisive. Cole taught her the importance of diction and enunciation, Doris Day provided some of her early repertoire, and all of them introduced her to the endless possibilities of jazz phrasing—especially Vaughan and Sinatra. She also loved the immensely popular Joni James, particularly her rendition of "The Nearness of You." The Chicago-born daughter of Italian immigrants, James topped the pop charts at the age of twenty-two. Her voice was young, vulnerable, slightly melancholy, and like Benjamin, she was partial to slow ballads. They also shared a similar look—dark hair, dark eyes, and a pretty face exuding more virginal innocence than coquettish sexuality.[9]

Benjamin could not afford records, songbooks, or sheet music, so she kept a pencil and note pad hidden inside the phonograph in order to jot down lyrics. It wasn't easy since she was under constant surveillance. "My grandmother would say, 'What are you doing there? You have to get on with the ironing' or whatever. So it was all done in secret. And even I was singing in secret . . . I had no ambitions to be a great singer. I didn't think about it. But I found out that when I sang I forgot whatever pain, whatever traumas, I was dealing with. I went into another world."[10] The cinema was another source of escape, as well as a rich musical resource. On Saturdays, Ma Benjamin gave the girls a little money and dispatched them to one of the local "bioscopes" so that she could indulge in her only vice—playing the horses. Young moviegoers were treated to cartoons, an episode of Dick Tracy, and a double feature of American westerns and musicals.

Sponsors frequently held talent contests at intermission during the Saturday matinees. One afternoon, encouraged by her sister, eleven-year-old Beattie took the stage and sang "I Wonder Who's Kissing Her Now?" It was an interesting choice. An old pop song originally written for a 1909 musical, *The Prince of Tonight*, it had taken on a new life in 1947—the year Beattie turned eleven—when Twentieth Century Fox released the movie, *I Wonder Who's Kissing Her Now?* Perry Como's recording of the tune reached #16 on Billboard's pop charts.[11] The spectacle of a skinny eleven-year-old girl singing

> I Wonder who's looking in to her eyes?
> Breathing sighs! Telling lies!
> I wonder who's buying the wine?
> For lips that I used to call mine

caught the audience's attention. She walked away with the grand prize: eight movie tickets.[12]

Benjamin entered many more talent contests, unbeknownst to her grandmother, took some voice lessons in opera, and joined the school choir. Although she displayed impressive vocal skills, the choir director never assigned her a solo. "I asked him why," she later recounted, "and he said, 'Because you sweep. You slide up and down the note, instead of staying directly on it.' That meant nothing to me at the time, but, in retrospect, it shows that I was unconsciously trying to imitate the black American singers I heard on the radio."[13]

Yes, Brother, Anything American

Benjamin was not alone in her efforts to imitate black American singers. For over half a century, African American music has been perhaps the greatest single influence on popular culture outside of South Africa itself. Cape Town, the gateway to the Atlantic and Indian oceans, and a major port for U.S. and European imports, had long been an entrepôt for American culture. African American and

Afro–West Indian seamen passed through regularly, and some ultimately chose to make Cape Town their home.[14] The popularity of American minstrelsy inspired the Cape's own Coloured minstrel tradition, the Coon Carnival. New Orleans–style jazz and other forms of American popular music came by way of gramophone records and became popular in the Cape during the early 1920s. Queenstown in the Eastern Cape earned the nickname "Little Jazz Town" due to the proliferation of New Orleans–style bands active there. During the 1930s, with the onset of swing music, jazz-based dance ensembles became the rage. Most of these bands fashioned themselves in the image of the African American bands they heard on the radio, saw in "soundies" at the bioscopes, or read about in magazines. Challenged by these upstart swing bands, established Cape Coloured orchestras began incorporating jazz alongside traditional folk forms (*vastrap* and *ghoema*) and standard ballroom fare of foxtrots, waltzes, and square dances. By the 1950s, many of the Coloured bands moved closer to modern jazz, exchanging guitars, violins, and banjos for saxophones and brass.[15]

For much of this period, however, jazz's center of gravity was in Sophiatown, an African suburb of Johannesburg. Nicknamed "Little Harlem" and South Africa's Chicago by its patrons, Sophiatown was overrun with popular bands such as the Harlem Swingsters, the Jazz Maniacs, the Merry Blackbirds, the Rhythm Clouds, the Pitch Black Follies, and the African Hellenics. They performed at nightclubs and dance halls, fronted female vocalists like Dolly Rathebe, Dorothy Masuku, Thandi Klaasen, Miriam Makeba and the Skylarks—all of whom became huge stars in South Africa. The bands' musical and sartorial style mirrored African Americans portrayed in films such as *Stormy Weather* and *Cabin in the Sky*.[16] Sophiatown boasted a vibrant black intelligentsia, but it was primarily a working-class community whose social and economic conditions deteriorated under apartheid, especially as pass laws limited mobility and the municipality increased transportation fares—all on the eve of the state's planned destruction of the township under the Western Areas Resettlement

Act of 1953. The Resettlement Act required that all residents relocate to the newly created Southwest Townships (Soweto), and there they were to be divided by language group.[17] Sophiatown's destruction, in addition to new regulations forbidding Africans from playing or patronizing venues where liquor was served, killed the big bands. Even established small bands had a hard time finding adequate rehearsal space and played very few gigs. (Some of the musicians complained of having to rehearse in local classrooms, tram sheds, dilapidated abandoned buildings, and bathroom stalls!)[18]

The fantastical world of popular culture and the political realities projected two very different images of South Africa. On the one hand, the dance halls, nightclubs, and traveling variety shows displayed the glamour and brilliance of a thriving music scene.[19] On the other hand, the country was in a state of war—a war that preceded the National Party's rule in 1948. Indeed, apartheid should be understood as a response to heightened opposition, especially during the mid-1940s, when the ANC Youth League pushed its parent organization to support mass uprisings against consumer and transportation racism. In the face of greater repression and deteriorating economic conditions under the National Party, the ANC launched the Defiance Campaign in 1952—a nationwide series of strikes, "stay-at-homes," pass burnings, and mass demonstrations. Though unable to roll back apartheid laws, the ANC's membership grew from 7,000 to 100,000 in 1952.

Both images of South Africa came together in the pages of a new magazine called *Drum,* launched in 1951. A white-owned monthly pitched to African and Coloured readers, *Drum*'s largely black editorial staff turned a pictorial styled after *National Geographic* into a powerful voice of South African modernity. They understood their audience. As one prospective reader demanded: "Give us jazz and film stars, man! We want Duke, Satchmo and hot dames. Yes, brother, anything American."[20] And they delivered, celebrating urban style, American cinema, and jazz. *Drum*'s main music writer, pianist and composer Todd Matshikiza, fashioned a jazz-inflected writing style so distinctive it came to be known as "Matshikese."[21] His regular column, "Music for Moderns," acknowledged American influences but encouraged South African musicians to pay attention to their own indigenous urban music. He argued relentlessly that the fusion of jazz and township music was the path to creating "the African form of expression. The African idiom."[22] Just as highlife captured the imagination of urban West Africans, township music—namely kwela (or pennywhistle jive) and mbhaqanga—competed with jazz in the realm of popular music. Both forms derived from marabi, an urban dance music that originated in the 1920s. Like jazz, it was played in the shebeens—local drinking holes where home-brewed beer was served.[23] Mbhaqanga combined marabi chord progressions, indigenous melodies, and jazz improvisation. The word itself is Zulu for a kind of steamed bread made from maize. Musicians referred to it as both a source of "daily bread" and something homemade. Ironically, because the South African Broadcasting Corporation—state-run radio—promoted mbhaqanga heavily in the 1950s through a regular feature called "This Is Bantu Jazz," political activists and even some musicians dismissed it as *msakazo,* or "broadcast," and associated it with state repression and the policy of "develop along your own lines."[24]

Given the intense debates raging over jazz, township music, and the pros and cons of American cultural influence, it is telling that Benjamin never credits South African singers with having influenced her. After all, African vocalists were in great demand in the early 1950s. This was the golden age, when the Skylarks, the Manhattan Brothers, and the African Mills Brothers reigned supreme, when former nightclub singers such as Miriam Makeba, Dolly Rathebe, and Dorothy Masuka not only transformed township ditties into popular protest songs but symbolized a new, urban, female sexuality. Glamorous photos and profiles of these women dominated the pages of *Drum,* propelling them to national stardom. But Benjamin had no desire to play sex kitten, and township music was not her cup of tea. So she shunned cheesecake photos and stayed committed to jazz, singing standards and old American and English ballads, often at slow tempos—creative choices that contributed to her marginalization.

In 1952, Benjamin enrolled in a two-year program at the Cape Town Teachers' Training College. Her desire to sing still burned within her, but she chose the practical path of becoming a schoolteacher. But during her two-year enrollment, she continued to sing in talent shows and, most important, fell in love with a fellow student named Sam Isaacs. He was a bona-fide jazz musician, a drummer about eight years older who was pursuing a graduate degree in music. "That was my first love," she reminisced. "And then he found out that I could sing." He had a regular trio gig at a whites-only skating rink on Tuesdays and Wednesdays, and Benjamin used to prop herself up on a box and listen to them through a window. "Their sound was George Shearing, the George Shearing sound; so I think that was where I started to get leanings."[25] Isaacs introduced her to more recording artists and a wider range of jazz styles, but their relationship ended by the time she graduated.

Benjamin began teaching right away, but she and her sister, Joan, also made the fateful decision to leave their grandmother and move in with their mother, Eva. After years of searching, she had found her mother living in Cape Town, remarried, and raising several younger children. The move proved traumatic at first. "It was so hard to leave my grandmother. And she couldn't understand why, after all she did for us. But you know what, your mother is your mother. And I wanted to know her." It turned out to be a blessing in disguise. Unlike her grandmother, Eva encouraged her daughter's musical ambitions. She had an upright piano in her house and, to Benjamin's surprise, she played a little ragtime—mostly old American songs like "Chicago" and "Up the Lazy River," and only in the key of C or F. "I was just amazed. Then I realized, okay it was the diamond rush and the Americans went there and wherever they go they take their culture. And she, as a young girl, was a domestic and she worked in their houses and she heard and she played by ear. A lot of wrong notes but she played by ear."[26] Evelyn earned most of her income as a dress-maker and occasionally took domestic work, but every so often she was "asked to play in the local hotels and rent parties."[27]

From about 1955 to 1957, Beattie Benjamin lived something of a double life. She spent her weekdays teaching elementary students in Athlone, Cape Town, where she was the consummate educator—organized, informed, diligent, and readily accessible. But come Friday night, she and Joan hit the nightclubs—the Naaz, Mermaid, Zambezi, the Catacombs, or on occasion Weizmann Hall in Sea Point.[28] Coloured musicians performing at the smaller venues would invite her to sing. Since she couldn't read music, they helped her determine key, taught her the importance of tempo, expanded her repertoire, and offered general advice about ways to improve her performance. The "lessons" often lasted into the wee hours of the morning. "I call it my night school," she mused, "because I learned all the standards . . . Sometimes they'd give me records. After singing with them we did not know how to get home to our area because we had no transport so we'd have to hang with these guys until one of them who had a car would say we're ready to take you home. Then we'd go to one of their houses in the early hours of the morning and they would play Charlie Parker, Stan Getz, Ellington . . . and you know, they'd play jazz. And I got to hear these things."[29]

Her music education took a formal turn when guitarist Kenny Jephtah introduced her to pianist Henry February. Ten years her senior, February was a native of Cape Town and one of the most respected jazz musicians in the city. His father, a prominent church organist, encouraged his son to take up piano, but Henry remained a reluctant student until high school—about the time he discovered Teddy Wilson and Nat King Cole. While admiring Benjamin's talents, he recognized she had work to do and was a strict and demanding taskmaster. Every week she left with a stack of new music to learn, new artists to check out, and a swirl of ideas about melody, rhythm, accent, and sound.[30] She was good enough to join Kenny Jephtah's band, a drumless trio modeled after Nat King Cole's group, with

Jephtah on guitar, February on piano, and Johnny du Toit on bass. February's idea was to write arrangements akin to Cole's but with a female vocalist.[31] They performed fairly regularly on Saturday afternoons at the Holy Cross Hall in District Six, often accompanied by saxophonist Jimmy Adams.[32]

Like so many South African schoolteachers of her generation, Benjamin was a young intellectual living through a period of intense political turmoil. She spent her free evenings in the local public library, where the talented pianist and drummer Vincent Kolbe was head librarian. She immersed herself in African American history and literature, devouring works by noted authors such as Richard Wright, W. E. B. Du Bois, and Langston Hughes, not to mention Billie Holiday's memoir, *Lady Sings the Blues*, just before the government banned it. "There wasn't such a strong ban on U.S. literature then," she remembered, "so I was able to read a good deal about black Americans, and I felt a bond with them, with their longing to be free."[33] She also participated in the library's "bohemian" culture, which included membership in the Jazz Appreciation Club, a small listening and discussion group organized by Kolbe.[34] Many of these young educators were active in the Teachers' League of South Africa (TLSA), a Cape-based organization dedicated to the overthrow of apartheid. Founded in 1913 initially to protect Coloured interests, the TLSA had been radicalized by wartime militancy, the Defiance Campaign, and the regime's racist assault on education.[35] Although Benjamin was not an active member, as both a high school student and as a teacher she admired their work. And like most of her colleagues, she understood all too well that the Bantu Education Act (1953) was just the first salvo in the regime's racial overhaul of the school system. A few years later, the legislature passed the Coloured Persons Education Act, further separating white and Coloured education and forcing Coloured schools to register with the government.

Her burgeoning political consciousness sprang not just from books and conversations, but out of her daily battles with discrimination and oppression. "I sang in the nightclubs in the white areas, where black and so-called 'colored' entertainers were allowed to perform but were not allowed to mix with the customers. We had to sit in the kitchen during intermissions, just as black musicians were having to do in the American South." Consequently, she began to question the utility of a "Coloured" identity, noting how it obscured the brutal realities of white supremacy by creating a mythic racial hierarchy among nonwhites. Benjamin recognized how the classification divided "Coloureds" from "blacks," though neither group could escape the indignities of apartheid. "Black is not a color, it's an experience. And in South Africa, there are only two possible experiences. I was never privileged to know what the white one was. That makes me black."[36]

In 1957, just when she felt she needed to get away from Cape Town and take a break from teaching, Arthur Klugman hired her to join his new traveling show, Colored Jazz and Variety. Saxophonist Jimmy Adams was also part of the entourage. A Coloured follow-up to the African Jazz and Variety show, the troupe of dancers, musicians, acrobats, and comedians traveled all over southern Africa, performing before half-sold auditoriums filled with indifferent and even hostile audiences. Benjamin usually held the room with popular tunes like "Over the Rainbow" and "Mr. Wonderful," but she had never encountered such tough crowds or such terrible working conditions. "That was my first on-the-road for the music. I can't begin to explain; that was horrendous. We drank sugar water and ate dry bread to survive most of the time."[37] Although Benjamin gained valuable experience, the entire production was a commercial failure. Klugman abandoned the show in Rhodesia, leaving the entire band stranded—no money, no transportation, no work. The immigration authorities put them on a train and dropped the group just across the South African border. In order to raise the fare needed to get to Johannesburg, Jimmy Adams organized a dance. "There was no electricity," he remembered. "It was just me, my bassist, and we had a banjo."[38]

Safely in Johannesburg, Benjamin and Adams were befriended by the alto saxophonist Kippie Moeketsi and a baby-faced trumpeter named Hugh Masekela—two key figures who, along with Benjamin's future husband, were on the verge of revolutionizing modern jazz in South Africa. "Kippie," born Jeremiah Moeketsi, was only nine years older than Benjamin but was already considered a living legend. A formidable voice on clarinet and saxophone, he performed with several leading Sophiatown bands, including Todd Matshikiza's celebrated Harlem Swingsters. After the Swingsters broke up, Moeketsi joined the Shantytown Sextet, a band led by tenor saxophonist Mackay Davashe that backed the popular vocal group the Manhattan Brothers and the young singer Miriam Makeba.[39] Moeketsi was still working with the Shantytown Sextet when Benjamin and Adams arrived in Johannesburg, and Masekela was the newest (and youngest) addition to the band. Masekela had already achieved some fame as a member of the Huddleston Jazz Band, an ensemble named for Father Trevor Huddleston, a former headmaster of St. Peter's Secondary School (which Hugh attended). Father Huddleston was an outspoken critic of apartheid who refused to cooperate with the Bantu Education Act. He was also responsible for providing Masekela with his first trumpet and encouraging his music career. Masekela became a remarkable soloist partial to fat tones and singing melodic lines, his influences ranging from African American trumpeter Clifford Brown to South Africa's own Elijah Nkwanyana.[40]

Kippie's generosity toward Benjamin and Adams belied his reputation for being notoriously difficult and moody. But his favors weren't always doled out evenly. Kippie gave each of them a pound every day so they could eat, but he invited only Adams to rehearse with his big band. Impressed with his playing, Kippie offered to take Adams to Lourenço Marques (Maputo), Mozambique, to play a Christmas engagement. At first, Kippie wasn't interested in bringing Benjamin. Adams stepped up and lobbied on her behalf. "What about Beattie? She is a vocalist, I can't leave her here!" The band's pianist had limited skills, so Adams sat at the piano and accompanied her for an impromptu audition. Kippie hired her immediately. Before they could leave, however, they had to solve one problem. "Beattie had a dress on that she made herself. And I borrowed my clothes from somebody. We didn't have clothes, we didn't have money. And I said to Kippie, please lend us some money so we can buy clothes and I will pay you back after the shows." With the money Kippie advanced, they were both able to buy decent outfits, and the gig generated enough income for Adams to pay back the advance and purchase train tickets to Cape Town.[41]

I Got It Bad

Benjamin returned home in 1958 weary, a little wiser, and more committed than ever to modern jazz. She had seen the dark side of highly commercialized entertainment and realized how easy it was to lose the essential artistry of music in the hustle to make a profit. She settled back into her old life of teaching during the week and singing on the weekends, but this time she achieved a little recognition. Write-ups about her began to appear in the local papers. More and more bands and local variety shows wanted to hire her. The attention became too much for the headmaster of her school, who demanded that she choose between her singing career and her teaching job. She chose to sing.

Her decision was hardly a fait accompli. On the contrary, she came very close to leaving music, and for reasons having to do with gender. Being a woman in the masculine realm of jazz and popular music meant navigating a stifling, condescending, sexually dangerous, exploitative world dominated by men. On the road with Klugman, she was vulnerable and often had to depend on men (such as Adams) to protect her or even vouch for her musicianship. And unlike her male counterparts, she was expected to exude sex appeal on stage. Although she earned fellow musicians' respect the legitimate way—through her voice, imagination, and hard work—the late-night listening sessions left her vulnerable to sexual advances, especially

since she had to rely on others for transportation. Her growing reputation as an outstanding singer was no deterrent to the propositions,
which seemed to increase over time. At one point she temporarily
quit music. "I got disgusted and I said I'm not doing this because all
the guys just want to sleep with me in the end. I don't want to sleep
with anyone. So I gave up . . . And I would get blue and recover and
then get blue again. All of it just made me want to say goodbye to
this."[42]

She was just about to call it quits when she met a Swiss expatri-
ate named Paul Meyer. In 1958, Meyer had launched "Just Jazz," a
concert series at the Cape Town City Hall to benefit mentally ill
people living in backyards, or what was known derisively as the
"snake pits."[43] A graphic artist by trade, Meyer loved jazz and was
reputed to have one of the largest record collections in South Africa,
though he limited his acquisitions to black artists only. The same
could be said about the women he dated. A diminutive man with
blond hair, blue eyes, and "a film star's looks," his proclivity for black
women was second only to his love of jazz. According to one of his
acquaintances, he fled Johannesburg for Cape Town "when his romantic relationships across racial lines attracted unwelcome police
attention."[44]

Meyer approached Benjamin and told her he loved her voice
because she sang like Billie Holiday. This intrigued her, as she had
not yet read *Lady Sings the Blues* and only possessed a passing knowledge of Holiday's recordings. Meyer, in turn, invited her to his place
to listen to some of Holiday's music. "He had a red sport car and he
came into this colored area with his sport car and he would come
and pick me up and take me into the white area. And me in all my
innocence, thinking this is just a nice guy; besides I want to hear
these records." He would bring her to his house in the coastal suburb
of Camps Bay and play records by Billie Holiday, Bessie Smith, and a
host of black female vocalists she had not heard. "I went there once
or twice and everything was cool. I had never drank alcohol, I had
never smoked cigarettes. I was just so puritan it was unbelievable. So

everything was fine; he was so nice and he played me these things and it was mind-boggling to hear all of this."[45]

Meyer also wanted to introduce Benjamin to a friend of his, a pianist by the name of Dollar Brand—later known as Abdullah Ibrahim.[46] The prospect of meeting Ibrahim didn't impress her, however. "I heard that he was a rebel and that nobody liked him and his music was different and all that sort of thing."[47] Then one night, during one of her visits to Meyer's place, he started making sexual advances toward her. When she politely demurred, he became more aggressive. "I kept saying, 'You just have to take me home. I don't want to come here any more.' And I'm realizing, who am I going to complain to? I'm in the wrong area. I can't call cops—not that I would have had to, but he was being very aggressive. He was just a little guy, but he was saying, 'Come on, come on, I slept with Miriam Makeba!'"[48]

Just as she was preparing to fight her way out of it, there was a knock on the front door and in walked a very tall, lanky, serious-looking, brown-skinned man in miners' boots. It was Ibrahim. There was no time for introductions. "I just said, please would you help me? Would you get in the car with me and have this guy take me back?"[49] Meyer took her home, and she did not think she would see Meyer or Ibrahim again. But a few weeks later, Meyer begged her to sing in his next concert, "Just Jazz Meets Ballet," to be held in January 1959. She would be a featured artist, and he had already arranged for a pianist to accompany her. "I said, 'listen here, I'm not singing anymore,'" but she eventually relented. When she arrived for rehearsal, she saw the man who saved her from Meyer's clutches sitting at the piano. She introduced herself, again, and he asked,

"So, now, what are you doing?"

"I'm a singer and I'm working with Ellington's music," she replied.

"You are?" He was shocked. He loved Duke and few, if any, vocalists with whom he had worked knew his music.

"What song?" he asked.

"I'm working on 'I Got It Bad.'"

"What key?"

"The key of D." He paused for a moment, and then told her, "That will take some work. I mean, I just can't go into that song. I'm also working with Ellington but that's a very difficult key."[50] Not to be discouraged, Benjamin invited him over to her mother's house to work on the song since she had a decent piano. After a couple of rehearsals, they got it together in the key of D, and "I Got It Bad" was a smashing success. The *Golden City Post* waxed enthusiastic over her appearance, declaring Benjamin "Most promising singer for 1959."[51] Ibrahim, for his part, was selected "South Africa's best pianist" as a result of their performance.[52] Benjamin left "Just Jazz Meets Ballet" with more than a good review. "I was totally in love. I never met anyone like that. He just took over my life. Very strong, very different. I had leanings toward [his music] because I was sick of everything else. And I threw caution to the wind. Gave up my teaching job. Just went on the road with him."[53]

Different, indeed. Some musicians revered Ibrahim like a god, others avoided him like the plague. The critic Mike Phahlane, who described him as "the unpredictable mystery man of modern jazz," remembered the early days when club owners fired him regularly for playing music the patrons did not understand.[54] He rarely left home without his signature miners' boots, a satchel of sheet music, and a dog-eared copy of Shakespeare's *Julius Caesar*, from which he quoted passages at every opportunity. Gigs were few and far between, so he applied for a position as a clerk at the post office. Even though he had studied two years at Cape Town University, they hired him to sweep the floor. One writer described him as "the most persecuted man in Cape Town."[55]

Ibrahim was no stranger to poverty. Just two years older than Benjamin, Adolf Johannes Brand was raised in Kensington, a West Side slum in Cape Town, by his Basotho father and Khoisan (so-called Bushman) mother. His parents scraped by, setting aside enough money to pay for piano lessons. Besides the standard classical repertoire, he learned hymns and old "Negro" spirituals from his grandmother, an organist and founding member of the local African Methodist Episcopal Church. Like any kid running around the working-class neighborhoods of District Six, he absorbed local dance music. By some accounts, he discovered jazz by way of a 78 disc of Duke Ellington's recording of Billy Strayhorn's "Take the A Train." Duke became his obsession: he played "A Train" constantly on his grandmother's upright piano, and when "other kids were playing football or something, he would be listening to Duke Ellington records at the nearest record dealer's shop."[56] According to other accounts, he attributed his love of jazz to an ice cream truck that used to pass through the neighborhood blasting saxophonist Louis Jordan, the Honeydrippers, and Tiny Bradshaw through its loudspeakers. He began playing with a vocal group called the Streamline Brothers and even performed with local pennywhistle bands. But what sealed his fate as a musician was hearing Charlie Parker and Dizzy Gillespie on the radio. He earned the nickname "Dollar" because whatever little money he had was spent at a local music shop on American jazz records and stock arrangements by the likes of Tommy Dorsey, Glenn Miller, Artie Shaw, and, especially, Duke Ellington.[57]

Still, Ibrahim was not one of those musicians obsessed with the United States. "The American jazz I heard on the radio and on records," he explained, "was only an extension of the music I was already playing." It was never "simply American music—it was Ellington!" He considered Ellington more "the wise old man of the village" than the *American* jazz artist.[58] In other words, jazz was at its heart African music, and the story of South African jazz was not a matter of American influence but one of "parallel developments. There is a hardcore, basic musical literature that is common to both countries. Africa is the fountainhead."[59]

Ibrahim was only seventeen when he went on the road with the Streamline Brothers. After two years in Johannesburg, in 1953 he moved back to Cape Town, where he played with a few different groups and took small pick-up gigs, including one with Kippie Moeketsi.[60] Moeketsi was so impressed with the young pianist that when Todd Matshikiza left the Shantytown Sextet in the summer of 1958 to compose the music for the African jazz opera *King Kong,* he—along with saxophonist Christopher "Columbus" Ngcukane— insisted that Ibrahim take over piano duties.[61] On the road with the sextet, Moeketsi and Ibrahim were inseparable. Ibrahim shared Moeketsi's fascination with Charlie Parker and bebop, and his dream to "modernise African music."[62] "It was just [him] and a couple of other guys," recalled Ibrahim, "who were really interested in the modern sound. As it was, it was tragically hard to get work playing jazz. We'd play crazy things that would chase the other musicians away."[63] One of those "other guys" that stuck around was Hugh Masekela. The young trumpeter practically sat at Moeketsi's and Ibrahim's feet, absorbing all he could about modern jazz: "They would teach me the complicated chord structures for the latest Thelonious Monk and Charlie Parker compositions and songs from the limitless book of Duke Ellington, Abdullah's favorite . . . If I didn't make any money, at least I received a musical education I could never have afforded from these two musical geniuses during our fateful summer tour."[64] The three men vowed to form a group of their own at some point in the near future.

Masekela wasn't the only "student" on the tour. Ibrahim credits Moeketsi with introducing him to the music of Thelonious Monk. The effect was life-changing. "Kippie would talk to me about Monk before I'd heard of any of his records. I was saying: 'Monk? What's this Monk thing?' And then, man I heard the music and I said 'aaaaaah! I can dig this . . . so this is Monk!' Kippie would be scream-ing about how Monk was playing the same type of sound you could hear in so-called tribal music up in the Northern Transvaal."[65] Ibra-him returned from the tour playing as if he had been possessed by Monk's sound and spirit. Even Cape Town's young modernists had trouble hearing what he was trying to do. Bassist Sammy Maritz re-members that the effect of Monk's music on Ibrahim was decisive: "So much so, that when he played, nobody understood it."[66]

Benjamin understood it. She gravitated immediately to Ibrahim's modern sound, his chord voicings, and his phrasing—elements they both heard in Ellington's piano playing. A few weeks after their debut performance, with the encouragement of Paul Meyer, she decided to make a record. She asked Ibrahim to accompany her, put together a trio, and produce the date. She wasn't interested in recording a couple of sides for a 78; she had enough material for an LP, and she thought she could benefit from the momentum generated by her "Just Jazz Meets Ballet" performance. Ibrahim readily agreed, secured a studio in Cape Town, and hired bassist Joe Colussi and Donald Stegmann on drums. On August 11, 1959, the group laid down eight complete tracks, all standards ("Bewitched," "Fine and Dandy," "But Not for Me," "I'll Take Romance," "Almost Like Being in Love," "It Could Happen to You," "My Funny Valentine" [two takes]) except for a redux of Ellington's "I Got It Bad." The LP was to be titled *My Songs for You,* and had it been released, it would have been the first jazz LP in South African history. Paul Meyer had even employed his graphic design skills to mock up the jacket, but it was not to be. Besides the predictable problem of finding a distributor amid rising racial tensions and state repression, the session just wasn't up to par. "I thought, this is so awful," Benjamin concluded. "The bass player is playing wrong notes!"[67]

If Benjamin had had a stronger rhythm section and *My Songs for You* had been released, her life might have been very different. She may have gotten some radio play, opportunities to tour South Africa, a substantial write-up in *Drum* or *Zonk!* or some of the other popular arts and culture magazines, and offers to make more recordings. She may have even fronted her own band with Ibrahim backing her—though Abdullah had his own plans, and they did not include backing up a vocalist, even one he loved madly. Instead, Benjamin slid back into obscurity and slipped into a powerful musical partnership in which her partner was the dominant figure. Together they organized a Sunday night jazz series at the Ambassadors School of Dancing in the Cape Town suburb of Woodstock. The owner, Dave Saunders, gave Benjamin and Ibrahim the run of the place, and they opened it up to jazz musicians of all persuasions and people of all races. They served no food or drink, and, ironically, no one danced, yet the people came in droves—Africans, Coloureds, Indians, and whites. "Nobody made any money," Benjamin recalled, "but it was a center of expression, and it was beautiful."[68] The state did not think it was so beautiful. Although the Sunday night jazz programs continued for many months, they were ultimately banned for violating apartheid laws.

Many different musicians played at the Ambassadors, but the main attraction was the Dollar Brand Trio. No one had heard a band like this in Cape Town. They played exceedingly difficult pieces by Ellington, Monk, and Bird, as well as Ibrahim's original compositions, and as a rhythm section their synchronicity bordered on telepathic. On bass, Ibrahim hired the extraordinary Johnny Gertze, a multi-instrumentalist equally proficient on guitar, clarinet, trumpet, drums, and piano.[69] Ibrahim's drummer was Makaya Ntshoko, a professional boxer turned musician who had learned his instrument under the tutelage of the legendary Phaks Joya.[70] Benjamin occasionally sang with the band, but her appearances were infrequent. Although audiences appreciated her slow, languid ballads, most of the young jazz aficionados piled into the Ambassadors to hear the Dollar Brand Trio and those sitting in, the horn players who took off on uptempo bebop numbers.

As Ibrahim's reputation grew, he was summoned to Johannesburg in October to play a concert with Moeketsi, Masekela, and Masekela's cousin—a phenomenal trombone player named Jonas Gwangwa who had been part of the original Huddleston Band. Their reputation was also rising. The trio of horn players had recently returned from an eight-month tour of the country providing music for the critically acclaimed *King Kong*.[71] After the tour ended, Mocketsi, Masekela, and Gwangwa made history by cutting two LPs with white American pianist John Mehegan, marking the debut of South African jazz on a long-playing disc. A Julliard professor and respected musician who had recorded with Charles Mingus and Lionel Hampton, Mehegan had traveled to South Africa to lecture, promote his new book, *Jazz Improvisation,* and help nurture the jazz scene there.[72] For many African musicians, Mehegan's visit provided an occasion to shine an international spotlight on South Africa's burgeoning jazz scene, as well as expose the blatant violation of human rights under apartheid. Mehegan did both: he gathered the best talent and insisted on recording them, and he openly criticized the racial barriers that arrested the music's development. He praised Masekela, Gwangwa, and Moeketsi, whom he described as "three magnificent African jazzmen in Johannesburg," singling out Moeketsi as "one of the greatest jazz musicians in the world today."[73] Still, his plaudits were tempered by a slight tone of condescension, particularly when he declared that he could not find a decent black drummer in all of South Africa. For the record date, he hired a white drummer named Gene Latimore, whose heavy-handed, monotonous swing patterns weighed down the boppish flights of the three horn players. Nevertheless, the group produced some fine recordings of jazz standards, a blues in all twelve keys, and a marabi-inspired original written by Mackay Davashe.[74]

The concert, held at Selbourne Hall on October 13, 1959, was a smashing success. Since Ibrahim's regular rhythm section could not make the trip, they hired Mongezi Samson Velelo and Early Mabuza on drums. For Ibrahim and Moeketsi, who had been talking about forming a band since their days with the Shantytown Sextet, this was a dream come true. Ibrahim had even named the group: the Jazz Epistles. As he told one journalist, he chose the name because "he is a teacher and like the early Christian teachers, he believes that he is writing his Epistles."[75] Hubris, for sure, but the band lived up to its name. They regaled the crowd with near-flawless renditions of "Cherokee" and "Delilah," as well as tunes by Charlie Parker, Thelonious Monk, Dizzy Gillespie, Clifford Brown, and Duke Ellington—delivered in rapid-fire succession.[76]

No one left Selbourne Hall disappointed, except perhaps Benjamin. She had accompanied her boyfriend on the long journey to Johannesburg only to watch the band from the wings. It must have been doubly painful to witness the Jazz Epistles back four different female vocalists: Thandie Khumalo (later Thandie Klaasen), Thoko Mgcina, "Mummy Girl" Nketle, and Abigail Kubeka. Each one sang standards such as "Stella by Starlight," "Easy Street," and classics by Gershwin, Johnny Mercer, and Harold Arlen—in other words, the kinds of tunes Benjamin performed.[77] As if to rub salt in her wounds, *Drum* magazine covered Ibrahim's close collaboration with Thoko Mgcina, whom he reportedly deemed "the best in the country."[78]

Not long after the couple returned to Cape Town, Ibrahim invited Moeketsi, Masekela, and Gwangwa to join his trio at the Ambassadors. The three men jumped at the chance, in part because Johannesburg was becoming politically intolerable and economically unsustainable. "Work was drying up all over the country," Masekela remembered.[79] Neither the success of *King Kong* nor Mehegan's influence could generate work for musicians in Johannesburg. The political climate certainly contributed. In August 1959 the trials began of 156 South African activists who had been arrested and charged with treason soon after drafting the ANC's Freedom Charter. The Pan Africanist Congress had formed the previous year under the militant leadership of Robert Sobukwe, who escalated opposition to the pass laws. The situation was tense, as confrontations between the state and the movement escalated in frequency and ferocity.[80] Meanwhile, the Dollar Brand Trio was playing to a packed house every night.

With just enough money for train tickets to Cape Town, Moeketsi, Masekela, and Gwangwa spent the first few nights sleeping on the floor in the back of the club and spending most of their days rehearsing. They practiced from ten in the morning until seven at night, working through tunes by Monk, Dizzy Gillespie, Miles Davis, Charlie Parker, Fats Waller, and Duke Ellington. "We also composed our own modern tunes," Masekela recalled, "a cross between mbhaqanga and bebop."[81] All the musicians and jazz lovers packed into the Ambassadors for a glimpse of what was being deemed the greatest jazz ensemble in South African history. Vincent Kolbe mused, "When

Abdullah played those Monk chords, it said a lot about the state of Africa at that time. When people went to concerts, it was like coming to a church service. And it wasn't to forget life and be happy-happy. The music of that time had got a lot of soul in it. The Jazz Epistles' music is beautifully soulful."[82] Chris McGregor, a progressive white pianist who would go on to found another historic South African jazz ensemble, the Blue Notes, saw the arrival of Moeketsi, Masekela, and Gwangwa as a catalyst for new developments in Cape Town: "It was a period of jazz explosion."[83] The authorities also found the happenings at the Ambassadors explosive. As they began to crack down on racial mixing, even the presumably more liberal Cape started to become a difficult place for jazz musicians to work.

In January, the entire band returned to Johannesburg. Ibrahim convinced Benjamin to come along for an extended stay. She readily agreed, both to support Ibrahim and the band but also hoping to reignite her own career. "I just like totally changed," Benjamin remembered. "I didn't have any fears about anything and it was rough and it was very hard. Relying on the generosity and the love of friends who love the music, they put us up, we slept on the floor, and had no money. It was all for the music."[84] She continued to sing, but the oft-repeated claim that she was a member of the Jazz Epistles is an overstatement. As Benjamin later explained, "whenever they had work, I was with them," though not always on stage.[85] The fact is, a female vocalist was not part of the Jazz Epistles' core identity, especially as they began to compose their own music. Perhaps she could have formed her own group or worked with other artists during these formative years with Ibrahim, but she chose not to. Thus, at the very moment when Benjamin decided to turn professional, inspired in part by Ibrahim's musical vision and example, her own aspirations took a backseat.

As Benjamin's fledgling career stalled, the Jazz Epistles took Johannesburg by storm. Club dates suddenly opened up and the white-owned South African label, Gallo Records, offered them a rare opportunity to make an LP. Notorious for exploiting African musicians,

Gallo paid the band a measly seventy-six pounds and no royalties to do the date.[86] Despite the terms, on January 22, 1960, the sextet assembled at Gallo Studios and laid down eight dazzling tracks in just three hours—all original music.[87] They played no jazz standards or vocal numbers of any kind, effectively excluding Benjamin from contributing. Instead, the LP was an explosive, masculine display of virtuosity and mastery. The compositions were structurally complex and demanding, involving shifting time signatures and tempos, and dissonant harmonies. Ibrahim's pieces, "Uka-Jonga Phambili" (Xhosa for "look forward") and "Vary-oo-um," employ Monkish chord voicings and encourage soloists to break free of the chord changes. Moeketsi's "Blues for Hughie," which opens hauntingly with a unison bass and trumpet duo, is not a standard blues but a sixteen-bar AABB form in a minor key. Masekela's composition "Dollars Moods" is a twenty-eight-bar boppish romp that shifts from a ten-bar A section in ⁴⁄₄ time to a six-bar bridge in waltz time.

The best-known and perhaps most successful tune of the date was Kippie Moeketsi's "Scullery Department." A brilliant example of what musicologists call an asymmetric time-line pattern, the piece opens with Ibrahim and Ntshoko playing in ⁶⁄₄ rhythm, but the horns entering with a melody line in ⁴⁄₄ time, thus displacing the down beat, or the "one." Their performance swings despite sudden shifts in dynamics and rhythm. Freedom is the operative word here; their improvisational flights are equal to anything Ornette Coleman or Charles Mingus was doing at the time. The story behind the song's title, "Scullery Department," also speaks to the group's politics of masculinity. Its music and aggressive performance style were assertions of dignity and manhood in a racist world that thought of them as boys and servants. One night, while playing at an exclusively white Johannesburg nightclub, the management insisted that they take their break in the kitchen. This wasn't the first time. They had worked in other venues where they had to take their breaks on fire escapes or in alleys. But on this occasion, Moeketsi complained to Ibrahim, "By right, you know Dollar, this is all nonsense—this idea of us being taken into the kitchen when there's a break . . . 'Are we kitchen "boys." Aren't we here to entertain the people?'" In a mocking reply, Ibrahim described them as the scullery department. The two men then approached the owner's son and demanded that they take their meal in the club with the customers. After some argument, the management relented and that was the last time they were in the kitchen.[88]

A couple of weeks later, Ibrahim was back at Gallo Studios to record a trio LP. The session consisted of an eclectic mix of standards, music by Thelonious Monk, South African composers Todd Matshikiza and Mackay Davashe, and three of Ibrahim's original compositions. Once again, he did not invite Benjamin to participate in the session, though he did include an original Monkish blues he had written for her titled "Blues for B."[89]

When *Jazz Epistle—Verse I,* the first all-black jazz LP in South African history, was released in the early summer of 1960, Gallo pressed a mere five hundred copies and did nothing to promote the record.[90] It sold out in no time, quickly becoming something of a collector's item. Gallo held on to Ibrahim's trio recording for over two years. It was finally released as *Dollar Brand Plays Sphere Jazz* in 1962, well after Ibrahim and Benjamin had fled the country.[91] Gallo's reluctance to promote such revolutionary music may have been a consequence of the political climate. By the time *Jazz Epistle—Verse I* was ready for release, the world had changed. On March 21, 1960, the Pan Africanist Congress organized peaceful protests against the pass laws in the township of Sharpeville, in the Transvaal, and in Langa, a township in the Cape and Makaya Ntshoko's hometown. Some protesters burned their pass books, others simply showed up without passes and offered themselves up for arrest. In Sharpeville, the police opened fire on the demonstrators, killing at least sixty-nine people including eight women and ten children, though the unofficial count was much higher. The massacre sparked more protests, strikes, and violent uprisings all across the country. Nine days later the ruling Nationalist Party declared a state of emergency and detained over 18,000 people. The United Nations responded immediately, condemning the violence and the South African government. Whatever vestiges of democracy existed in South Africa were swiftly crushed after Sharpeville. The state passed laws banning all African organizations and permitting ninety-day detentions without legal process. Torture and outright murder for those confined became commonplace. Between 1963 and 1965 alone, at least 190 Africans were hanged. In response, both the ANC and PAC decided that peaceful means were no longer possible; they formed underground guerrilla wings and launched an armed struggle.[92]

The Sharpeville Massacre effectively killed the Jazz Epistles and dealt a devastating blow to jazz in general. A nationwide tour of the Epistles scheduled for April was canceled, and Masekela and Gwangwa turned their attention to finding safe passage out of the country. The state of emergency and the apartheid regime's enforcement of the Separate Amenities Act effectively barred African and Coloured musicians from playing in white venues.[93] A growing number of South African artists considered the prospect of exile, including Benjamin. "After Sharpeville," she explained, "that's when we had to leave . . . Jazz was actually considered by that government subversive music, because it brought the races together and we would be mixed on the stage because we had African musicians and white musicians."[94]

Even if they had wanted to leave, Benjamin and Ibrahim did not have the money. The couple decided to go back to Cape Town, where Ibrahim and his trio briefly enjoyed a hero's welcome. They had conquered Johannesburg, put out a record of staggering imagination, and returned at a moment when it seemed as if the Cape Town jazz scene was on an upswing. The welcome was short-lived, however. The Ambassadors and similar venues were now under constant surveillance, and Ibrahim's reputation for being difficult and temperamental certainly did not help him. Critic Frank Barton described Ibrahim's trio as "the lone wolves of the Cape." "They play it their way," he wrote in a *Drum* magazine article celebrating Cape Town's jazz renaissance, "and if the customers don't like it then that's tough on the customers. But don't ask The Dollar to play something different, or he may slam the piano lid and go home."[95]

He eventually stopped playing the Ambassadors because, in his words, "they gone all square"—though the frequent raids and police surveillance probably influenced his decision. He continued to play where he could and worked with Benjamin more often now that they were back in familiar territory. To try to make ends meet, the couple launched the Dollar Brand School of Music. The venture proved disastrous. Despite Benjamin's knowledge and talents, she was little more than a glorified secretary, while Ibrahim, the master teacher, played the role of the aloof artist. He attracted few if any students, and he did not see the need to actively recruit any. "The money don't count," he told one writer. "It's the art."[96]

Their main priority, however, was leaving South Africa. Once again, Paul Meyer—perhaps out of guilt, genuine friendship, or both—offered valuable assistance. He had recently returned home to Switzerland and offered to help them relocate to Zurich. On January 21, 1962, Cape Town's jazz community held a huge farewell benefit concert at the Ambassadors to raise the money for two one-way tickets.[97] A couple of weeks later, Ibrahim and Benjamin packed a few precious belongings and the warmest clothes they could find and left the sun-splashed beaches of Cape Town for the snow-covered streets of Zurich.

Sometimes I Sing

Meyer helped them secure housing at the International Student House and used his contacts to find gigs. Without his trio, Ibrahim had to work solo or join various pick-up bands to make money. Although club dates were hard to come by at first, Benjamin ended up working more than she had in South Africa—both as a soloist and in a duo with Ibrahim. They played in Berne, Geneva, Lausanne, and various small towns around Switzerland, Germany, and Scandinavia—namely Oslo, Stockholm, and Helsinki—and Ibrahim toured briefly with Swiss tenor saxophonist Chester Gill. The couple made it to Copenhagen a few times at the Montmarte jazz club, where they met a number of notable African American musicians, including Don Byas, Dexter Gordon, Kenny Drew, Ben Webster, Bud Powell, and Kenny Dorham. They even had a stint with a Swiss-based calypso group.[98] As exciting as these times were, Benjamin found it hard to adapt to Zurich. "I can remember how very cold it was, the wonder of seeing snow for the first time, the culture shock I experienced, the longing for the sun and the tenderness and warmth of my people affected me a great deal and after a few days 'I longed for home.' But there was no turning back."[99]

Fortunately, Ibrahim's playing so impressed the owner of Zurich's Club Africana that he offered him a regular engagement and contributed a bit to help defray travel costs for Makaya Ntshoko and Johnny Gertze.[100] By late fall of 1962, Ibrahim happily reunited with his trio and moved both men into International Student House. They spent most of their days rehearsing at the Club Africana in preparation for the nightly gigs. Benjamin continued to enjoy guest appearances with the band, though by now she had invested more energy in promoting Ibrahim's career than her own. When she learned that the Duke Ellington Orchestra would be appearing at Kongresshaus in Zurich on February 19, 1963, she made sure to secure a ticket, hoping to meet her idol and convince him to catch the Dollar Brand Trio's last set before heading off to the next city.[101]

Benjamin made her way backstage during intermission and practically begged Duke to swing by the Club Africana after the concert. Intrigued as much by her looks and charm as by her commitment to her husband's music, he listened to her case but made no promises. What convinced Ellington to accept her invitation was the news that Ibrahim had no recording contract. As an A&R man for Reprise Records, a fledgling three-year-old label founded by Frank Sinatra, Duke was always on the prowl for new talent.[102]

They arrived just as the owner was about to lock up, allowing the

Dollar Brand Trio to treat Ellington to a private impromptu concert. Clearly impressed, Duke then turned to Benjamin and asked if she managed the group or was married to one of the band members. No, she replied, but quickly added, "But I sing sometimes." Ellington smiled and insisted, "Then you must sing." Duke's warmth and encouragement wiped away her fears and calmed her nerves, enabling her to deliver a tender rendition of "I'm Glad There Was You." He loved it. Before he headed back to his hotel in those early morning hours, he invited the trio *and* Benjamin to record LPs for Reprise and arranged for a recording session at Barclay Studios in Paris on February 24. He provided train tickets and made sure they arrived on the 23rd in time for the Ellington Orchestra's concert at the Olympia Theater.[103] This left them only four days to prepare, but the sheer weight of meeting the man whom they both idolized, the artist whose music had brought them together in the first place, made them feel invincible.

The session reinvigorated Benjamin's dedication to her own music and supplied a much-needed boost to her confidence. Ellington treated her and Ibrahim as equals, and he even asked her to record first. The great Billy Strayhorn showed up for the date and accompanied her on "Your Love Has Faded" and "A Nightingale Sang in Berkeley Square." And Duke himself commandeered the piano when she sang his tunes, "I Got It Bad" and "Solitude." Ibrahim's trio backed her on the remaining eight titles—all standards. Pizzicato violinist Svend Asmussen, having just recorded with Ellington two days earlier, also dropped by the studio that morning and accompanied Benjamin on every track.

The results are remarkable. Singing with a slight vibrato and a crystalline tone, Benjamin displays astounding maturity and control for a twenty-six-year-old singer who worked infrequently. Her choice of very slow tempos required enormous patience and imaginative phrasing, but it also allowed her to create a field of emotion—to give the impression that she had lived every lyric. She shined on "Darn that Dream" and "A Nightingale Sang in Berkeley Square," revealing slight traces of Billie Holiday, and mastered "Spring Will Be a Little Late This Year," whose wide intervals seemed to suit her voice perfectly. Her collaborations with Ellington and Strayhorn were gorgeous, particularly on "Solitude," which may be the session's high point. Although she limited her repertoire to slow ballads, about two-thirds of the way into "I Could Write a Book," "Man I Love," and "Soon," the band doubles the tempo, demonstrating her ability to "swing" and breaking up what had become a uniform cadence.

Ellington adored Benjamin's voice and thought the session went well. So did Benjamin, who would mark February 24, 1963, as one of the most important days of her life. Unfortunately, Frank Sinatra and the men running Reprise disagreed. Months later, Ellington delicately informed Benjamin that the bosses elected to shelve the recording because they did not think it was "commercial enough for a vocal album." Benjamin was devastated. Another unreleased LP, another chance at visibility lost. Duke cushioned the news with encouraging remarks. "When they tell you it's not commercial enough," he advised, "you must have something going on there. You keep doing what you're doing—you're my singer from Africa."[104] She had never had the opportunity to hear the recording, and when she asked about the tapes many years later, she was told they had been destroyed. Fortunately, the recording engineer, Gerhard Lehner, secretly made a duplicate of the session.[105] David Hadju, Strayhorn's biographer, discovered the tape, which set in motion the release of the session in 1997 on CD with the title *A Morning in Paris*. The CD drew a flurry of attention and critical praise, though thirty-four years overdue.[106]

Ibrahim did not suffer the same problem. On the contrary, his three-hour session with just his band was released amid great fanfare as *Duke Ellington Presents the Dollar Brand Trio*. And although the band plays brilliantly, one is hard-pressed to call this LP "commercial." Ibrahim had composed all but one song on the album, and that song was Thelonious Monk's famously difficult "Brilliant Corners."

And even his original pieces possessed strong Monk and Ellington influences. "The Stride" is chock-full of Monkish chord voicings, off-beat phrasing, distinctive bass countermelodies, and rapid shifts in time signature. "Ubu Suku" (the Evening) knits together phrases from two favorite Monk standards: the first bar of "I'm Getting Sentimental Over You" and the second bar of "You Are Too Beautiful." Duke's influence looms just as large. "Jumping Rope" and "Dollar's Dance" are clear nods to Ellington's playful sense of swing as well as the most avant-garde elements of his piano style, while "Kippi," a lovely ballad in tribute to his friend and former bandmate, opens with a quote from Ellington's "Rockin' in Rhythm."[107]

What made Ibrahim's LP commercially viable and Benjamin's not? For one thing, the Dollar Brand Trio performed mostly original compositions, giving listeners something fresh and unfamiliar. Second, while they never strayed from the modern jazz idiom, their African roots made them slightly more exotic—made evident by the subtle references to Africa in a couple of the song titles. Third, the Dollar Brand Trio created a sound that stood at the crux of hard bop and the jazz avant-garde. The era of the "New Thing" had achieved some recognition when Reprise released *Duke Ellington Presents the Dollar Brand Trio,* the same year trumpeter Bill Dixon organized the infamous "October Revolution," a series of avant-garde concerts at the Cellar Cafe in New York's Upper West Side. And more often than not, the "New Thing" was considered a man's thing, as musicians and critics at the time interpreted dissonant harmonies and startling rhythmic displacements as distinctively "masculine."[108]

Benjamin, on the other hand, sang familiar love songs, songs that had been covered many times over by singers she herself adored—including Sarah Vaughan, Ella Fitzgerald, and Billie Holiday. Unlike Ibrahim, or for that matter Miriam Makeba—now a huge star in the United States and Europe—Benjamin was too light-skinned and too committed to the jazz idiom to come across as African (read: exotic), despite her pronounced Cape Town accent.[109]

There were aspects of the recording that limited its commercial value as well. She might have benefited from a few medium- and up-tempo pieces, as well as from jazz interpretations of South African music. This alone would have distinguished her from all other torch singers. And the addition of Sven Asmussen's violin, while musically interesting, at times threatened to overwhelm the subtleties of Benjamin's voice. On "Lover Man" and "I'm Glad There Is You," for example, his heavy-handed improvisations are more of a distraction than a complement.

In other words, Benjamin's creative choices and her illegibility in the worlds of jazz and popular music may have contributed to Reprise executives' short-sighted decision to shelve her LP. Ellington was right: she was not a commercial singer and had no intention of becoming one. She had already chosen a different path back in 1958, if not earlier, that entailed putting her own uniquely modern spin on early to mid-twentieth-century popular songs. Everything she sang would be a reflection of her roots—in Cape Town, Johannesburg, Saint Helena, Mauritius, the Philippines—but only insofar as these places continued to live through her. At this point in her career few listeners could discern these elements in her music, partly because she had no recordings in circulation, and partly because she had not yet begun to compose her own music.

Ellington was one who had discerned what she was doing, what made her stand apart from the rest, what made her "my singer from Africa." His support never wavered. He secured invitations for the couple to appear at the prestigious Antibes–Juan-les-Pins Jazz Festival in 1963, the Molde Jazz Festival (Norway), and the Ascona festival (Switzerland) the following year, and he personally invited Benjamin to sing with the Ellington Orchestra on several occasions between 1965 and 1972—most famously at the 1965 Newport Jazz Festival where she performed "Solitude" and "In a Mellow Tone" as an encore.[110] Ibrahim also acknowledged Sathima's unique sound—a decidedly South African sound grounded in the modern, urban landscape of Cape Town and Johannesburg, in the nightclubs and the bohemian jam sessions, in the bioscopes and church halls. But Ibrahim had his own music to make, and he pursued his creative path with a singularity of purpose. Benjamin would later reflect, "You have to remember when you live with someone like Abdullah, it's very hard to pull yourself out from under and say, 'You know what? I want to do this.' And I think for a long time I was very intimidated. Once I started to break out, it became easier as the years went on."[111]

Breaking out took some time. They left Zurich and moved to England briefly, where they finally married in February 1965. Then Ellington's invitation to Newport turned into a three-year stay in New York City, resulting in the demise of the Dollar Brand Trio.[112] Between 1968 and 1971, they moved between Europe, South Africa, and Swaziland, during which time Ibrahim made several recordings, converted to Islam, and with Benjamin's assistance opened the Marimba Music School in Mbabane, Swaziland.[113] Benjamin, by contrast, made no recordings (except for a single track on one of Ibrahim's unreleased transcription records), and made even fewer appearances with her husband as his music moved in a freer, more experimental direction.[114] In 1971, she did give birth to her son, Tsakwe. Over time, she felt abandoned, especially during their European sojourns. "I don't like Europe very much," she confessed. "I felt very alienated there, but I used my time wisely. I would go to libraries. I would read. I investigated all the religions of the world. I used my time wisely, maybe because I was so alone. That's just something we have to do to survive. And that's where the work was."[115]

The combination of solitary study, reflection, motherhood, and travel back and forth to southern Africa inspired her to write poetry and compose her own music. In 1974 she composed "Music" as a tribute to her husband. The entire lyric consisted of a short poem repeated:

> Music
> is the spirit
> within you

> deep within you
> Find your sound
> Then let it flow
> Free
> and Easy
> and Out.

She also composed "Africa," an homage to the continent and a celebration of her return. The lyrics speak to the end of her long exile, her joy in coming

> home
> To feel my people's warmth
> to shelter 'neath your trees
> To catch the summer breeze
> Africa.

The next year she penned "African Songbird" to honor the memory of Duke Ellington, who had passed in 1974. Her minimalist lyrics invite all of us to "Sing/naturally/like a bird." All three songs are essentially poems set to uncluttered melodies, whose simplicity, strong swing, and transcendent spirituality bear a strong kinship with the compositions of singer and songwriter Abbey Lincoln. By the mid-1970s, Benjamin strongly identified with Lincoln, who she called her musical "sister."[116] Lincoln, whose 1973 LP *People in Me* included a paean to the continent titled "Africa," had also survived a musical partnership with a dominant man (Max Roach) and had moved from singing torch songs to political songs, finally composing her own.[117]

Ironically, Benjamin's burst of creative energy attracted Ibrahim's attention and brought them closer together. After moving back to South Africa in 1973, Ibrahim and Rashid Vally co-founded The Sun record label (also known by the Arabic name, As-Shams), and he offered to arrange, produce, and record all three of her compositions.

The session took place in March of 1976 at Gallo Studios in Johannesburg, backed by an ensemble made up of two drummers, three bass players, the African American trumpeter Billy Brooks, and the popular South African saxophonist Basil Coetzee, led by Ibrahim on electric piano. Faced with the task of filling an LP with just three songs, the soloists stretched out on "Africa," turning it into a twenty-one-minute virtuoso performance.[118]

Ibrahim and Vally wasted no time putting out *African Songbird*, which hit South African record shops in the summer of 1976. At forty years old, Benjamin finally saw the release of her first LP. It was a landmark recording for other reasons as well. *African Songbird* not only unveiled her talent as a composer but it revealed her deep and abiding interest in the freedom struggle in South Africa. Her interest became a full-blown engagement in June 1976, after some 20,000 schoolchildren of Soweto rose up to protest the state's decision to teach math and social studies in Afrikaans instead of English. Once again, the police retaliated against the protesters. The damage this time around was worse than Sharpeville: between 300 and 500 Africans were killed and over 2,000 were wounded.[119] At the time of the Soweto Uprising, Benjamin was about four months pregnant with her second child, a daughter who they named Matsidiso ("Tsidi" for short). A few months after she was born, they fled South Africa— again—and returned to New York, where they settled into the Chelsea Hotel and became politically active on behalf of the African National Congress. Among other things, Benjamin initiated the Secacha Pioneers, a group of young ANC members in exile who met each Saturday afternoon to sing freedom songs and discuss the situation in South Africa. She opened her home to students, dignitaries, and exiled activists. And she participated in countless concerts and fundraisers in support of the ANC. As a result of Benjamin's and Ibrahim's activities as cultural workers for the liberation movement, the South African state revoked their citizenship, leaving them no choice but to become U.S. citizens.[120]

The political work notwithstanding, Benjamin confronted many difficult challenges in New York. Now that she was responsible for keeping house and raising two young children, her music hit a temporary roadblock. Inspired by *African Songbird*, she had begun composing more and thinking about ways to incorporate "Cape Town rhythms," the distinctive shuffle beat common in the popular dance music back home. In 1979, she approached Ibrahim about making an all-Ellington LP. "I was going to record *Sathima Sings Ellington*, and I booked a downtown studio and I assumed Abdullah would do it. Then at the last minute he said 'I'm not doing that.'" She was devastated. In hindsight, it compelled her to take more control over her music, but at the time "it made me feel like I wasn't good enough or he was too good."[121] He agreed to produce the record, but left the task of putting together a band to Benjamin, who ended up hiring an outstanding trio consisting of Onaje Allen Gumbs on piano, bassist Bill 'Vishnu' Wood, and drummer John Betsch.

Even more significant, she released *Sathima Sings Ellington* on her *own* label, Ekapa Records, which she also launched in 1979 with Ibrahim's help. She felt she had no choice, having lost her main musical collaborator of twenty years and feeling the obligations of motherhood. "I was at home with two small children," she told critic Sally Placksin a few years after founding Ekapa, "and I really started feeling very left out because I couldn't move, and I think it really happened out of sheer urgency to do something musically . . . The important thing is I felt I had to keep in touch musically with what was happening. Since there were no other venues for me, and I wasn't able to travel, the record in a way could do a little bit of traveling for me."[122]

Her records did quite a bit of traveling for her. Having taken control of her career, she slipped out from Ibrahim's shadow, developed new relationships in motherhood and in the antiapartheid movement, and found her voice—or at least found a way to project her voice amid the din of the jazz police and the African purists. Between 1979 and 2006, she released eight discs: *Sathima Sings Ellington, Dedications, Memories and Dreams, Windsong, Lovelight, South-*

ern Touch, Cape Town Love, and *Musical Echoes.* Each of these recordings received rave reviews, and *Dedications* was nominated for a Grammy in 1982. A mix of standards, old Tin Pan Alley songs, and original compositions, these recordings reveal the full range of her talent as a singer, songwriter, and bandleader. Her controversial "Liberation Suite" (1982) consists of three compositions, "New Nations a-Coming," "Children of Soweto," and "Africa." It departs sharply from most "political music" intent on representing the conditions of black South Africans. Originally inspired by a visit to Mozambique in 1982 on behalf of the ANC, she deliberately created pieces that imagine a liberated future grounded in love rather than in the current crises. "You can see the joy [the Mozambicans] feel in just having their country back, even though there's a lot of work to be done."[123]

Benjamin found joy in the most oppressive circumstances because she was part of a generation who lived through some of the worst ravages of apartheid and managed to create some of the most beautiful and joyous music on the planet. Indeed, in spite of spending most of her professional life in exile, Benjamin's distinctive musical and political voice was formed during the first decade of official apartheid, just as South Africa's vibrant urban popular culture was under siege all over the country. In response, many black and Coloured artists and intellectuals turned to either modern jazz or township music (or both) as the way forward, in opposition to the retrograde "native" policies of the new regime. It was in this context that former nightclub singers such as Miriam Makeba, Dolly Rathebe, and Dorothy Masuka embraced township music and created popular protest songs. At the same time, these singers symbolized a new, urban, female sexuality; glamorous photos and profiles of them in *Drum* magazine contributed to their popularity and to Benjamin's marginalization. Benjamin shunned cheesecake photos and stayed committed to jazz, singing standards and old American and English ballads, often at slow tempos and in a style akin to Billie Holiday and Sarah

Vaughan. Moreover, she gravitated to artists dedicated to jazz, such as Abdullah Ibrahim, whose passion for Thelonious Monk made him a kind of rebel among South African musicians—though a highly respected outcast.

And yet, while her once outcast husband became one of South Africa's best-known jazz musicians, she has spent the better part of her life working in relative obscurity, struggling to be seen and heard. As I've suggested, essentialist notions of culture had rendered Benjamin illegible—not African enough for some, not American enough for others, and certainly not commercial enough for a market that traffics in familiar, digestible commodities. Perhaps most important, Sathima Bea Benjamin was not *man* enough to sustain her own music on her terms—at least not until she launched Ekapa Records, began booking her own gigs, and seized control of all aspects of her career. In other words, in her long struggle for visibility, gender was decisive. She was initiated into a world where she put up with sexual harassment from musicians on whom she depended for practical skills, gigs, even transportation. She escaped a near-rape by her benefactor, Paul Meyer—and he was considered one of the "good" guys. As a female balladeer in an era when South Africa's modernists sought ways to express the cry of freedom and the cadences of mass resistance, Benjamin's sensitive love songs were often drowned out. Even her relationship with Abdullah Ibrahim—her closest collaborator and most enthusiastic supporter—had at times a stifling effect. One poignant story speaks volumes of the depths of her marginalization. Although she had spent the better part of a decade working for the ANC's cultural wing and composing paeans to the movement, including "Winnie Mandela, Beloved Heroine" and her three-part "Liberation Suite," Benjamin was not invited to perform at President Nelson Mandela's inauguration in 1994. Ibrahim was, however, and in her words she had to "steal" one minute from his five allotted minutes so that she could sing for her new president.[124]

Today, Benjamin no longer has to "steal" time from her husband. In the land of her birth, at least, she has finally earned the kinds of accolades befitting an artist of her stature. In October 2004, South African president Thabo Mbeki honored her with the Order of Ikhamanga Silver Award in recognition for her "excellent contribution as a jazz artist," as well as for her contribution "to the struggle against apartheid." More recently, Don Yon made her the subject of a sensitive documentary film, *Sathima's Windsong*.

Benjamin may have struggled for visibility, but she was never invisible. No matter what obstacles stood in her way, she never abandoned the music. She honed her skills surrounded by musicians who saw themselves as modern, urban, cosmopolitan people whose tastes and cultural influences knew no boundaries. America spoke—via jazz, blues, and a hip politics of style—and Africa listened. But what they heard was filtered through their experience—in the townships, the dance halls, the embattled community centers, the rent parties, the mass demonstrations—and transformed into music that was both local and global, native and international. So while America spoke and Benjamin listened, she spoke back again, creating what she calls "musical echoes." Those echoes reverberate, from Saint Helena to Cape Town, Mauritius to Manhattan, Swaziland to Switzerland. Her distinctive interpretations of jazz standards, Ellingtonia, English theater songs, and original tone poems are South African by virtue of the fact that her core musical knowledge and aesthetic sensibilities were forged in South Africa. Even in exile her native land remained her point of reference. "It's a spiritual embrace," is how she put it, "so I'm always home. It's like I took Africa within, and that's the coming home. I'm here, but Africa is with me all the time."[125]

Coda

On November 13, 2010, a capacity audience filled the Tribeca Performing Arts Center in Manhattan to commemorate the fiftieth anniversary of Randy Weston's suite, *Uhuru Afrika*. Before Weston and his twenty-six-piece orchestra struck a single note, the entire auditorium was on its feet applauding, shouting, some even crying. No one seemed to care that the band had taken the stage an hour late, or that an overwhelmed box-office staff was still wrestling with lines of would-be concertgoers. Men, women, and some kids draped in kente, mud cloth, dashikis, and djellabas, sporting kofi hats and head wraps, proudly displayed their identification with Africa. Most had not been born when Weston first recorded *Uhuru Afrika,* though quite a few were old enough to have bought the LP's first pressings and may have even worked on behalf of African independence. Amid the predictable sea of black faces was a rainbow of colors and nationalities—whites, Latinos, and a fairly large contingent of Asian Americans. Once the music started, generational, ethnic, and racial differences evaporated. For the next hour, the entire room swayed as one to the rhythm.

The music that night sounded as fresh and new and timeless as it had a half-century earlier. The band was composed of younger musicians, many of whom were just children when Weston assembled the first *Uhuru Afrika* orchestra. Besides Weston, only percussionist Candido Camero and drummer Charlie Persip had participated in the original recording date. Weston also hired more Africans from the continent to play traditional instruments—notably Ghana's Kwaku Obeng on balaphon and Gambia's Muhamedou Salieu Suso on the kora. Their participation transformed *Uhuru Afrika* from a paean written *for* Africa to a trans-Atlantic expression of a single African voice. In other words, Africa and (African) America spoke—together—and, hopefully, the world listened.

The concert called attention to the cultural distance traveled since 1960. Of course, the jazz world still has its purists who insist that the ability to swing is distinctively American and has nothing to do with Africa, but they represent a shrinking minority. Today the meeting of modern jazz and African music is commonplace. Jazz can be found in virtually all parts of Africa while popular African music (sometimes known as "Afro-pop" or "World Beat") competes for dominance in an expanding global market. August venues such as Jazz at Lincoln Center in New York have hosted performances by African artists, such as percussionist Yacub Addy, whose fusions of jazz and African music build on the foundation established by Weston, Warren, and Abdul-Malik. Hugh Masekela's fusions of jazz, soul, funk, and township music have made him South Africa's best-known instrumentalist and a global icon. Meanwhile, Cape Town, Johannesburg, and Durban are counted among the world's leading centers of jazz. Once famous for its exiled jazz community, South Africa has become home to a number of leading American musicians, most notably saxophonist René McLean.

But what of the *political* distance traveled since 1960? When Weston proudly reminded his audience that *Uhuru Afrika* was written as a tribute to African independence, his words met tepid applause and polite indifference. The halcyon days when the new African nations held the promise for a new future, a democratic, spiritual, and decidedly post-Western modernity, seemed so long ago. Gone were those revolutionary times that inspired Weston's suite and his experiments with highlife, Ahmed Abdul-Malik's dream to make sacred Arab music swing, Guy Warren's efforts to meld the hippest African rhythms with modern jazz, and Sathima Bea Benjamin's struggle to give beauty and human dignity a voice against a backdrop of apartheid and racial subjugation. The era of hope and possibility has given way to a period characterized by "Afro-pessimism"—a demoralizing fear that Africa's economic and political problems are beyond repair.[1] The continent has suffered continuous economic decline, massive poverty, unemployment, and health crises caused by the persistent exploitation of Africa's resources by multinational corporations, enormous debt, financial dependency, severe ecological degradation, political instability and war, and rapid urbanization without sufficient infrastructure or resources. Although corruption by indigenous elites and wars, assassinations, and coups—often casualties of CIA covert action and Cold War rivalries between the United States and the former Soviet Union—contributed to the current crises facing many African nations, the core problems can be traced to colonialism. Africa was exploited for its raw materials, often through forced labor, taxation, land expropriation, and other forms of subjugation. Except for South Africa, the economies were never diverse, consumer markets were underdeveloped, and the new African nations had virtually no accumulated capital. From the beginning, Africa depended on foreign investment, and to attract such investment had to produce for a world market and offer "ideal" conditions for profit—cheap labor, wage controls, deregulated environment, low taxes, and few claims on the wealth being generated by foreign companies. Increasingly, African nations relied on loans from the World Bank and the International Monetary Fund, and when governments could not meet their debt obligations, their lenders imposed structural adjustment programs—real wage reductions, privatization of state-owned enterprises, elimination of price controls and state subsidies, liberalization of trade, currency devaluation, and a slew of austerity measures that made the poor even poorer. Meanwhile, democracy suffered under military regimes and dictators who skimmed billions from state coffers for their personal Swiss bank accounts.

The artists discussed in this book were not oblivious to Africa's challenges. Warren lived through Nkrumah's overthrow and Ghana's economic struggles, and Weston saw the effect of military rule during his 1967 tour, but even then Africa's future still looked hopeful. The optimism of the 1960s did not last, however. In 1977 Lagos, Nigeria, hosted the Second World African Festival of Arts and Culture, known by its acronym FESTAC. A follow-up to the First World Festival of Negro Arts held in Dakar in 1966, FESTAC represented a crossroads where an era of Pan-African unity and optimism ended and the consolidation of power by undemocratic repressive regimes, dominance of global capitalism, and the continent's downward economic spiral began. It also coincided with, if not underscored, the commercial decline of jazz compared to pop, soul, funk, and rock music during the 1970s. Ironically, one of the few subgenres of jazz that experienced growth in the 1970s was groove-based African jazz fusion by the likes of Cannonball Adderley, Hugh Masekela, James Mtume, Pharoah Sanders, and Fela Kuti.[2] As police repression, agent provocateurs, and internal dissension brought down black militant organizations, Black Power slogans and Pan-Africanist sentiment were alive and well throughout the African diaspora in the late 1970s. The black world was primed for a world celebration of African culture.

But many radical Nigerian intellectuals and activists, most visibly playwright Wole Soyinka, actor Herbert Ogunde, and Fela Kuti, did not believe their country was in a position to host a month-long festival involving thousands of dancers, writers, scholars, visual artists, actors, and musicians from around the world. A military junta led by Lieutenant-General Olusegun Obasanjo ruled Nigeria and bankrolled FESTAC with substantial oil revenue. In a country still recovering from civil war and renowned for government corruption, investing a large chunk of state revenues for a cultural event when the country needed to attend to problems of health, education, democracy, and the economy seemed like a gross misuse of funds. Moreover, Nigerian critics complained that the organizers' selections did not accurately represent the modern, sophisticated character of contemporary West African culture, but rather reinforced stereotypes of Africa. The Obasanjo regime did succeed in laying bare the sharpening class divisions in the country and the state's repressive nature. Besides pricing tickets so high as to exclude the vast majority of Lagosians, police were instructed to use public flogging and other forms of intimidation to punish traffic violators in order to reduce congestion.[3]

The flamboyant Fela had become the Nigerian government's most popular and vociferous critic. He had built a significant following among the youth and was planning a presidential bid once the military regime permitted democratic elections. He boycotted the festival, distributed thousands of antigovernment pamphlets, and staged a counter-FESTAC at his club, the Shrine. Each night he performed political songs such as "Upside Down," criticizing Africa's disorganization and corruption; "Yellow Fever," which called out Nigerian women who use skin-lighteners; and the wildly popular "Zombie," a scathing attack on Nigeria's military. Between verses he gave speeches denouncing the country's leaders and calling for revolution.[4] Dozens of musicians dropped by the Shrine and jammed with Fela and his Afrika 70 band, including Stevie Wonder, saxophonist Archie Shepp, the Art Ensemble of Chicago, and members of Sun Ra's Arkestra (despite Sun Ra's order to stay away from Fela).[5]

Randy Weston also made an appearance at the Shrine. He was living in Paris at the time but had come to FESTAC as part of the U.S. delegation. He was aware of the festival's critics, its level of disorganization, and its unwieldiness (with so many acts, Weston was allowed only one very brief performance), but he also recognized FESTAC's historic importance. He was not disappointed. In his memoir he described it as "one of the most amazing experiences of my life."[6] His time at the Shrine was the most amazing part of it, not only because of the incredible music and the overflowing crowds but because Fela turned the club into a political stage. He asked Weston to sit in with his band, introducing him as "my brother from America." Holding his hand as they stood on stage together, Fela launched into a tirade against Nigeria's ruling clique. Fela's words left him in awe: "he's cursing out the military—and there were military guys in the club . . . Man, Fela was fearless, but I was sweatin' . . . what this guy *didn't* call the government."[7]

Fela's protest against national corruption and multinational exploitation, held amid the world's largest single gathering of African and Afro-diasporic arts, laid bare the problems facing modern Africa. Through his music, words, and the cultural space he created, Fela reminded the Afro-coifed delegates who greeted each other with raised-fist Black Power salutes that the majority of citizens in the host country—let alone Africa—had no power. The era of praise songs for the new African nations was over. In the struggle for the soul of the continent, Fela believed the artist must become the critic, the musician must sing and play the truth. But his government exacted a dear price. Six days after FESTAC's closing ceremonies, the military attacked Fela's compound—the self-proclaimed Kalakuta Republic—and burned everything to the ground. A major cultural institution was destroyed, thousands were displaced, and Fela's mother, socialist and beloved political activist Funmilayo Ransome-Kuti, was so badly hurt in the attack that she subsequently died of her injuries.[8]

The attack devastated Fela's organization, but it did not stop him. He intensified his political critique with songs such as "Sorrow, Tears, and Blood" (1977), "Vagabonds in Power" (1979), "International Thief Thief" (1979), "Authority Stealing" (1980), and "Coffin for Head of State" (1981). He also continued the tradition of trans-Atlantic collaboration, recording a vitally important LP with jazz vibraphonist Roy Ayers in 1980 titled *Music of Many Colors*. Ayers had just completed a three-week tour of Nigeria opening for Fela and the Afrika 70, and the two men decided to make a joint musical statement promoting liberation for Africa and the entire black world. The results were "Africa—Center of the World" and "2000 Blacks Got to Be Free," both tracks containing explicit political lyrics sung over infectious dance rhythms.[9] The latter track predicted that by the year 2000, Africa would finally be united and free and the entire black world would be knowledgeable and respectful of their homeland. To fulfill this dream, however, black people around the world had to be united.

Fela died three years before the new millennium, though it must have been clear to him then that Africa would not be free in 2000. The continent's debt burdens grew exponentially in the years after

FESTAC, along with poverty, violence, and the spread of AIDS and other health crises. On the other hand, Africa claimed key victories during the last twenty years: South Africans overthrew apartheid, some of the worst civil wars ended, several states achieved a semblance of political stability, and the devastating genocide in Rwanda in 1994 gave way to a truth commission that intended to bring justice to its victims and heal the nation. The very forces of globalization that have caused so much misery have also contributed to what has been called the "African renaissance." Global movements for social justice and an international boycott helped bring down apartheid; globalization of culture nurtured a new generation of modern African artists in all fields—visual arts, music, theater, film, and dance—who used the world as their palette in order to create innovative, hybrid works of art; and the ease of communication and transnational circulation of culture, ideas, and bodies facilitated intercultural collaboration.

Indeed, as a result of waves of African immigration—generated by war, neoliberalism, and structural adjustment policies—the kinds of collaborations that fifty years ago required trans-Atlantic travel and cultural exchange programs now occur in almost any major city and with greater frequency. Cornetist and composer Graham Haynes began working with Cameroonian drummer Brice Wassy as early as 1990. Working in both Paris and New York, Haynes and Wassy put together groups consisting of African, Arab, and Indian musicians and instrumentation, and created a jazz-based hybrid music that defied categorization.[10] Craig Harris, a phenomenal trombonist and composer who has worked with Abdullah Ibrahim, Randy Weston, and Sun Ra's Arkestra during FESTAC, recognized that his own Harlem community was fast becoming an African city. New York is currently home to well over 100,000 Africans, mostly from Mali, Senegal, Ghana, Somalia, Nigeria, and the Congo, and a large proportion of these residents are concentrated around West 116th Street in Harlem. Harris's interest in indigenous music from around the globe was already evident in his mastery of the didjeridoo, the instrument of northern Australia's aboriginal people. In the mid-1990s, he began working with several West African musicians in the community—particularly master kora players from Mali and Senegal. Simultaneously, he collaborated with African American poet Sekou Sundiata on two major theater works: *The Return of Elijah,* about the trans-Atlantic slave trade; and *Udu,* a powerful musical exposé of contemporary slavery in Mauritania. The music for *Udu* was performed in part by a troupe of West African musicians based in New York.[11] David Murray, another Weston collaborator who is a master of the tenor saxophone and bass clarinet, has long incorporated African percussion in his music. His travels to Paris and Guadeloupe, in particular, put him in direct contact with African and Afro-Caribbean musicians, resulting in several ground-breaking projects, including "M'Bizo Suite," written for the late South African bassist Johnny Dyani, and his powerful collaborations with Gwo Ka drummers of Guadeloupe. His composition "Africa" (2007), featuring singer Taj Mahal, shares an affinity with earlier paeans to the continent, except that Ishmael Reed's haunting lyric draws on metaphors of illness to lament an Africa on her death bed.[12]

In short, the musical *and* political dialogue between Africa and America continues, and jazz—along with hip-hop, reggae, Afro-beat, makossa, rai, zouk, and countless styles and genres—remains a vibrant language. But like everything else, the conversation has changed and will change again. The essential qualities of the music have not. Jazz knows no borders or boundaries; it is a music with an ear toward the future but rooted in the past; a music of lamentation and hope, pain and exhilaration, crisis and resistance, and above all . . . freedom—*uhuru!* Jazz speaks and will continue to speak, from every continent, every city, every culture around the globe. And before we answer, let us listen—listen to the music and listen *for* the music, wherever it might be. It will not solve global economic crises or end conflicts, but it can do what it has always done—free our imaginations, animate the marvelous, activate our spirit, and illuminate an improvised path we've never heard (or seen) before.

Notes

Prelude

1. "Crow Jim," *Time* 80, no. 16 (October 19, 1962), 59–60.
2. Guy Warren, "Open Letter to *Time* Magazine," reprinted in Warren, *I Have a Story to Tell* (Accra: New Guinea Press, 1962), 169–170.
3. For a fascinating discussion of Africa in the imagination of jazz musicians during this era and earlier, see Norman Weinstein, *A Night in Tunisia: Imaginings of Africa in Jazz* (New York: Limelight Editions, 1993).
4. Richard Iton, *In Search of the Black Fantastic: Politics and Popular Culture in the Post–Civil Rights Era* (New York: Oxford University Press, 2008); also Ingrid Monson, *Freedom Sounds: Civil Rights Call Out to Jazz and Africa* (New York: Oxford University Press, 2007), 145.
5. Penny Von Eschen, *Satchmo Blows Up the World: Jazz Ambassadors Play the Cold War* (Cambridge, MA: Harvard University Press, 2006); Monson, *Freedom Sounds*, 110–113.
6. Iton, *In Search of the Black Fantastic*, 50.
7. These topics have been explored in great detail elsewhere. See Luigi Onori, *Il Jazz e l'Africa: Radici, miti, suoni* (Nuovi Equilibri, 2004); Gerhard Kubik, *Africa and the Blues* (Jackson: University Press of Mississippi, 1999); Pascal Bokar Thiam, *From Timbuktu to the Mississippi Delta: How West African Standards of Aesthetics Shaped the Music of the Delta Blues* (San Diego: Cognella, 2011); Samuel A. Floyd, *The Power of Black Music: Interpreting Its History from Africa to the United States* (New York: Oxford University Press, 1996); Fredrich Kaufman and John Guckin, *The African Roots of Jazz* (Sherman Oaks, CA: Alfred, 1979); Karlton E. Hester, *From Africa to Afrocentric Innovations Some Call "Jazz,"* 4 vols.

(Ithaca: Hesteria Records and Publishing, 2000); Monson, *Freedom Sounds;* Weinstein, *A Night in Tunisia.*

8. Aimé Césaire, *Discourse on Colonialism* (New York: Monthly Review Press, 2000). These sentiments, fueling the idea that Africans at the dawn of independence were "the saviors of humanity," are beautifully captured in Manthia Diawara's brilliant exegesis, *In Search of Africa* (Cambridge, MA: Harvard University Press, 1998), 6–7.

9. Veit Erlmann, *Music, Modernity and the Global Imagination: South Africa and the West* (New York: Oxford University Press, 1999), 9.

10. Recently, Leonard Brown put together a powerful collection of essays and interviews exploring the relationship between the black freedom movement and the spiritual quest embodied in John Coltrane's music. Of course, it is impossible to write about John Coltrane without delving into his own spiritual quest, but the Brown collection represents perhaps the best example of the kinds of questions and relationships I am pursuing here. See Leonard Brown, ed., *John Coltrane and Black America's Quest for Freedom: Spirituality and the Music* (New York: Oxford University Press, 2010).

11. I am indebted here to political scientist Cedric Robinson, whose book *The Terms of Order: The Myth of Political Leadership* (Albany: State University of New York Press, 1980), offers a brilliant critique of the Western presumption—rooted as much in Marxism as in liberal democratic theory—that mass movements reflect social order and are maintained and rationalized by the authority of leadership. He concludes with what amounts to a wholesale rejection of all universalist theories of political and social order. Although he is looking at politics, I find his analysis useful for understanding culture, art, and various social movements.

1. The Drum Wars of Guy Warren

1. *The Boy Kumasenu,* dir. Sean Graham (Gold Coast Film Unit, 1951). Incidentally, throughout the film's soundtrack, both highlife and jazz are used to represent the city.

2. The most accurate description of Kofi Ghanaba's modified drum kit is in Royal Hartigan, "Ghanaba and the Heritage of African Jazz," *Annual Review of Jazz Studies* 9 (1997–1998), 146.

3. *Sankofa*, dir. Haile Gerima (Mypheduh Films, 1993).

4. Kofi Ghanaba, interview with author, August 13, 2004.

5. On Dafora's life and work, see John Perpener, *African American Concert Dance: The Harlem Renaissance and Beyond* (Urbana: University of Illinois Press, 2001), 101–127; Marcia Heard and Mansa K. Mussa, "African Dance in New York City," in *Dancing Many Drums: Excavations in African American Dance,* ed. Thomas F. DeFrantz, 143–149 (Madison: University of Wisconsin Press, 2002); Maureen Needham, "*Kykunkor, or the Witch Woman:* An African Opera, 1934," in DeFrantz, *Dancing Many Drums,* 233–249.

6. Robert Martin, "African Festival at Carnegie Hall," *New York Times,* December 1, 1943; John Martin, "The Dance—Novelties," *New York Times,* December 12, 1943.

7. Gillespie, quoted in Ingrid Monson, *Freedom Sounds: Civil Rights Call Out to Jazz and Africa* (New York: Oxford University Press, 2007), 110; see also Dizzy Gillespie, with Al Fraser, *To Be or Not to Bop: Memoirs of Dizzy Gillespie* (New York: Da Capo Press, 1985), 290.

8. "Efrom Odok, Draft Registration Card, 1942, United States, Selective Service System," *Selective Service Registration Cards, World War II: Fourth Registration,* National Archives and Records Administration; "Swing Is African," *Amsterdam News,* January 21, 1939; "Says 'Swing' Based on African Rhythms," *Pittsburgh Courier,* January 21, 1939; "African Drummers Set for Recital," *Atlanta Daily World,* December 7, 1943. See also Heard and Mussa, "African Dance in New York City," 143.

9. "African Drummers Set for Recital."

10. Ibid.

11. "Swing Is African"; "Says 'Swing' Based on African Rhythms."

12. John Martin, "The Dance—Events of the Week," *New York Times,* March 11, 1945; John Martin, "The Dance—Plenty of Activity," *New York Times,* February 11, 1945. This little-known performance ought to be considered a landmark in jazz history, for it predates the Gillespie-Pozo collaboration—usually credited for being the first meeting of modern jazz and African drums—by two years.

13. Tiroro, *The Haitian Drummer* (Smithsonian Folkways COOK05004); Joseph H. Howard, *Drums in the Americas: The History and Develop-*

ment of Drums in the New World from the Pre-Columbian Era to Modern Times (New York: Oak, 1967).

14. From the liner notes to Thurston Knudson, *Primitive Percussion: African Jungle Drums* (Reprise R 600), which was released in 1961. The series of 78s they recorded and released in 1941 include Thurston Knudson and Augie Goupil, *Conga Kongo* (Dla2383); *Rhumba Uganda* (Dla2381); and *Samba Tembo* (Dla2382).

15. *African and Afro-American Drums: Vols. 1 and 2* (Ethnic Folkways Album, FE4502). I'm grateful to master drummer Neil Clarke for bringing this album to my attention.

16. Ibid., vol. 2, Program Notes, 4.

17. Gillespie, *To Be or Not to Bop,* 317–325; Alyn Shipton, *Groovin' High: The Life of Dizzy Gillespie* (New York: Oxford University Press, 1999), 199–202. The Gillespie-Pozo collaboration was not the first time West African–derived drums entered the realm of jazz. Latin jazz bands had already begun using various African percussion instruments, and it was bandleader Mario Bauza who first introduced Pozo to Gillespie. And during the 1920s and 1930s, the island of Cuba was undergoing a kind of Afro-Cuban cultural renaissance, "Afro-Cubanismo," celebrating black rural folk music like the son, or the rumba, and so on. Jazz was also big and some of the Cuban dance bands combined these forms—groups like the Los Hermanos Castro, La Orquesta Casino de la Playa, and others. See especially Robin D. Moore, *Nationalizing Blackness: Afrocubanismo and Artistic Revolution in Havana, 1920–1940* (Pittsburgh: University of Pittsburgh Press, 1997).

18. Appeared on *Horace Silver Trio and Spotlight on Drums: Art Blakey—Sabu* (Blue Note 1625).

19. Ibid., quote from liner notes.

20. If Blakey actually did travel to Africa, he could not have been there more than a few months because during this period he was recording for Blue Note in the United States. Blakey's complicated relationship to African music is discussed in great detail in Ingrid Monson, "Art Blakey's African Diaspora," in *The African Diaspora: A Musical Perspective,* ed. Monson (New York: Garland, 2000), 329–252.

21. Guy Warren, interview with Les Tompkins, June 1962, reprinted in Warren, *I Have a Story to Tell,* 175.

22. Letter to the editor, *Accra Daily Graphic*, June 1978, personal archives of Kofi Ghanaba.

23. Letter from Mrs. Elizabeth N. Lartey to Guy Warren, December 20, 1971, archives of Kofi Ghanaba.

24. Letter from Richard Akwei to Guy Warren, June 20, 1956, archives of Kofi Ghanaba.

25. Kofi Ghanaba, interview with author, August 12, 2004; Hartigan, "Ghanaba and the Heritage of African Jazz," 145–146.

26. Ghanaba, interview with author, August 12, 2004. See also Warren, *I Have a Story to Tell*, 13; John Collins, *Highlife Time* (Accra: Anansesem, 1994), 134.

27. Ghanaba, interview with author, August 12, 2004; Hartigan, "Ghanaba and the Heritage of African Jazz," 145–146.

28. See John Collins, *E. T. Mensah: The King of Highlife* (London: Off the Record Press, 1986), 1–4; John Collins, *West African Pop Roots* (Philadelphia: Temple University Press, 1992), 17–31; Sonny Oti, *Highlife Music in West Africa* (Lagos: Malt House Press, 2009).

29. Kofi Ghanaba and Max Roach, conversation, tape in author's possession.

30. Ghanaba, interview with author, August 12, 2004.

31. Ibid.

32. Ibid.; Warren, *I Have a Story to Tell*, 19; Hartigan, "Ghanaba and the Heritage of African Jazz," 146.

33. Ghanaba, interview with author, August 12, 2004.

34. In 1947, the Tempos consisted of Joe Kelly (tenor and vocals), E. T. Mensah (sax, trumpet), Guy Warren (drums), Pop Hughes (sax), Bossman (bass), Peter Johnson (guitar), Von Cofie (piano). Collins, *E. T. Mensah,* 15.

35. Ghanaba, interview with author, August 13, 2004; he tells a similar story in Collins, *E. T. Mensah,* 16.

36. Hartigan, "Ghanaba and the Heritage of African Jazz," 146; *Melody Maker* (June 10, 1950); Warren, *I Have a Story to Tell,* 74–75.

37. Mike Phillips and Trevor Phillips, *Windrush: The Irresistible Rise of Multi-Racial Britain* (New York: HarperCollins, 1998); Ian R. G. Spencer, *British Immigration Policy since 1939: The Making of Multi-racial Britain* (London: Routledge, 1997), 49–56. On the thriving Caribbean

jazz scene, see Alan Robertson, *Joe Harriot: Fire in His Soul* (London: Northway, 2003), 18–28.

38. Ghanaba, interview with author, August 16, 2004. Ted Heath did record "Haitian Ritual" in 1955 on *At the London Palladium, Vol. 3* (De LK4097), but Graham recorded it first, in 1953, on his LP *Caribbean Suite* (Esquire [E]20–023).

39. Ghanaba, interview with author, August 13, 2004; on the station's history, see "ELBC—A Brief History: An Overview of the Liberia Broadcasting System (LBS) Past, Present and Future," available at http://www. liberiabroadcastingsystem.com/about.php.

40. Ghanaba, interview with author, August 12, 2004. Alexander worked at Walter Reed Hospital in Chicago for several years. She was about three years older than Warren and was raised in Chicago by her cousins. U.S. Census, *1930: Population Schedule: Illinois, Cook County—Chicago,* Enumeration District 158.

41. Ghanaba, interview with author, August 12, 2004.

42. Ibid.

43. Warren, *I Have a Story to Tell,* 14–15.

44. Ibid., 16.

45. Ghanaba, interview with author, August 15, 2004.

46. Ghanaba, interview with author, August 12, 2004; Warren, *I Have a Story to Tell,* 17–18. As a consequence of their relationship, Saunders put together an "African review" as a vehicle to introduce jazz and African music to Chicago's public school children. Theodore (Red) Saunders, interview with Don DeMichael, March 7, 1978, Chicago, p. 124.

47. See Art Hodes, "Sittin' In: Looking at Red," *Down Beat* 34, no. 16 (1967), 18.

48. John Collins, "Fela and the Black President Film—A Diary," in *Fela: From West Africa to West Broadway,* ed. Trevor Schoonmaker (New York: Palgrave, 2003), 66.

49. Baker is not mentioned in either the original liner notes or Warren's memoir, though his participation in the session was noted in passing in a brief article in the *Chicago Defender* about a year after the LP had been released. "Eddie Baker Trio Scores Hit," *Chicago Defender,* June 3, 1957. Warren confirmed Baker's presence in an interview with me, and again in a set of revised and corrected liner notes he planned to include in his

updated memoir. This and other documents are gathered in a folder titled "All the Published Music Albums of Ghanaba, Formerly Known as Guy Warren of Ghana," in author's possession.

50. "African Personality in Drumming," *Ghana Times* (May 7, 1960); Warren, *I Have a Story to Tell*, 115.

51. Both quotes in Warren, *I Have a Story to Tell*, 79.

52. Ghanaba, interview with author, August 15, 2004.

53. Ibid.

54. Warren, *I Have a Story to Tell*, 28.

55. Ghanaba, interview with author, August 12, 2004.

56. Chief Bey, panel discussion, "The African Drum: A Symposium," New York University, October 2003, recording in author's possession; Heard and Mussa, "African Dance in New York City," 144. Ismay Andrews was originally born in British Guiana in 1883 and grew up in Philadelphia. See U.S. Census, 1910: *Population Schedule—Philadelphia Ward 14, Philadelphia, Pennsylvania;* Enumeration District 0203.

57. Babatunde Olatunji, with Robert Atkinson, *The Beat of My Drum: An Autobiography* (Philadelphia: Temple University Press, 2005), 140.

58. Warren, *I Have a Story to Tell*, 32–33. Initially, Brown was not available for the date so Warren's producer, Nat Shapiro, suggested another trombonist named Ferdinand "Al" Alcindor. After no less than twelve rehearsals, Warren dismissed the Juilliard-trained Alcindor as an "idiot" and fired him before recording a single track. While Alcindor never distinguished himself as a trombone player, his son, Ferdinand Lewis Alcindor, Jr.—better known as Kareem Abdul-Jabbar—distinguished himself on the basketball court.

59. From liner notes by Guy Warren, The Guy Warren Soundz, *Themes for African Drums* (RCA Victor LSP-1864).

60. Ibid., quote from liner notes.

61. It was recorded on October 22, 1959, and released on Thelonious Monk, *Alone in San Francisco* (Riverside RLP-12–312). On Warren and Monk's relationship, see Robin D. G. Kelley, *Thelonious Monk: The Life and Times of an American Original* (New York: Free Press, 2009), 244–245.

62. Warren, liner notes, *Themes for African Drums.*

63. "A Legacy of Better Health," *University of Arkansas Medicine* (Fall 2003), 42; "UA Receives $3 Million Bequest, Largest Ever in School History,"

Arkansas Gazette, August 3, 1979; "Marie Howells," *Social Security Death Index.* Born in a town bearing her family name (Wilson, Arkansas), her father, Robert E. Lee Wilson, would honor his daughter by naming a neighboring town Marie.

64. Ghanaba, interview with author, August 14, 2004.

65. Ibid.

66. Ibid.

67. See Monson, "Art Blakey's African Diaspora," 334–335; Art Blakey, *Orgy in Rhythm: Vols. 1 and 2* (Blue Note 56586), recorded March 7, 1957, had Blakey, Arthur Taylor, Jo Jones, and "Specs" Wright on drums and tympani; Sabu Martinez (bongo and timbales); "Patato" Valdez and Jose Valiente (congas); Ubaldo Nieto (timbales); Evilio Quintero (cencerro, maracas, tree log); Herbie Mann (flute); Ray Bryant (piano); and Wendell Marshall (bass).

68. Guy Warren, interview with Les Tompkins, June 1962, reprinted in Warren, *I Have a Story to Tell,* 183.

69. "Nigerian Students Given Big Ovation in Atlanta," *Atlanta Daily World,* April 27, 1950. On his original intentions and move to Morehouse, see Olatunji, *The Beat of My Drum,* 87.

70. Leroy Aiken, "'Africa No Longer Dark Land,' Says Nigerian Student in Speech," *Atlanta Daily World,* February 2, 1954; "'Africa Yesterday, Today, and T'morrow' to Be Olatunji's Topic at Mt. Calvary," *Atlanta Daily World,* January 30, 1954.

71. Olatunji, *The Beat of My Drum,* 95–96, 117–118; "Musical Group in Performance," *Atlanta Daily World,* May 1, 1954.

72. Olatunji, *The Beat of My Drum,* 123–128.

73. Ibid., 138–143.

74. "Jungle Drum Beats Out a Cultural Message to Pupils," *New York Times,* May 30, 1958; "Dance Summer," *New York Times,* July 20, 1958; "Nigerian Student Plays Drums Here," *New York Times,* October 19, 1958; Olatunji, *The Beat of My Drum,* 132–134.

75. The story of Olatunji's initial limitations is not new. Eric Charry's introduction to Olatunji's memoir says as much (see Olatunji, *The Beat of My Drum,* 4). However, there had been long-simmering resentment over the fact that Olatunji received virtually all of the credit for *Drums of Passion* while Bey, Duvall, and Joe were ignored. The tensions flared

at "The African Drum: A Symposium," held at New York University in October 2003. Organized in the wake of Olatunji's death (April 2003), all three men were in attendance and shared their stories of working with the group.

76. "Ghana Ball Reflections: Windy City Smart Set Hails Forming of West African Republic," *Chicago Defender,* March 23, 1957; "Ancient Nigerian Rhythms Beat at Ghana Ball," *Chicago Defender,* March 12, 1957.

77. Olatunji, *The Beat of My Drum,* 136–137.

78. Warren had heard this charge many times before. Critic Leonard Feather once caught him at the African Room and said to him, "Why don't you change your name from Guy Warren to an African name?" At the time, Warren did not see the point because he had worked so hard to establish himself under his existing name, but years later, upon further reflection, he declared, "it was a good suggestion which I didn't accept or welcome at that point in time. But then again, when the personality really changed and the music really changed I felt . . . that carrying the name Guy Warren was not appropriate at all." Ghanaba, interview with author, August 14, 2004.

79. Exchange reprinted in Warren, *I Have a Story to Tell,* 137.

80. Quote from liner notes.

81. *African Rhythms: The Exciting Soundz of Guy Warren and His Talking Drums* (Decca DL-4243).

82. *Emergent Drums* (Columbia 33SX 1584); *Native Africa,* Vol. 1 (KPM 1053); *Native Africa,* vol. 2 (KPM 1054); *Afro-Jazz* (EMI/Columbia SCX-6340); *The African Soundz of Guy Warren of Ghana* (EMI Records Fiesta FLPS-1646).

83. *Herbie Mann at the Village Gate* (Atlantic 1380).

84. Art Blakey and the Afro-Drum Ensemble, *The African Beat* (Blue Note BLP 4097). Recorded January 24, 1962. The personnel included Solomon G. Ilori, a Nigerian (pennywhistle, talking drum); Chief Bey (conga, telegraph drum, double gong); Montego Joe (Bambara drum, double gong, corboro drum, log drum); Garvin Masseaux (chekere, African maracas, conga); James Ola Folami, also from Nigeria (conga); Robert Crowder (bata drum, conga); Yusef Lateef (oboe, flute, tenor sax, cow horn, thumb piano); and bassist Ahmed Abdul-Malik. Surprisingly, the tympani player is trombonist Curtis Fuller.

85. Quoted in liner notes to *The African Beat.*

86. Robert Shelton, "Shifting Tides in African Music," *New York Times*, November 1, 1959.

87. Warren, *I Have a Story to Tell*, 119–122. He reprinted several letters from fans and defenders of his music from the United States and within Ghana, some directly responding to criticisms of his 1960 performance of "The Third Phase."

88. *Emergent Drums* (Columbia 33SX 1584) [U.K.]; *Afro-Jazz* (Columbia SCX 6340) [U.K.]. Warren recorded a two-LP set, *Native Africa* (KPM 1053 and KPM 1054).

2. The Sojourns of Randy Weston

1. Randy Weston, with Willard Jenkins, *African Rhythms: The Autobiography of Randy Weston* (Durham, NC: Duke University Press, 2010), 18.

2. U.S. Selective Service System, *Selective Service Registration Cards, World War II: Fourth Registration*, 1942, Roll WW2_2370851, National Archives.

3. Passenger and Crew Lists of Vessels Arriving at New York, New York, 1897–1957: Year, 1924; Microfilm roll T715_3513; Line 3, pg. 146, National Archives.

4. UNIA citations; on the Fourth International Convention of the Negro Peoples, see Robert Hill, ed., *The Marcus Garvey and Universal Negro Improvement Association Papers*, vol. 5 (Berkeley: University of California Press, 1987); Amy Jacques Garvey, ed., *The Philosophy and Opinions of Marcus Garvey* (Dover, MA: Majority Press, 1986), 101.

5. On the S.S. *Esperanza*'s ship manifest, Frank Weston indicated that Brooklyn was his final destination.

6. Vivian Moore and her mother, Octavia Marable, appear twice on the 1920 Census; once at their employer's address in Elizabeth City, and again at the home of Samuel Marable, Octavia's husband and Vivian's stepfather. It is possible that she was divorced in 1920 because one entry lists her as married, the other as divorced. She had no children, and if she had siblings they did not live in the same household. U.S. Bureau of the Census, *Fourteenth Census of the United States, 1920: Fort Monroe,*

Elizabeth City, Virginia, Enumeration District 30, p. 16B; U.S. Bureau of the Census, *Fourteenth Census of the United States, 1920: Chesapeake, Elizabeth City, Virginia,* Enumeration District 28, p. 17B.

7. U.S. Bureau of the Census, *Fifteenth Census of the United States, 1930, Brooklyn, Kings, New York,* Enumeration District 667, p. 7B; Weston, *African Rhythms,* 5.

8. Weston, *African Rhythms,* 18; Randy Weston, interview with author, July 30, 2003.

9. Weston, *African Rhythms,* 16; U.S. Selective Service System, *Selective Service Registration Cards, World War II.* On Frank Weston's draft registration card, he lists the business at 340 Sumner Avenue as a barbershop. It may have been a barbershop at first, but he quickly turned it into a luncheonette. Randy clearly remembers that space and location as Trios. Randy Weston, interview with author, July 30, 2003.

10. Arthur Taylor, *Notes and Tones: Musician-to-Musician Interviews* (New York: Da Capo Press, 1993), 20.

11. Weston, *African Rhythms,* 23–35; Randy Weston, interview with author, July 30, 2003.

12. Randy Weston, Lecture/Interview, Duke Ellington Society, New York Chapter, 1967, cassette deposited in New York Public Library; Ira Gitler, "Randy Weston," *Down Beat* (February 27, 1964), 16.

13. Tommy Watkins, "Escapading in Brooklyn," *Amsterdam News,* October 10, 1942; Gitler, "Randy Weston," 16.

14. Ahmed Abdul-Malik, interview with Ed Berger, "Jazz from the Archives," WBGO, recorded January 30, 1984, tape at Institute for Jazz Studies, Rutgers University, New Brunswick, NJ (hereafter IJS).

15. Weston, *African Rhythms,* 60; also Randy Weston, interview with author, August 20, 2001; Gitler, "Randy Weston," 16.

16. Electronic Army Serial Number Merged File, 1938–1946 [Archival Database], World War II Army Enlistment Records, National Archives; Milton R. Bass, "The Lively Arts," *Berkshire Evening Eagle,* December 28, 1954; Weston, *African Rhythms,* 28–35.

17. Weston, *African Rhythms,* 53.

18. Ibid., 26; Randy Weston, Lecture/Interview, Duke Ellington Society; Randy Weston, interview with author, July 30, 2003.

19. "'Jazz Encyclopedia' Questionnaire: Randy Weston" (typescript form, 1954), Vertical Files, IJS; Gitler, "Randy Weston," 16; Weston, *African Rhythms,* 38–41.

20. Weston, *African Rhythms,* 43–46; Gitler, "Randy Weston," 17; Randy Weston, interview with author, July 30, 2003. In his memoir, Weston gives 1952 as his first year going to the Berkshires, but in an interview he gave to the *Berkshire Evening Eagle,* he unequivocally identifies 1951 as his first year there. Given that the interview was conducted in 1954, it is probably pretty accurate. Milton R. Bass, "The Lively Arts."

21. Weston, *African Rhythms,* 45–46.

22. Jeremy Yudkin, *The Lenox School of Jazz: A Vital Chapter in the History of American Music and Race Relations* (South Egremont, MA: Farshaw, 2006), 16–33.

23. Randy Weston, interview with author, July 30, 2003. See also Weston, *African Rhythms,* 48–49; Gitler, "Randy Weston," 17.

24. Initially funded by a Guggenheim award Stearns received in 1950, *The Story of Jazz* was published by Oxford University Press in 1956. On Stearns and the "Jazz Roundtables," see John Gennari, *Blowin' Hot and Cool: Jazz and Its Critics* (Chicago: University of Chicago Press, 2006), 144–153; Yudkin, *The Lenox School of Jazz,* 28–29; *Music Inn: A Documentary Film,* produced and directed by Ben Barenholtz (Projectile Arts, 2007).

25. "Berkshire Jazz Roundtable," *Christian Science Monitor,* August 15, 1953; "Prof. James in Afro-American Music Talks," *Atlanta Daily World,* July 11, 1962; Randy Weston, interview with author, July 30, 2003.

26. Stephanie Barber, quoted in *Music Inn: A Documentary Film.*

27. Randy Weston, interview with author, February 22, 1999; Gitler, "Randy Weston," 17.

28. "Berkshire Jazz Roundtable."

29. Weston, *African Rhythms,* 49; Randy Weston, interview with author, February 22, 1999.

30. Advertisement, "Attention Please! African Recreation Center," *Amsterdam News,* December 3, 1949. Odok is also discussed in Chapter 1.

31. Quotation from Bilal Abdurahman, *In the Key of Me: The Bedford Stuyvesant Renaissance, 1940s–60s Revisited* (Brooklyn: Contemporary Visions, 1993). The self-published text has no page numbers.

32. Peter Kihss, "Negro Extremist Groups Step Up Nationalist Drive," *New York Times,* March 1, 1961; and see Chapter 3 for a discussion of the African Quarter, Brooklyn's first African restaurant.

33. "'Jazz Encyclopedia' Questionnaire: Randy Weston."

34. Quoted in Nat Hentoff, "The Continuous Growth of Randy Weston," *International Musician* (November 1964), 21–22.

35. On Monk and Weston's relationship, see Robin D. G. Kelley, *Thelonious Monk: The Life and Times of an American Original* (New York: Free Press, 2009), 98, 119, 165, 185, 191.

36. Weston, *African Rhythms,* 59.

37. Rick Kennedy and Randy McNutt, *Little Labels—Big Sound: Small Record Companies and the Rise of American Music* (Bloomington: Indiana University Press, 1999), 107–110; Jesse Hamlin, "A Life in Jazz," *Columbia College Today* (November 2004), available at www.college.columbia.edu/cct/nov04/features2.php; Orrin Keepnews, *The View from Within: Jazz Writings, 1948–1987* (New York: Oxford University Press, 1988), 120.

38. Randy Weston, interview with author, February 22, 1999; Gitler, "Randy Weston," 17. Keepnews's approach reflected a growing trend emerging in the 1950s to "mainstream" or canonize jazz. Thus Riverside's first modern LP, *Cole Porter in a Modern Mood* (Riverside RLP 2508), was in essence a mainstreaming project. See Mark Tucker, "Mainstreaming Monk: The Ellington Album," *Black Music Research Journal* 19, no. 2 (1999), 231–232.

39. *The Randy Weston Trio with Art Blakey* (Riverside RLP 2515). "Zulu" is similar to Monk's compositions in that the harmonic motion in the A and B sections consists of chromatically descending 7th chords with flat 5ths, while the C section is an eight-measure vamp of an altered 7th chord.

40. Liner notes, *The Modern Art of Jazz* (Dawn DLP-1116).

41. "Basie Tops in Big Band Mag Voting," *Chicago Defender,* August 27, 1955.

42. *Get Happy with the Randy Weston Trio* (Riverside RLP 12–203).

43. Randy Weston/Cecil Payne, *Jazz A La Bohemia* (Riverside RLP 12–232); Weston, *The Modern Art of Jazz* (Dawn DLP-1116); *Piano à la Mode* (Jubilee 1060).

44. Randy Weston, *With These Hands . . . The Randy Weston Trio with Cecil Payne* (Riverside RLP 12–214).

45. Weston, quoted in Taylor, *Notes and Tones*, 23.

46. Weston, *African Rhythms*, 82–83. It is not clear when in 1958 Weston began work on the piece, but he did debut an excerpt from what he was then calling "Bantu Suite" at the Newport Jazz Festival on July 5, 1958. He performed with his trio—Jamil Nasser on bass and Wilbert G. T. Hogan on drums. See *New Faces at Newport* (MGM [E]EP687). Besides his memoir, there are many sources in which he identifies 1958 as the year he began working on *Uhuru Afrika*. See, for example, "Nous Sommes Tous Africains," *L'Autre Afrique* 25 (31 July–3 September 2002), 14; Randy Weston, Lecture/Interview, Duke Ellington Society, New York Chapter, 1967.

47. For a profile of Melba Liston, see Erica Kaplan, "Melba Liston: It's All from My Soul," *The Antioch Review* 57, no. 3 (Summer 1999), 415–425; Dalia Pagani, "Melba Liston: Interview," *Cadence* (May 1984), 5–12.

48. Randy Weston, Lecture/Interview, Duke Ellington Society, New York Chapter, 1967.

49. Randy Weston, *Little Niles* (United Artists UAL 4011). It should be noted that the sextet for this session would make up the core of his historic big band responsible for *Uhuru Afrika*. The band consisted of trumpeters Ray Copeland and Idris Sulieman (who replaces Copeland on one tune, "Babe's Blues"), Melba Liston on trombone, saxophonist Johnny Griffin, Jamil Nasser on bass, Charlie Persip on drums, and of course, Weston.

50. They performed at the Market Place Gallery for an art opening, the Village Gate, and the Vanguard, to name a few. Jesse H. Walker, "Theatricals," *Amsterdam News*, March 14, 1959; Jesse H. Walker, "Theatricals," *Amsterdam News*, May 9, 1959; Arnold Rampersad, *The Life of Langston Hughes*, vol. 2 (New York: Oxford University Press, 2002), 280.

51. Once Weston decided to include a ki-Swahili translation in the suite, the final line was altered and "Uhuru" was inserted next to "Freedom." Thus the final line reads: "Out of yesterday's night, Uhuru/Freedom! Uhuru! Freedom!"

52. Weston, *African Rhythms*, 89–90.

53. Advertisement, "Jazz for Civil Rights," *Amsterdam News*, September 26,

1959; "Jazz Stars Will Play for NAACP," *Amsterdam News,* September 26, 1959.

54. Billed as "The Story of Jazz," these lecture-performances were so successful that Pepsi Cola agreed to sponsor a national tour of colleges and universities. Langston Hughes ended up replacing Stearns after he suffered a heart attack. The program came to an abrupt end after Pepsi Cola withdrew funding around 1961–1962. Randy Weston, Lecture/Interview, Duke Ellington Society, New York Chapter, 1967; Weston, *African Rhythms,* 52; advertisement, *Chicago Tribune,* October 1, 1961.

55. Weston, *African Rhythms,* 83.

56. Ibid., 85–86; Randy Weston, interview with author, August 20, 2001.

57. Richard Jennings and UN Staff Recreation Council Jazz Society, *Twenty-Five Years of the UNSRC Jazz Society, April 1959–April 1985: Special Issue of "The World of Jazz"* (New York: United Nations, 1985), 3–9. Hanson's talk is discussed on p. 9.

58. Randy Weston, interview with author, February 22, 1999; Weston, *African Rhythms,* 92–95.

59. Billy Taylor and Quincy Jones followed with their take on *My Fair Lady,* as did Oscar Peterson; Eddie Costa and later the Manhattan Jazz All-Stars took on *Guys and Dolls;* and Miles Davis and Gil Evans scored a big hit with *Porgy and Bess* in 1958. United Artists, in particular, was committed to this format, having just recorded *Porgy and Bess—Highlights* featuring singer Diahann Carroll and Andre Previn, and *The Jazz Soul of Porgy and Bess* by Billy Potts and an all-star band. See, for example, Tim J. Anderson, *Making Easy Listening: Material Culture and Postwar American Recording* (Minneapolis: University of Minnesota Press, 2006), 92–93; John Szwed, *So What: The Life of Miles Davis* (New York: Simon and Schuster, 2002), 164–165; Jack Chambers, *Milestones I: The Music and Times of Miles Davis to 1960* (New York: Beech Tree Books—William Morrow, 1983), 290–291; Diahann Carroll, *Porgy and Bess—Highlights* (United Artists UAL4021); Billy Potts and His Orchestra, *The Jazz Soul of Porgy and Bess* (United Artists UAL4032).

60. The story of how Weston came to record *Destry Rides Again* is told in Weston, *African Rhythms,* 94–95. In a strange ironic twist, six years later Harold Rome would write the music for *The Zulu and the Zayada,* a play set in Johannesburg about a friendship between two displaced

people, a Jewish grandfather who came to South Africa to live with his son after having been uprooted at least twice, and a local Zulu whose native land was expropriated by whites. It featured some leading black male actors, including Lou Gossett, Ossie Davis, and Yaphet Kotto. Rome was enthusiastic about the play because he had been an avid collector of African art since 1939, and he developed an interest in African music—even before he scored the cowboy comedy, *Destry Rides Again.* Although they apparently never met, Weston and Rome had much in common. See Ken Bloom, *The Routledge Guide to Broadway* (New York: Routledge, 2007), 227.

61. Frederick Dannen, *Hit Men: Power Brokers and Fast Money Inside the Music Business* (New York: Vintage, 1991), 31–40; Phil Ramone, with Charles Granata, *Making Records: The Scenes Behind the Music* (New York: Hyperion, 2007), 23–24.

62. Taylor, *Notes and Tones,* 23; Weston, interview with author, July 30, 2003.

63. Randy Weston Lecture/Interview, Duke Ellington Society, New York Chapter, 1967; Weston, interview with author, August 20, 2001.

64. Charlie Persip, quoted in Weston, *African Rhythms,* 99.

65. Weston, *African Rhythms,* 93.

66. Langston Hughes, liner notes, *Uhuru Afrika* (Roulette Records SR65001). For excellent musical analyses of *Uhuru Afrika,* see Ingrid Monson, *Freedom Sounds: Civil Rights Call Out to Jazz and Africa* (New York: Oxford University Press, 2007), 149–152; and Jason J. Squinobal, "West African Music in the Music of Art Blakey, Yusef Lateef, and Randy Weston" (Ph.D. diss., University of Pittsburgh, 2009). See also Norman Weinstein, *A Night in Tunisia: Imaginings of Africa in Jazz* (New York: Limelight Editions, 1993), 110–112.

67. Weston, *African Rhythms,* 6–7.

68. Taylor, *Notes and Tones,* 23; Weston, *African Rhythms,* 93, 98–99; Monson, *Freedom Sounds,* 149. On Martha Flowers, see Maya Angelou, *Singin' and Swingin' and Gettin' Merry Like Christmas* (New York: Bantam Books, 1977), 115.

69. His trio at the time consisted of Jamil Nasser on bass and Wilbert G. T. Hogan on drums. See *New Faces at Newport.*

70. Hughes, liner notes, *Uhuru Afrika.*
71. Weston, *African Rhythms,* 93.
72. Ibid.
73. As Weston once explained in a 1980 interview, he always included the blues in his repertoire "so people can recognize that there's actually no difference in the musics. It's like I'm developing the language of the African talking drums on piano." Lem Lyons, *The Great Jazz Pianists, Speaking of Their Lives and Music* (New York: Da Capo, 1983), 213.
74. Hughes, liner notes, *Uhuru Afrika.*
75. "Reviews and Ratings of New Albums," *Billboard* (May 8, 1961), 31. See also the review in *Metronome* 78, no. 9 (1961), 40.
76. Ludo De Witte, *The Assassination of Lumumba* (London: Verso Books, 2001); William Blum, *Killing Hope: U.S. Military and CIA Interventions since World War II* (London: Zed Books, 2003), 156–162.
77. Kihss, "Negro Extremist Groups Step Up Nationalist Drive." Among the individuals singled out for their role in the UN protests, Kihss mentions singer Abbey Lincoln, a leader of the Cultural Association for Women of African Heritage and one of the principal organizers of the protests. She argued that militant protest was the only option available, denouncing "crumb-crunching, cocktail-sipping Uncle Tom leadership paid by the colonialists."
78. For an excellent discussion of *We Insist! Max Roach's Freedom Now Suite* (Candid CJM8002), see Monson, *Freedom Sounds,* 171–183.
79. In March 1962, for example, critic Ira Gitler published a highly defensive critique of black protest politics in jazz in the guise of a review of Abbey Lincoln's album *Straight Ahead.* Gitler disparaged her militant politics, criticized the fact that there were no white musicians on the date, and called her "naive" for her support of African nationalism. In Gitler's mind, this album and the current trends in jazz were precursors to a powerful black separatist movement. He warned, "we don't need the Elijah Muhammed [*sic*] type thinking in jazz." Ira Gitler, "Racial Prejudice in Jazz," *Down Beat* (May 24, 1962), 24. The controversy led to a panel discussion titled "Racial Prejudice in Jazz," the results of which were printed in *Down Beat.*
80. Taylor, *Notes and Tones,* 23.

81. "Disc Albums Banned in South Africa," *Chicago Defender,* October 17, 1964; "South Africa Bans Lena Horne Disc," *Amsterdam News,* October 3, 1964.

82. According to Weston, the invitation was the result of a series of fortuitous events. Initially, he wasn't on Davis's radar. However, Weston's former girlfriend, Jean Krentz, was working with AMSAC at the time, and she personally made the case to Davis, showing him Weston's various LPs and demonstrating his knowledge of and interest in the continent. Weston shared this story with me in interviews and tells it in his memoir, *African Rhythms,* 102–103. However, the archives tell a slightly different story, revealing that Davis had known about Weston for quite some time but had kept him at arm's length for months before accepting him.

83. On the founding of AMSAC and CIA support, see Hugh Wilford, *The Mighty Wurlitzer: How the CIA Played America* (Cambridge, MA: Harvard University Press, 2008), 197–224; Lawrence P. Jackson, *The Indignant Generation: A Narrative History of African American Writers and Critics, 1943–1960* (Princeton: Princeton University Press, 2010), 462–463; Brenda Gayle Plummer, *Rising Wind: Black Americans and U.S. Foreign Affairs, 1935–1960* (Chapel Hill: University of North Carolina Press, 1996), 256; Dan Schechter, Michael Ansara, and David Kolodney, "The CIA as an Equal Opportunity Employer," in *Dirty Work 2: The CIA in Africa,* ed. Ellen Ray, William Schaap, Karl Van Meter, and Louis Wolf (Secaucus, NJ: Lyle Stuart, 1979), 50–69; Penny Von Eschen, *Race Against Empire: Black Americans and Anti-Colonialism, 1937–1957* (Ithaca, NY: Cornell University Press, 1997), 175; James Smethurst, *The Black Arts Movement: Literary Nationalism in the 1960s and 1970s* (Chapel Hill: University of North Carolina Press, 2005), 120; John J. Munro, "The Anticolonial Front: Cold War Imperialism and the Struggle against Global White Supremacy, 1945–1960" (Ph.D. diss., University of California, Santa Barbara, 2009), 404–410.

84. Von Eschen, *Race Against Empire;* Plummer, *Rising Wind,* 167–297; Hollis R. Lynch, *Black American Radicals and the Liberation of Africa: The Council on African Affairs, 1937–1955* (Ithaca, NY: Center for Research in Africana Studies, 1978); Gerald Horne, *Communist Front? The Civil*

Rights Congress, 1946–1956 (Rutherford, NJ: Fairleigh Dickinson University Press, 1988).

85. A. C. Thompson to John A. Davis, June 22, 1961, Box 22, AMSAC Papers, Moorland-Spingarn Research Center, Howard University, Washington, D.C. [hereafter AMSAC Papers]. On Thompson, see "Seeks New UN Commission on South Africa," *Amsterdam News,* January 19, 1957; Thomasina Ford, "On the Town," *Amsterdam News,* December 26, 1959.

86. A. C. Thompson to John A. Davis, September 13, 1961, Box 22, AMSAC Papers.

87. Randy Weston to John A. Davis, September 23, 1961, Box 22, AMSAC Papers.

88. John A. Davis to Calvin H. Raullerson, September 13, 1961, Box 2, AMSAC Papers.

89. Memorandum, Yvonne O. Walker to Calvin H. Ralluerson, October 9, 1961, Box 2, AMSAC Papers.

90. The first mention of Weston's participation in the Lagos trip appears in a November 20 memo, although he did not sign a contract until November 22. Memorandum, Yvonne O. Walker to Calvin H. Ralluerson, November 20, 1961, Box 2, AMSAC Papers; Agreement between American Society of African Culture and Randy Weston, November 22, 1961, Box 22, AMSAC Papers.

91. "Draft of Program Participants as It Appears as of December 4—(per J. K. B.)," Box 2, AMSAC Papers; AMSAC Festival Program, King George V Stadium, Lagos, Nigeria, December 18 and 19, 1961, Box 4, AMSAC Papers. The "Afro-American jam session" quote comes from cablegram, Yvonne O. Walker to Calvin Raullerson and James Baker, November 29, 1961, Box 2, AMSAC Papers.

92. "U.S. Negroes, Nigerians Begin Own Cultural Program During 2-Day Meet," *Chicago Defender,* December 2, 1961; "33 U.S. Negroes Off for 2-Day Cultural Program in Nigeria," *Chicago Defender,* December 12, 1961; Morris Kaplan, "U.S. Negro Artists Go to Africa to Join in Cultural Exchange," *New York Times,* December 14, 1961; "African-American Cultural Exchange," *Ebony* (March 1962), 87; Gitler, "Randy Weston," 36; Weston, *African Rhythms,* 103–104.

93. Langston Hughes commented on the poor attendance at the morning

panels. Langston Hughes, response, Lagos Festival Participant Questionnaire, Box 4, AMSAC Papers.

94. "U.S. Negroes, Nigerians Begin Own Cultural Program"; "33 U.S. Negroes Off for 2-Day Cultural Program"; "African-American Cultural Exchange."

95. AMSAC Festival Program, King George V Stadium, Lagos, Nigeria, December 18 and 19, 1961, Box 4, AMSAC Papers.

96. Quoted in Rampersad, *The Life of Langston Hughes,* 2:348. The African American press, in contrast, described Hampton's performance as a rousing success. "Lionel Hampton Heads Star Group in Africa," *Chicago Defender,* January 6, 1962. Hampton's finale was deemed so "bad" that when Davis set out to make an LP of the performances for commercial and educational release, he and his staff decided, after much hand wringing, to exclude his set from the disc. See memo from John A. Davis to James K. Baker, January 12, 1962, Box 4, AMSAC Papers; memo from James K. Baker to John A. Davis, May 22, 1962, Box 4, AMSAC Papers.

97. "U.S. Negroes, Nigerians Begin Own Cultural Program"; "33 U.S. Negroes Off for 2-Day Cultural Program"; "African-American Cultural Exchange." The fact that some of the Nigerian names were misspelled in the program could not have helped their credibility. Mike Falana, for example, appeared as Mike Falani.

98. Quoted in Rampersad, *The Life of Langston Hughes,* 2:348; "African-American Cultural Exchange."

99. Both quotes from "African-American Cultural Exchange," 88.

100. All quotes from responses by Willis James, Oliver Jackson, and Al Minns, Lagos Festival Participant Questionnaire, Box 4, AMSAC Papers.

101. Langston Hughes, response, Lagos Festival Participant Questionnaire, Box 4, AMSAC Papers.

102. Natalie Hinderas, response, Lagos Festival Participant Questionnaire, Box 4, AMSAC Papers.

103. Randy Weston, "Notes on AMSAC's Proposed Program for 1963–1964," Box 22, AMSAC Papers.

104. Quoted in Gitler, "Randy Weston," 36.

105. John S. Wilson, "American Jazzmen Overseas," *New York Times,* July 14, 1957.

106. Chief Bassey Ita, *Jazz in Nigeria: An Outline Cultural History* (Lagos: A Radical House Publication, 1984), 14–15; Jack O'Dell, interview with author, October 25, 2010.

107. Sonny Oti, *High Life Music in West Africa* (Lagos: Malthouse Press, 2009), 179; Christopher Alan Waterman, *Jùjú: A Social History and Ethnography of an African Popular Music* (Chicago: University of Chicago Press, 1990), 42–45, 83; Benson Idonije, "Remembering Bobby Benson," available at http://www.championsfornigeria.org/cfn/index.php?option =com_content&view=article&id=129:remembering-bobby-benson-of -africa&catid =1:latest&Itemid=2. Most accounts of Bobby Benson state that he was a member of "the Negro Ballet," but the actual name of the group was "Les Ballets Nègres." For a brief description of the troupe, see Alison Donnell, ed., *Companion to Contemporary British Culture* (London: Routledge, 2002), 122.

108. Ita, *Jazz in Nigeria,* 18–26, 45; for a comprehensive gathering of interviews, essays, tributes, and photos documenting the life and work of Steve Rhodes, see http://www.livingprojectslimited.com/steverhodes/ home.htm.

109. Quoted in Ita, *Jazz in Nigeria,* 26.

110. All three quotes from "Satchmo in West Africa," *Drum* (February 1961), 25.

111. Ivan Annan, "Are West Africans Squares? In Ghana We Certainly Are," *Drum* (February 1961), 29.

112. Nelson Ottah, "Are West Africans Squares? We Haven't Got the Concentration," *Drum* (February 1961), 29.

113. Weston, *African Rhythms,* 106.

114. Randy Weston to Bobby Benson, January 10, 1961 [*sic*], in Randy Weston's possession. The letter was obviously written in 1962.

115. Flyer, "Ndugu Ngoma Presents, Pianists Unlimited, Saturday October 12, 1963"; Activities of Randy Weston, October 24, 1963, both documents in Box 22, AMSAC Papers; Gitler, "Randy Weston," 36; "Dizzy Heads Board for Jazz Society," *Amsterdam News,* April 29, 1961. Weston also devoted much of his time to playing benefits for a variety of political causes. Just months after he returned from Africa, he participated in a benefit for the radical black publication, *Freedomways.* "Magazine to Mark First Year at Dance," *Amsterdam News,* June 2, 1962. For a more

thorough discussion and accounting of Weston's benefit performances, see Monson, *Freedom Sounds.*

116. Promotional flyer for The Story of Jazz in Music and Dance, n.d., Box 22, AMSAC Papers.

117. "Prof. James in Afro-American Music Talks."

118. AMSAC Membership Form, Randy Weston, Box 22; Randy Weston to John A. Davis, August 16, 1962, Box 22, AMSAC Papers.

119. Randy Weston to John A. Davis, November 11, 1963, Box 22; Randy Weston, "Notes on AMSAC's Proposed Program for 1963–1964," p. 2, Box 22, AMSAC Papers.

120. Ibid., pp. 1–2.

121. Ibid., pp. 2–4.

122. John A. Davis to Randy Weston, December 17, 1963, Box 22, AMSAC Papers.

123. Weston retained much of the personnel from the *Uhuru* sessions, but with notable changes in the percussion section. Only drummer Charlie Persip played on both dates. The band consisted of Ray Copeland (trumpet), Quentin Jackson (trombone), Julius Watkins (Fr. horn), Aaron Bell (tuba); Booker Ervin (tenor); Budd Johnson (soprano, tenor); Randy Weston; Peck Morrison (bass); Charlie Persip (drums); Archie Lee (congas); other percussion by Frankie Dunlop and George Young. Randy Weston, *Music from the New African Nations Featuring the Highlife* (Colpix CP 456).

124. "Highlife, More Afro-Asian Rhythms, Jazz Up Jazz Scene Says Weston," *Music Vendor,* July 13, 1963.

125. "Elton Fax and Randy Weston in Lagos: AMSAC and NIGERSAC Co-Sponsor Symposia," *AMSAC Newsletter* 5, no. 11 (June 1963), 1; "Randy Finds Rapport with the Brethren," *Pittsburgh Courier,* July 13, 1963; "Randy Weston Scores in Africa," *Chicago Defender,* July 3, 1963; Weston, *African Rhythms,* 104–106.

126. *Lagos Sunday Post,* May 19, 1963.

127. "Randy Finds Rapport with the Brethren"; "Elton Fax and Randy Weston in Lagos," 1.

128. Quoted in "Elton Fax and Randy Weston in Lagos," 1.

129. Gitler, "Randy Weston," 36.

130. Bayo Martins to Randy Weston, April 7, 1965, Box 22, AMSAC Papers.

131. Weston to Bayo Martins, June 20, 1965, Weston to Yvonne O. Walker, June 20, 1965, Box 22, AMSAC Papers.

132. See "Randy Weston & Orchestra at Village Gate," July 11, 1963, press release; Georgia Griggs, "AN INVITATION TO HEAR . . . RANDY WESTON AT THE VILLAGE GATE," typescript press release, July 1963, in author's possession.

133. All quotes from Statement of Purpose about "History of Jazz" Concerts During Negro History Week, February 7–14, 1965, Box 22, AMSAC Papers; Dick Read, "The New Scene," *Crisis* (March 1966), 151–154.

134. Statement of Purpose about "History of Jazz" Concerts; flyer, A "History of Jazz" Concert by the Randy Weston Sextet, Countee Cullen Library, February 17, 1965; flyer, A "History of Jazz" Concert by the Randy Weston Sextet, Halsey Junior High School, February 16, 1965, Box 22, AMSAC Papers.

135. Taylor, *Notes and Tones*, 19.

136. Read, "The New Scene," 153; see also Carole Levine, "Teen-agers Tune in on Jazz Man's Lesson," *Newark Star-Ledger*, December 11, 1966.

137. Rampersad, *The Life of Langston Hughes*, 1:400.

138. Edward Kennedy Ellington, *Music Is My Mistress* (New York: Da Capo Press, 1976), 337. See also Von Eschen, *Satchmo Blows Up the World*, 150.

139. Hoyt W. Fuller, "Festival Postscripts," *Negro Digest* (June 1966), 83; see also Hoyt W. Fuller, "World Festival of Negro Arts," *Ebony* (July 1966), 102.

140. "Memorial Jazz for Haynes," *Amsterdam News*, December 11, 1965.

141. Weston, *African Rhythms*, 115–116; Georgia Griggs, "With Randy Weston in Africa," *Down Beat* (July 13, 1967), 16.

142. This brief survey draws on the following sources: David and Marina Ottaway, *Algeria: The Politics of a Socialist Revolution* (Berkeley: University of California Press, 1970), 174–195; John Douglas Ruedy, *Modern Algeria: The Origins and Development of a Nation* (Bloomington: Indiana University Press, 2005), 205–207; Blum, *Killing Hope*, 198–200; Ahmad A. Rahman, *The Regime Change of Kwame Nkrumah* (New York: Palgrave Macmillan, 2007); Kevin K. Gaines, *African Americans in Ghana: Black Expatriates and the Civil Rights Era* (Chapel Hill: University of North Carolina Press, 2006), 165–166, 219–248 passim; Amadu

Sessay, Charles Ukeje, et al., *Post-War Regimes and State Reconstruction in Liberia and Sierra Leone* (Dakar: Council for the Development of Social Science Research in Africa, 2009), 27–33; Andrea L. Stamm, Dawn E. Bastian, and Robert A. Myers, compilers, *Mali* (Oxford: Clio Press, 1998), 134–135; Giordano Sivini, *Resistance to Modernization* (New Brunswick, NJ: Transaction, 2007), 35–38; Jeggan Colley Senghor, *The Politics of Senegambian Integration, 1958–1994* (Bern, Switzerland: Peter Lang, 2008), 124–125; David A. Yates, *The Rentier State in Africa: Oil Rent Dependency and Neocolonialism in the Republic of Gabon* (Trenton, NJ: Africa World Press, 1996), 112–117; Christopher S. Clapham, *Africa and the International System: The Politics of State Survival* (Cambridge: Cambridge University Press, 2002), 95–96; Michael B. Oren, *Six Days of War: June 1967 and the Making of the Modern Middle East* (New York: Rosetta Books, 2003).

143. Weston, *African Rhythms*, 119.

144. Griggs, "With Randy Weston in Africa," 16–17; Randy Weston, interview with author, July 30, 2003. In all other accounts, Niles is described as fifteen years old, but he was born August 12, 1950, making him sixteen during the first three months of 1967. Azzedin Weston Resume, ca. 1977, in author's possession.

145. Weston, *African Rhythms*, 123.

146. Ibid., 123; see also Griggs, "With Randy Weston in Africa," 17. The best account of the tour, besides Weston's own memoir, can be found in Von Eschen, *Satchmo Blows Up the World*, 171–177.

147. Dr. E. Otis Pratt, "Caught in the Act: Randy Weston, Freetown University," *Down Beat* (June 29, 1967), 46.

148. Quoted in Von Eschen, *Satchmo Blows Up the World*, 173.

149. Quoted in Griggs, "With Randy Weston in Africa," 16. Griggs did not identify the instrument at the time, calling it an African zither. Further research suggests that it could have only been an mvet. The term *mvet* also refers to a spoken or sung epic tradition associated with the Fang, Beti, and Bulu peoples in Gabon and Cameroon. See Gerhard Kubik, *Theory of African Music*, vol. 2 (Chicago: University of Chicago Press, 2010), 68–70; Stephen Belcher, *Epic Traditions of Africa* (Bloomington: Indiana University Press, 1999), 51–55.

150. Weston, *African Rhythms*, 121; Griggs, "With Randy Weston in Africa," 39.

151. Griggs, "With Randy Weston in Africa," 38–39; Valerie Wilmer, *Jazz People* (New York: Da Capo, 1977), 83–84.

152. Von Eschen, *Satchmo Blows Up the World*, 173–176.

153. Report reprinted in Weston, *African Rhythms*, 134.

154. Ibid., 134.

155. Randy Weston Lecture/Interview, Duke Ellington Society, New York Chapter, 1967.

156. Weston, *African Rhythms*, 139; Randy Weston, interview with author, August 20, 2001.

157. Weston, *African Rhythms*, 128; Toyin Falola and Matthew M. Heaton, *A History of Nigeria* (Cambridge: Cambridge University Press, 2008), 174–180.

158. Weston, *African Rhythms*, 138–140.

159. Weston's years in Morocco are beyond the scope of this book. The best scholarly treatment of Weston's Moroccan sojourn and ongoing collaboration with the Gnawa is Deborah Anne Kapchan, *Traveling Spirit Masters: Moroccan Gnawa Trance and Music in the Global Marketplace* (Middletown, CT: Wesleyan University Press, 2007).

160. The impact of this collaboration is certainly evident in LPs such as *Blue Moses* (CTI6016), *Tanjah* (Polydor PD5055), *Blues to Africa* (Freedom [E]FLP40153), *The Healers* (Cora (F) 0), and *Blue* (1750 Arch S1802), among others.

3. Ahmed Abdul-Malik's Islamic Experimentalism

1. "Abdul-Malik, Ahmed," questionnaire for Leonard Feather's Encyclopedia of Jazz, 1959, typescript, Institute for Jazz Studies, Rutgers University, New Brunswick, NJ (hereafter IJS). He repeats the same story in Ahmed Abdul-Malik, interview with Ed Berger, "Jazz from the Archives," WBGO, recorded January 30, 1984, tape at IJS; and in most of the liner notes to his LPs. See, for example, *The Eastern Moods of Ahmed Abdul-Malik* (NJLP 8298).

2. U.S. Census, 1930: *Population Schedule, Kings County, Brooklyn*, Enumeration District 24–571; *Polk's Brooklyn (N.Y.) City Directory, 1933–1934* (New York: R. L. Polk and Co., 1934); Certificate of Death, Jonathan Tim, #3482; *Local 802 of AFM Directory* (Newark: International Press, 1948), 125.

3. U.S. Census, 1930: *Population Schedule, Kings County, Brooklyn*, Enumeration District 24–571; *Polk's Brooklyn (N.Y.) City Directory 1933–1934;* Randy Weston, interview with author, August 20, 2001.

4. "Abdul-Malik, Ahmed," questionnaire for Leonard Feather's Encyclopedia of Jazz. The Vardi School, also known as the Vardi Conservatory, was a small, short-lived institution founded by violinist Joseph Vardi and his wife, Anna, a concert pianist who trained in Vienna and Petrograd. They ran the school out of a studio in Carnegie Hall. They taught many African American students during the 1930s and held scholarship competitions in Harlem at the YMCA. See ads in *New York Times,* September 18, 1927; *Amsterdam News,* June 5 and 12, 1937; Wilnette K. Mayers Scores, "Music Notes," *Amsterdam News,* June 5, 1937.

5. Quoted in liner notes to *The Eastern Moods of Ahmed Abdul-Malik* (NJLP 8298).

6. Certificate of Death, Jonathan Tim, #3482.

7. "Abdul-Malik, Ahmed," questionnaire for Leonard Feather's Encyclopedia of Jazz; Ahmed Abdul-Malik, interview with Ed Berger, January 30, 1984; Bill Coss, "The Philosophy of Ahmed Abdul-Malik," *Down Beat* (July 4, 1963), 14.

8. Ahmed Abdul-Malik, interview with Ed Berger, January 30, 1984.

9. Randy Weston, with Willard Jenkins, *African Rhythms: The Autobiography of Randy Weston* (Durham, NC: Duke University Press, 2010), 60; also Randy Weston, interview with author, August 20, 2001; Ira Gitler, "Randy Weston," *Down Beat* (February 1964), 16.

10. Kambiz GhaneaBassiri, *A History of Islam in America: From the New World to the New World Order* (Cambridge: Cambridge University Press, 2010), 208; see also Simon Ross Valentine, *Islam and the Ahmadiyya Jama'at: History, Belief, Practice* (New York: Columbia University Press, 2008).

11. Robert Dannin, *Black Pilgrimage to Islam* (New York: Oxford University Press, 2002), 35–38, 58–60; Richard Turner, "The Ahmadiyya Mission to Blacks in the United States in the 1920s," *Journal of Religious Thought* 44, no. 2 (Winter–Spring 1988), 50–66; Richard Turner, *Islam in the African American Experience* (Bloomington: Indiana University Press, 1997).

12. Christopher W. Chase, "Prophetics in the Key of Allah: Towards an Understanding of Islam in Jazz," *Jazz Perspectives* 4, no. 2 (August 2010),

165; Dannin, *Black Pilgrimage to Islam*, 58; "Moslem Musicians: Mohammedan Religion Has Great Appeal for Many Talented Progressive Jazz Men," *Ebony* (April 1953), 104–111; Claude Clegg III, *An Original Man: The Life and Times of Elijah Muhammad* (New York: St. Martin's Press, 1998); Arthur Taylor, *Notes and Tones: Musician-to-Musician Interviews* (New York: Da Capo Press, 1993), 251; Mike Hennessey, "The Enduring Message of Abdullah ibn Buhaina," *Jazz Journal International* 30 (1977), 6; Eric Porter, "'Dizzy Atmosphere': The Challenge of Bebop," *American Music* (Winter 1999), 437.

13. According to the union directory, in 1947 and 1948 Abdul-Malik went by Jonathan Timm and lived at 687 Halsey St., Apt. 33, Brooklyn. The following year's directory, 1949, a bass player named "Ahmad H. Abdul-Malik" is living at the same address on Halsey Street. *Local 802 of AFM Directory* (Newark: International Press, 1947), 118; *Local 802 of AFM Directory* (Newark: International Press, 1948), 125; *Local 802 of AFM Directory* (Newark: International Press, 1949).

14. Dannin, *Black Pilgrimage to Islam*, 58; "Moslem Musicians," 108. Leslie Gourse, *Art Blakey: Jazz Messenger* (New York: Schirmer Trade Books, 2002), 40. Gourse claims he converted to Islam after returning from two years in Africa in 1949, but earlier interviews indicated that he had already launched a Muslim Mission with Talib Dawud in 1947.

15. Chase, "Prophetics in the Key of Allah," 166–167; Porter, "'Dizzy Atmosphere,'" 437; "Art Blakey Interview: Part I (taken and transcribed by Bob Rusch)," *Cadence* 7 (July 1981), 10–11. While the "seventeen" varied, original members included Sahib Shihab (Edmund Gregory) on alto; tenor players Musa Kaleem (Orlando Wright) and Sonny Rollins; Haleen Rasheed (Howard Bowe) on trombone; trumpeters Kenny Dorham (another convert who had adopted the name Abdul Hamid), Ray Copeland, and Little Benny Harris; Cecil Payne on baritone sax; Bud Powell, Kenny Drew, and later Walter Bishop, Jr. (Ibrahim Ibn Ismail) held piano duties at different times; and Gary Mapp on bass. Steve Schwartz and Michael Fitzgerald, "Chronology of Art Blakey (and the Jazz Messengers)," available at http://www.jazzdiscography. com/Artists/Blakey/chron.htm; Henderson, "Idrees Sulieman Interview," 6. Gourse mistakenly claims the Messengers began in 1949, after Blakey allegedly returns from Africa, but clearly the group is being ad-

vertised as the Messengers as early as January 1948, and all other indications suggest they were in existence for much of 1947. Gourse, *Art Blakey*, 36–38.

16. "Moslem Musicians," 107.

17. Ibid., 108.

18. Lynn Hope, *Morocco* (Saxophonograph RBD 508, 1985).

19. Bilal Abdurahman, *In the Key of Me: The Bedford Stuyvesant Renaissance, 1940s–60s Revisited* (Brooklyn: Contemporary Visions, 1993), n.p.; "Bilal Abdurahman," *Marquis Who's Who*, 2009 (Farmington Hills, MI: Gale, 2010); liner notes, *The Music of Ahmed Abdul-Malik* (New Jazz 8266).

20. Ahmed Abdul-Malik, interview with Ed Berger, January 30, 1984.

21. "Abdul-Malik, Ahmed," questionnaire for Leonard Feather's Encyclopedia of Jazz, 1959.

22. The band consisted of Freddie Washington (piano), Shad Collins (trumpet), Prince Robinson (clarinet), Sam Taylor (tenor saxophone), Billy May (drums), and Abdul-Malik (bass). They recorded old Dixieland classics "At the Jazz Band Ball" and "Tin Roof Blues" but there is no evidence these recordings were ever released. See *Tom Lord Discography*, Session W 146–4, CD Rom.

23. Quote from "Abdul-Malik, Ahmed," questionnaire for Leonard Feather's Encyclopedia of Jazz, 1959. In the document he identifies the school as the Cairo Oriental Institute of Music, but the precise name at the time was the Arab Music Institute, having been renamed in the early 1930s. However, depending on how old the gentleman might have been, he could have been a student when the school was still called the Royal Oriental Music Institute. Anne Elise Thomas, "Intervention and Reform of Arab Music in 1932 and Beyond," paper delivered at Conference on Music in the World of Islam, Asilah, Morocco, August 8–13, 2007.

24. Dannin, *Black Pilgrimage to Islam*, 60; Melani McAlister, "One Black Allah: The Middle East in the Cultural Politics of African American Liberation, 1955–1970," *American Quarterly* 51, no. 3 (September 1999), 622–656; Vijay Prashad, *The Darker Nations: A People's History of the Third World* (New York: New Press, 2009), 51–52, 99–100; Caroline Attie, *Struggle in the Levant: Lebanon in the 1950s* (London: J. B. Tauris, 2004).

25. McAlister, "One Black Allah," 633.

26. Dannin, *Black Pilgrimage to Islam*, 60; Phil Casey, "Moslems Here Wary on Mid-East Comment," *Washington Post*, July 20, 1958; GhaneaBassiri, *A History of Islam in America*, 249.

27. "Mohammed El-Bakkar—Singer of Middle Eastern Songs Is Dead at 46," *New York Times*, September 9, 1959; Stanley Rashid, "Cultural Traditions of Early Arab Immigrants to New York," in *A Community of Many Worlds: Arab Americans in New York City*, ed. Kathleen Benson and Philip M. Kayal (New York: Museum of the City of New York, 2002), 77.

28. *Port Said* (Audio Fidelity AFSD-5833); *Sultan of Bagdad* (Audio Fidelity AFSD-5834); *Music of the African Arab* (Audio Fidelity AFSD-5858); *The Magic Carpet* (Audio Fidelity AFSD-5895); *Dances of Port Said* (Audio Fidelity AFSD-5922); *Exotic Music of the Belly Dancer* (Audio Fidelity AFSD-6154); *An Arabic Party with Mohammed El-Bakkar* (Orient SLPO-161).

29. Shawna Helland, "Ancient Ritual to Cabaret Performance," in *Moving History/Dancing Cultures: A Dance History Reader*, ed. Ann Dils and Ann Cooper Albright (Middletown, CT: Wesleyan University Press, 2001), 130–131.

30. "Abdul-Malik, Ahmed," questionnaire for Leonard Feather's Encyclopedia of Jazz, 1959. In 1959 he appeared on Djamal Aslan's LP, *Lebanon: Her Heart, Her Sounds* (20th Century Fox 3001). Of course, the Arab community in New York and elsewhere in the United States was not exclusively, or even predominantly, Muslim. I presume that Abdul-Malik had also worked with Arab Christians and possibly Arab Jews. And as an Ahmadiyya himself, he was probably treated with suspicion by fellow Sunni Muslims.

31. Helland, "Ancient Ritual to Cabaret Performance," 135.

32. Casey, "Moslems Here Wary on Mid-East Comment."

33. Randy Weston Trio with Cecil Payne, *With These Hands* (Riv RLP 12–214); Randy Weston, *Jazz a la Bohemia* (Riv RLP 12–232); Randy Weston, *The Modern Art of Jazz* (Dawn DLP 1116); Jutta Hipp Quintet, *Jutta Hipp with Zoot Sims* (Blue Note BLP 1530). On Jutta Hipp, see the forthcoming biography of Hipp by Katja von Schuttenbach.

34. Abdul-Malik's experience in Monk's quartet is well documented in my *Thelonious Monk: The Life and Times of an American Original* (New

York: Free Press, 2009). He explained to critic Joe Goldberg that no one paid attention to him until he started working with Monk. Joe Goldberg, liner notes, *The Music of Ahmed Abdul-Malik* (New Jazz 8266), recorded May 23, 1961.

35. Quoted in Ahmed Abdul-Malik, interview with Ed Berger, January 30, 1984.

36. Advertisement, *New York Times,* October 27, 1957; "Abdul-Malik, Ahmed," questionnaire for Leonard Feather's Encyclopedia of Jazz, 1959.

37. Quote from Abdurahman, *Songs in the Key of Me,* n.p.; "Stardust Time in Kings and Queens," *Amsterdam News,* October 24, 1959. The *Amsterdam News* article suggested that Abdul-Malik was co-owner of the African Quarter, but I've found no evidence to support this.

38. Ahmed Abdul-Malik, *Jazz Sahara* (Riverside 12–287). He had planned to use both Griffin and John Coltrane on the date, but Coltrane could not participate because of contractual obligations. Ahmed Abdul-Malik, interview with Ed Berger, January 30, 1984.

39. My understanding of the maqām derives from several sources, particularly Amnon Shiloah, *Music in the World of Islam: A Socio-Cultural Study* (Detroit: Wayne State University Press, 1995), 127–130. My understanding of specific maqāmāt comes from Cameron Powers, *Arabic Musical Scales: Basic Maqam Notation* (Boulder, CO: GL Design, 2005).

40. Johnny Griffin, interview with author, February 4, 2004.

41. Orrin Keepnews, liner notes, *Jazz Sahara: Ahmed Abdul-Malik's Middle Eastern Music* (Riv 12–267).

42. Miles Davis's LP, *Kind of Blue,* is generally thought to have begun the trend toward modes-based improvisation in jazz. See Richard Williams, *The Blue Moment: Miles Davis's* Kind of Blue *and the Remaking of Modern Music* (New York: W. W. Norton, 2010). Of course, modal approaches to jazz were not entirely new in 1958. George Russell had been considering the application of modes in jazz when he published *The Lydian Chromatic Concept of Tonal Organization* in 1953.

43. "*Jazz Sahara:* Review," *Billboard* (March 9, 1959), 52.

44. Advertisement, *New York Times,* October 19, 1959; Advertisement, *New York Times,* November 23, 1959.

45. Ahmed Abdul-Malik, *East Meets West: The Musique of Ahmed Abdul-Malik* (RCA Victor LSP-2015).

46. *Muhawara* translates as "dialogue" in Arabic, but in ki-Swahili, *Maharawa* translates as "mistresses."

47. The Five Spot in the East Village and the Village Gate proved to be the two main venues willing to hire Abdul-Malik's group. In fact, he and his band (Calo Scott, George Scott, Richard Williams, and Bilal Abdurahman) enjoyed a nearly three-week run at the Five Spot in November and early December 1960. See "Personnel Roster, Five Spot Café," notebook, 1960, personal papers of Joe Termini, courtesy of Toni Behm. The Village Gate tended to hire him for one night or a short week. See advertisements, *New York Times,* October 19, 1959; *New York Times,* November 23, 1959.

48. In May 1960, Ahmed Abdul-Malik recorded a session for *Leroy Parkins and His Yazoo City Band* (Bethlehem BCP6047, 11098), and in January 1961, participated in sessions that resulted in two Bob Wilber LPs: *The Bob Wilber All-Star Jazz Band* (Music Minus One MMO-1009) and *The Dixie Do It Yourself* (Music Minus One MMO-1010).

49. He can be heard on *Coltrane: The Complete 1961 Village Vanguard Recordings,* boxed set (Impulse 232).

50. This is not a direct quotation from Abdul-Malik, but rather his paraphrase. Liner notes, *The Music of Ahmed Abdul-Malik* (New Jazz 8266).

51. One of the earliest recorded examples is his LP, *Gone Native* (Savoy MG12175) made as part of the New York Jazz Ensemble in 1957. That same year, Mann appears on Art Blakey's *Orgy in Rhythm* (Blue Note BLP1554). On Mann's explorations of Afro-Cuban music, see Scott Yanow, *Afro-Cuban Jazz* (San Francisco: Miller Freeman, 2000), 70.

52. "Ethnic jazz" is Mann's term, quoted in John S. Wilson, "Through Africa with Drums and Flute," *New York Times,* December 27, 1959; Ingrid Monson, *Freedom Sounds: Civil Rights Call Out to Jazz and Africa* (New York: Oxford University Press, 2007), 121; Lisa Davenport, *Jazz Diplomacy: Promoting America in the Cold War Era* (Jackson: University Press of Mississippi, 2009), 80. Babatunde Olatunji, on the other hand, had only positive things to say about Mann. "He had no ego," Olatunji reported in his memoir. See Babatunde Olatunji, with Robert Atkinson,

The Beat of My Drum: An Autobiography (Philadelphia: Temple University Press, 2005), 194.

53. John S. Wilson, "Through Africa with Drums and Flute."

54. Quoted in Davenport, *Jazz Diplomacy,* 80. Tellingly, when the *Chicago Defender* interviewed Mann about his trip to Africa, he characterized it more or less as a "jazz safari" and spoke more about the photographs and films he took than the music he made or listened to. A. W. McCollough, "Describes African 'Jazz Safari,'" *Chicago Defender,* June 18, 1960.

55. One of the first notices in the press displaying the band's new name appeared in April 1960. "Top Stars to Help African Students," *Amsterdam News,* April 23, 1960.

56. I listened to the concert on http://www.wolfgangsvault.com/herbie-mann-sextet/.

57. Herbie Mann and the Afro-Jazz Sextet, *The Common Ground* (Atlantic LP1343).

58. "Afro Jazz Revue to Birdhouse Tomorrow," *Chicago Defender,* October 31, 1960. Chief Bey was a member of the group when they played at Birdland in November 1960. See *Wailin' Modernist: Herbie Mann Afro Jazziacs Group* (Alto AL723).

59. A recording of Mann's group performing "Isma'a" in Rio de Janeiro is available on Herbie Mann, *Jazz Committee for Latin American Affairs* (FM 403). The other band members were Zoot Sims and Al Cohn (tenor saxophone), Ronnie Ball (piano), Ben Tucker (bass), Dave Bailey (drums), and Ray Mantilla (percussion).

60. Coss, "The Philosophy of Ahmed Abdul-Malik," 15.

61. Ahmed Abdul-Malik, *Sounds of Africa* (New Jazz 8282).

62. Coss, "The Philosophy of Ahmed Abdul-Malik," 15.

63. *The Eastern Moods of Ahmed Abdul-Malik* (Prestige PR16003). The recording session took place on June 3, 1963.

64. Liner notes, *The Eastern Moods of Ahmed Abdul-Malik.*

65. Ahmed Abdul-Malik, *Spellbound* (STLP 8303). The session took place on March 12, 1964.

66. Ahmed Abdul-Malik, interview with Ed Berger, January 30, 1984.

67. Howard Thompson, "Jazz by Children Enlivens a Park in Brooklyn,"

New York Times, August 8, 1966; *Memorial Service for Ahmed Hussein Abdul-Malik, January 30, 1927–October 2, 1993* (Program, 1993).

68. From promotional flyer, "East Meets West, Featuring Ahmed Abdul-Malik, Innovator of North African and Jazz Fusions," n.d. (circa 1990); "World Music Institute Presents Tradition and Beyond, April 12 and 13 [1991], Washington Square Church, New York." Both documents are located in Vertical files, Institute for Jazz Studies, Rutgers University, New Brunswick, NJ.

69. Promotional flyer, "East Meets West, Featuring Ahmed Abdul-Malik." For Simon Shaheen's extensive biography, see http://www.simonshaheen.com/biography.

70. Simon Shaheen, interview with author, June 11, 2010.

4. The Making of Sathima Bea Benjamin

1. Jon Pareles, "Jazz: Sathima Bea Benjamin," *New York Times,* April 3, 1983; see also Jon Pareles, "Sathima Bea Benjamin with a Cape Town Beat," *New York Times,* February 21, 1986.

2. Sathima Bea Benjamin, interview with author, March 5, 2004.

3. Unless otherwise noted, the portrait of Sathima Bea Benjamin's childhood is drawn from the following sources: Sathima Bea Benjamin, interview with author, March 5, 2004; Sally Placksin, "To Me, Music Is Such a Direct Way for One Heart to Speak to the Other," in *Sathima Bea Benjamin: Embracing Jazz,* ed. Lars Rasmussen (Copenhagen: Booktrader, 2000), 11–12; "Sathima Writes," in Rasmussen, *Sathima Bea Benjamin,* 73; Carol Ann Muller, "Capturing the 'Spirit of Africa' in the Jazz Singing of South African-Born Sathima Bea Benjamin," *Research in African Literatures* 32, no. 2 (2001), 137; Francis Davis, "The Home and the World," in *Jazz and Its Discontents: The Francis Davis Reader* (Cambridge, MA: Da Capo Press, 2004); "Sathima Bea Benjamin: An African Songbird in New York," in *Rare Birds: Conversations with Legends of Jazz and Classical Music,* ed. Thomas Rain Crowe and Nan Watkins (Jackson: University Press of Mississippi, 2008), 103–104; Seton Hawkins, "Jazz, Community, and Gender: Sathima Bea Benjamin's 'Musical Echoes,'" B.A. honors thesis, Columbia University, 2005.

4. "Sathima Writes," 73; Carol Ann Muller, "Copies, Covers, and 'Colo[u]redness' in Postwar Cape Town," *Cultural Analysis* 3 (2002), 41.

5. Sathima Bea Benjamin, quoted in Davis, "The Home and the World," 120.

6. Sathima Bea Benjamin, interview with author, March 5, 2004.

7. Davis, "The Home and the World," 120.

8. Placksin, "To Me, Music Is Such a Direct Way," 12; Muller, "Capturing the 'Spirit of Africa,'" 138.

9. Sathima Bea Benjamin, interview with author, March 5, 2004; on Joni James, see Mark Rotella, *Amore: The Story of Italian American Song* (New York: Farrar, Straus and Giroux, 2010).

10. Sathima Bea Benjamin, interview with author, March 5, 2004.

11. "The Billboard Music Popularity Charts, Part III," *Billboard* (October 18, 1947), 27; Don Tyler, *Music of the Postwar Era* (Westport, CT: Greenwood, 2008), 108.

12. Sathima Bea Benjamin, interview with author, March 5, 2004; Carol Ann Muller, "Sathima 'Beattie' Benjamin Finds Cape Jazz to Be Her Home Within," in Rasmussen, *Sathima Bea Benjamin,* 26.

13. Quoted in Davis, "The Home and the World," 120. She has told this story many times, though she usually uses the word "scoop" to refer to what musicians usually call *melisma,* or ornamenting a single syllable by singing through different notes. See Placksin, "To Me, Music Is Such a Direct Way," 12; Muller, "Capturing the 'Spirit of Africa,'" 138; "Sathima Bea Benjamin: An African Songbird in New York," 104.

14. Alan Gregor Cobley, "'Far from Home': The Origins and Significance of the Afro-Caribbean Community in South Africa to 1930," *Journal of Southern African Studies* 18, no. 2 (1992): 349–370.

15. See Christopher John Ballantine, *Marabi Nights: Early South African Jazz and Vaudeville* (Johannesburg: Ravan Press, 1993), 4; Veit Erlmann, *African Stars: Studies in Black South African Performance* (Chicago: University of Chicago Press, 1991), 32; Colin Miller, "'Julle kan ma New York toe gaan, ek bly in die Manenberg': An Oral History of Jazz in Cape Town from the Mid-1950s to the Mid-1970s," in *Imagining the City,* ed. Sean Field (Cape Town: HSRC Press, 2007), 135–136; Hotep Idris Galeta, "The Development of Jazz in South Africa," available at http://www.jazzrendezvous.co.za/special/spe2006062701.php.

16. Gwen Ansell, *Soweto Blues: Jazz, Popular Music, and Politics in South Africa* (New York: Continuum, 2004), 64–104; Gerhard Kubik, *Africa and the Blues* (Jackson: University Press of Mississippi, 1999), 163; David Coplan, *In Township Tonight! South Africa's Black City Music and Theatre* (New York: Longman, 1985), 145–148; Don Mattera, *Memory Is the Weapon* (Grant Park, South Africa: African Perspectives, 2007); Rob Nixon, *Homelands, Harlem and Hollywood: South African Culture and the World Beyond* (London: Routledge, 1994), 11–42.

17. "My Kind of Jazz: Zakes Nkosi, Interviewed by Mothobi Mutloatse," in *Umhlaba Wethu: A Historical Indictment,* ed. Mothobi Mutloatse (Johannesburg: Skotaville, 1989), 114; Coplan, *In Township Tonight!* 162–163; "Kippie's Memories and the Early Days of Jazz: Kippie Moeketsi Speaks," *Ten Years of Staffrider, 1978–1988,* eds. Andries Walter Oliphant and Ivan Vladislavic (Johannesburg: Ravan Press, 1988), 362.

18. "Mr. Drum Listens to Jazz!" *Drum* 2, no. 8 (August 1952), 15; Todd Matshikiza, "Music for the Moderns," *Drum* 2, no. 7 (July 1952), 38–39. According to Matshikiza, Johannesburg had only two decent rehearsal spaces for black musicians, the Bantu Men's Social Centre and the Donaldson Community Centre, and use of the space was restricted to members only.

19. This image is captured in films like *Zonk! Song of Africa,* and *The Magic Garden*—films made in South Africa during the 1950s. See Peter Davis, *In Darkest Hollywood: Exploring the Jungles of Cinema's South Africa* (Athens: Ohio University Press, 1996); Todd Matshikiza, "Music for the Moderns," *Drum* 2, no. 4 (April 1952), 15.

20. Anthony Sampson, *Drum: A Venture into the New Africa* (London: Collins, 1956), 20. There has been much written on *Drum* magazine and its history. See, for example, Michael Chapman, ed., *The "Drum" Decade: Stories from the 1950s* (Pietermaritzburg, South Africa: University of Natal Press, 2001); Mike Nicol, *A Good-Looking Corpse: The World of* Drum—*Jazz and Gangsters, Hope and Defiance in the Townships of South Africa* (London: Secker and Warburg, 1991); Nixon, *Homelands, Harlem and Hollywood.*

21. Sampson, *Drum,* 28. For a fascinating critical analysis of *Drum,* jazz, and modernity as expressed in Matshikiza's writings, see Michael Titlestad, "Jazz Discourse and Black South African Modernity, with Spe-

cial Reference to 'Matshikese,'" *American Ethnologist* 32, no. 2 (2005), 210–221.

22. Todd Matshikiza, "Where's Jazz Going Now?" *Drum* (August 1957), 55.

23. Ballantine, *Marabi Nights*, 5–7; Kubik, *Africa and the Blues*, 164–167.

24. Gwen Ansell, *Soweto Blues*, 59–60; Coplan, *In Township Tonight!* 159–161.

25. Sathima Bea Benjamin, interview with author, March 5, 2004; see also Muller, "Sathima 'Beattie' Benjamin Finds Cape Jazz to Be Her Home Within," 26.

26. Sathima Bea Benjamin, interview with author, March 5, 2004.

27. Placksin, "To Me, Music Is Such a Direct Way," 11. Sathima also learned that her mother's mother, Francesca de la Cruz, was a schoolteacher and a talented singer who performed little operettas with a violinist.

28. For a good overview of the Cape Town jazz scene in the 1950s, see Miller, "'Julle kan ma New York toe gaan,'" 140.

29. Sathima Bea Benjamin, interview with author, March 5, 2004; Muller, "Sathima 'Beattie' Benjamin Finds Cape Jazz to Be Her Home Within," 28; "Sathima Bea Benjamin: An African Songbird in New York," 106.

30. Sathima Bea Benjamin, interview with author, March 5, 2004; Muller, "Sathima 'Beattie' Benjamin Finds Cape Jazz to Be Her Home Within," p. 29; Placksin, "To Me, Music Is Such a Direct Way," 12.

31. "Henry February, pianist bandleader interview," in Lars Rasmussen, ed., *Jazz People of Cape Town* (Copenhagen: Booktrader, 2003), 64–65.

32. Jimmy Adams interview, in *Jazz People of Cape Town,* ed. Rasmussen, 11.

33. Davis, "The Home and the World," 120.

34. Sathima Bea Benjamin, interview with author, March 5, 2004; Muller, "Covers, Copies, and 'Colo[u]redness,'" 33.

35. See Crain Soudien, "Teachers' Responses to the Introduction of Apartheid Education," in *The History of Education under Apartheid, 1948–1994: The Doors of Learning and Culture Shall Be Opened,* ed. Peter Kallaway (Cape Town: Pearson Education South Africa, 2002), 212–215; Mohamed Adhikari, *"Let Us Live for Our Children": The Teachers' League of South Africa, 1913–1940* (Cape Town: Buchu Books, 1993).

36. Davis, "The Home and the World," 120.

37. Sathima Bea Benjamin, interview with author, March 5, 2004.

38. Jimmy Adams interview, in *Jazz People of Cape Town,* ed. Rasmussen, 13.
39. "Kippie's Memories and the Early Days of Jazz," 362–363; Bloke Modisane, "Masterpiece in Bronze: Problem Child of Music," *Drum* 83 (January 1958), 47, 49, 51; Casey Motsisi, "Kippie—Sad Man of Jazz," *Drum* 129 (December 1961), 68–69, 71; see also Michael Titlestad, "'I Was Not Yet Myself': Representations of Kippie 'Charlie Parker' Moeketsi," *Social Identities* 9, no. 1 (2003), 25–36.
40. Hugh Masekela and D. Michael Cheers, *Still Grazing: The Musical Journey of Hugh Masekela* (New York: Crown, 2004), 59–67, 94. On Father Huddleston and the jazz band, see Mattera, *Memory Is the Weapon,* 84–93; Robin Denniston, *Trevor Huddleston: A Life* (New York: St. Martin's Press, 1999), 10–66; John Hughes, "South Africa Writes . . . Jazz Wins White Plaudits," *Christian Science Monitor,* February 5, 1958, 13; John S. Wilson, "Jazz: A Young African with a Horn," *New York Times,* October 20, 1964.
41. All quotes from Jimmy Adams interview, in *Jazz People of Cape Town,* ed. Rasmussen, 13.
42. Sathima Bea Benjamin, interview with author, March 5, 2004.
43. Rasmussen, ed., *Jazz People of Cape Town,* 19.
44. First quote: Masekela, *Still Grazing,* 78; second quote: Leonard Weinreich interview, in *Jazz People of Cape Town,* ed. Rasmussen, 263
45. Sathima Bea Benjamin, interview with author, March 5, 2004.
46. As Abdullah Ibrahim prefers his Muslim name, I will refer to him by this name throughout the text.
47. Sathima Bea Benjamin, interview with author, March 5, 2004.
48. Ibid. All of the published versions of Sathima's experience with Paul Meyer omit this story. Instead, Meyer is portrayed as a generous benefactor and a great friend. Also, in Muller's version, Meyer shows up on a motorcycle, not in a sports car. Placksin, "To Me, Music Is Such a Direct Way," 14; Muller, "Covers, Copies, and 'Colo[u]redness,'" 30.
49. If Benjamin had known about Meyer's reputation, she might have exercised greater caution. He had, indeed, slept with Miriam Makeba, much to the chagrin of Hugh Masekela. Masekela believed she used him as a cover to allow her to move in and out of Meyer's flat. Masekela, *Still Grazing,* 78–79.

50. Sathima Bea Benjamin, interview with author, March 5, 2004.

51. *Golden City Post*, January 25, 1959, reproduced in Muller, "Sathima 'Beattie' Benjamin Finds Cape Jazz to Be Her Home Within," 21.

52. Lars Rasmussen, ed., *Abdullah Ibrahim: A Discography, Second Edition* (Copenhagen: Booktrader, 2000), 9.

53. Sathima Bea Benjamin, interview with author, March 5, 2004.

54. Mike Phahlane, liner notes, *Dollar Brand Plays Sphere Jazz* (Gallo Continental ZB 8047).

55. Benson Dyantyi, "Crazy? Genius? Beatnik? Dollar Brand," *Drum* 106 (December 1959), 27–28.

56. Phahlane, liner notes, *Dollar Brand Plays Sphere Jazz*.

57. Jack Lind, "Dollar Brand," *Down Beat* (November 21, 1963), 13; Chris Austin (dir.), *Abdullah Ibrahim: A Brother with Perfect Timing* (Rhapsody Films, 1989); Liner notes, Dollar Brand, *Duke Ellington Presents the Dollar Brand Trio* (released 1964; Reprise R96111); Rasmussen, ed., *Abdullah Ibrahim*, 9; Graham Lock, "In Struggle, in Grace: Abdullah Ibrahim—Music, Revolution and Prayer," *The Wire* 8 (October 1984), 12–14; Faith Okuley, "Dollar Brand—African Wayfarer," *Down Beat* (April 4, 1968), 18, 45. Interestingly, Ibrahim's resume, dating back to about 1965, indicates that he began piano lessons at the age of twelve, and yet most other sources and interviews with him more commonly give the age of seven. Resume: Dollar Brand: Black South African Pianist/Composer, Vertical Files, Institute for Jazz Studies, Rutgers University.

58. Both quotes from Abdullah Ibrahim, "Music Is a Healing Force," in *Umhlaba Wethu*, ed. Mutloatse, 87; and Leonard Feather, "Ellington's South African Protégé," *Los Angeles Times*, May 6, 1979.

59. Feather, "Ellington's South African Protégé."

60. Lars Rasmussen, ed., *Cape Town Jazz 1959–1963* (Copenhagen: Booktrader, 2001), 11.

61. Ibid., 11; "Kippie's Memories and the Early Days of Jazz," 364–365.

62. Modisane, "Masterpiece in Bronze," 51.

63. Quoted in Lind, "Dollar Brand," 34; see also Dyantyi, "Crazy? Genius? Beatnik? Dollar Brand," 28.

64. Masekela, *Still Grazing*, 94.

65. Quoted in Donald McCrae, liner notes, Abdullah Ibrahim, *Blues for a Hip King* (Kaz CD 104). Ibrahim has consistently identified Monk as his

greatest influence and credited Kippie Moeketsi for introducing him. See Abdullah Ibrahim, "Monk in Harlem: A Short Brief on Some Aspects of the Music of Thelonious Monk," *DU: The Magazine of Culture* 3 (March 1994), 80; Jurgen Arndt, *Thelonious Monk und der Free Jazz* (Graz, Austria: Akademische Druck—u. Verlagsanstalt, 2002), 133–150; Lind, "Dollar Brand," 34.

66. Sammy Maritz, bassist, interviewed in *Jazz People of Cape Town*, ed. Rasmussen, 126. Singer Zelda Benjamin (no relation to Sathima Bea Benjamin) leveled even more severe criticism against Ibrahim for the way in which Monk influenced his style. Zelda Benjamin interview, in *Jazz People of Cape Town*, ed. Rasmussen, 39.

67. Sathima Bea Benjamin, interview with author, March 5, 2004. Benjamin actually recorded nine tracks, another take of "My Funny Valentine," but it was incomplete. For session details, see *Sathima Bea Benjamin*, ed. Rasmussen, 81; *Abdullah Ibrahim*, ed. Rasmussen, 137. Benjamin shared a copy of the session, recorded from the original acetate, with the author.

68. Quoted in Placksin, "To Me, Music Is Such a Direct Way," 14; see also Muller, "Sathima 'Beattie' Benjamin Finds Cape Jazz to Be Her Home Within," 22; Maxine McGregor, *Chris McGregor and the Brotherhood of Breath: My Life with a South African Jazz Pioneer* (Flint, MI: Bamberger Books, 1995), 15.

69. Vincent Kolbe interview, in *Jazz People of Cape Town*, ed. Rasmussen, 110; Harry Peacock interview, in *Jazz People of Cape Town*, ed. Rasmussen, 249.

70. Lami Zokufa interview, Frank Barton, "Cape Jazz Is Now the Tops," *Drum* 122 (May 1961), 47; Gwen Ansell, *Soweto Blues*, 118; Rasmussen, ed., *Jazz People of Cape Town*, 273.

71. Masekela, *Still Grazing*, 99–100; Ansell, *Soweto Blues*, 101–104. The band occupying *King Kong's* orchestra pit was called the Jazz Dazzlers, a revamped version of the Shantytown Sextet. *King Kong* was based on the true story of South African boxer Ezekiel Dhlamini, who, after a series of setbacks, was convicted of murdering his girlfriend in a jealous rage and killed himself rather than serve out his sentence. See Harry Bloom and Pat Williams, *King Kong: An African Jazz Opera* (London: Collins, 1961); Mona Glasser, *King Kong: A Venture in the Theater* (Cape Town:

Norman Howell, 1960); Cynthia Erb, *Tracking King Kong: A Hollywood Icon in World Culture* (Detroit: Wayne State University Press, 1998), 191–197; Nixon, *Homelands, Harlem and Hollywood,* 32–33; Anthony Sampson, "From Veld to City: The Bantu Drama," *New York Times,* May 22, 1960; Tom Hopkinson, "King Kong is Coming," *London Observer,* January 29, 1961; Joe Rogaly, "When the Afrikaners Clap to the Black Man's Jazz," *The Guardian* (London), June 16, 1960. Todd Matshikiza, *Chocolates for My Wife* (Cape Town: David Philip, 1982, orig. 1961), is a memoir about Matshikiza's London period when he traveled there with *King Kong.*

72. The full title of Mehegan's book is *Jazz Improvisation: Tonal and Rhythmic Principles* (New York: Watson-Guptill, 1959). It was the first in a trilogy of books on jazz piano improvisation. John Mehegan was not the first American jazz musician to make an official visit to, and take a tour of, South Africa after the imposition of apartheid. Under the auspices of the Jazz Foundation, clarinetist Tony Scott visited in August 1957, and the Bob Cooper-Bud Shank quartet with singer June Christy went in April 1958. John Mehegan, "Report from Africa," *Down Beat* (November 26, 1959): 22–24; "Scott, Red Hot," *Drum* 80 (October 1957), 40–43; Todd Matshikiza, "What Our Players Learned from the Jazz Prof.," *Drum* 104 (October, 1959), 58.

73. Mehegan, "Report from Africa," 23.

74. Masekela, *Still Grazing,* 100; Mehegan, "Report from Africa," 22–24; Matshikiza, "What Our Players Learned from the Jazz Prof.," 57, 59–60; Todd Matshikiza, "With the Lid Off," *Drum* 107 (January 1960), 13; Ansell, *Soweto Blues,* 98–100. Two LPs were issued as *Jazz in Africa: Vol. 1* (Continental CON-T 09) and *Jazz in Africa: Vol. 2* (Continental CON-T 10). The other musicians on the date were bassist Claude Shange, Ray Shange on pennywhistle, Samson Singo on mbira, and Indian pianist Chris Joseph substituting for Mehegan on a few songs.

75. Dyantyi, "Crazy? Genius? Beatnik?" 27.

76. David Coplan, *In Township Tonight!* 173; Rasmussen, ed., *Abdullah Ibrahim,* 194.

77. Rasmussen, ed., *Abdullah Ibrahim,* 194.

78. Dyantyi, "Crazy? Genius? Beatnik?" 26.

79. Masekela, *Still Grazing,* 101.

80. South African Democracy Education Trust, *The Road to Democracy in South Africa*, vol. 1, *1960–1970* (Cape Town: Zebra Press, 2004), 257–318, 341–343.

81. Masekela, *Still Grazing*, 102.

82. Vincent Kolbe interview, in *Jazz People of Cape Town*, ed. Rasmussen, 109–110.

83. McGregor, *Chris McGregor*, 13. Chris McGregor remembers bringing the band's front line to the College of Music, where he was studying, and the three horn players performed with his rhythm section (p. 13). On the Jazz Epistles' run at the Ambassadors, see also Rasmussen, ed., *Cape Town Jazz*, 12.

84. Sathima Bea Benjamin, interview with author, March 5, 2004.

85. Placksin, "To Me, Music Is Such a Direct Way," 14.

86. Masekela, *Still Grazing*, 104.

87. Ibid., 104; Rasmussen, ed., *Cape Town Jazz*, 11.

88. "Kippie's Memories and the Early Days of Jazz," 370.

89. See *Dollar Brand Plays Sphere Jazz*; Rasmussen, ed., *Abdullah Ibrahim*, 17.

90. Liner notes, *Jazz in Africa* (Continental CONT9); South African Audio Archive, available at http://www.flatinternational.org/template_volume.php?volume_id=116.

91. Phahlane, liner notes, *Dollar Brand Plays Sphere Jazz*.

92. The best account of the massacre is Tom Lodge, *Sharpeville: An Apartheid Massacre and Its Consequences* (New York: Oxford University Press, 2011); see also Philip Frankel, *An Ordinary Atrocity: Sharpeville and Its Massacre* (New Haven: Yale University Press, 2001).

93. Masekela, *Still Grazing*, 104–108; Rasmussen, ed., *Cape Town Jazz*, 7–8; Ansell, *Soweto Blues*. The common story is that the band broke up when Moeketsi, Gwangwa, and Masekela rejoined the cast of *King Kong* for its London premiere, but Masekela left for London in May, long before rehearsals for the London tour. Masekela, *Still Grazing*, 108; see also Leonard Ingalls, "African Musical Sets London Trip," *New York Times*, January 5, 1961; Hopkinson, "King Kong is Coming."

94. Sathima Bea Benjamin, interview with author, March 5, 2004; see also "Sathima Writes," in *Sathima Bea Benjamin*, ed. Rasmussen, 68.

95. Barton, "Cape Jazz Is Now the Tops," 46. Not surprisingly, Barton's an-

nouncement that jazz in the Cape surpassed Johannesburg did not go unanswered. See Mike Phahlane, "Nuts to That! Joburg Is Still the Only Jazz Town," *Drum* 122 (May 1961), 48–49.

96. "Dollar Brand Shows 'Em How," *Drum* 113 (July 1960), 19.

97. "S. A. Jazz Pianist to Go Abroad," *Cape Argus*, January 27, 1962; Muller, "Capturing the 'Spirit of Africa,'" 134; "Sathima Writes," 69.

98. Bruno Rub, liner notes, Bea Benjamin with Dollar Brand, *African Songbird* (The Sun As-Shams GL 1839); Rasmussen, ed., *Abdullah Ibrahim*, 9; "Sathima Writes," 69; Sathima Bea Benjamin, interview with author, March 5, 2004; Placksin, "To Me, Music Is Such a Direct Way," 14.

99. "Sathima Writes," 69.

100. According to Lars Rasmussen, Ibrahim signed a three-year contract promising four and a half months of work each year. Rasmussen, ed., *Abdullah Ibrahim*, 9.

101. The Ellington Orchestra's Zurich concert was recorded for broadcast and part of it released as *Duke Ellington 20th Death Anniversary* (Jazz Portraits CD 14564).

102. David Hadju, liner notes, Sathima Bea Benjamin, *A Morning in Paris* (Enja (G)ENJ-9309–2 [CD]); Muller, "Capturing the 'Spirit of Africa,'" 141; Placksin, "To Me, Music Is Such a Direct Way," 14–15; "Sathima Bea Benjamin: An African Songbird in New York," 107; Jack Lind, "Dollar Brand," 13. Virtually every review of the CD, *A Morning in Paris*, recounts some version of this story.

103. Placksin, "To Me, Music Is Such a Direct Way," 15; Hadju, liner notes, *A Morning in Paris*; Sathima Bea Benjamin, interview with author, March 5, 2004.

104. Hadju, liner notes, *A Morning in Paris*.

105. Ibid.; Muller, "Sathima 'Beattie' Benjamin Finds Cape Jazz," 31; "Sathima Bea Benjamin: An African Songbird in New York," 107–108.

106. Jules Epstein, "Sathima Bea Benjamin—Framework of a Legend," *Philadelphia Tribune*, March 14, 1997; Hazel Smith, "Sathima Bea Benjamin—What We Do Not Possess Is Not Lost," (New York) *Beacon*, March 5, 1997; Will Friedwald, "Missing Links," *Village Voice* 42, no. 16 (April 1997), 67; Dave Gelly, "Jazz: Do Bea, Do Bea, Do," *The Observer*, April 27, 1997, to cite just a few of the many reviews.

107. Dollar Brand, *Duke Ellington Presents the Dollar Brand Trio;* see also Lind, "Dollar Brand," 34.

108. For an extended discussion of gender and masculinity and the jazz avant-garde, see my essay, "New Monastery: Monk and the Jazz Avant-Garde," *Black Music Research Journal* 19, no. 2 (Fall 1999), 135–168.

109. In fact, in an incredibly nasty review of one of Benjamin's concerts, critic Stephen Holden dismissed her diction as "flawed," without any consideration for her accent. Stephen Holden, "Sathima Bea Benjamin," *New York Times,* June 4, 1992.

110. Will Friedwald, "Sathima Sings Ellington," in *Sathima Bea Benjamin,* ed. Rasmussen, 52; "Sathima Writes," 71; Denis-Constant Martin, "From Africa with Love: Sathima Bea Benjamin and Duke Ellington: A Discovery and a Revelation," also in *Sathima Bea Benjamin,* ed. Rasmussen, 39; Placksin, "To Me, Music Is Such a Direct Way," 15. She did not know all the lyrics to "In a Mellow Tone" at the time, so she ended up singing the first chorus twice. In addition to Newport, she performed with Ellington in Copenhagen, Vermont, and Maryland. Her final appearance with him was at a Jazz Vespers at St. Peter's Church in Manhattan on Christmas Eve, 1972.

111. Sathima Bea Benjamin, interview with author, March 5, 2004.

112. Makaya Ntshoko moved to Copenhagen for a while, where he became a highly sought-after drummer, eventually leading his own band. Tragically, Johnny Gertze became addicted to heroin and in 1968 was deported back to South Africa. Despite his enormous talent, he hardly worked. "He used to beg from people in the street and to sleep in the bush. It was a very sad story." He eventually succumbed to brain cancer in 1983. http://www.makayantshoko.com/biography.php. Harry Peacock interview, in *Jazz People of Cape Town,* ed. Rasmussen, 251; Vincent Kolbe interview, in *Jazz People of Capetown,* ed. Rasmussen, 110.

113. "Brand Leaves U.S.A., Finds Europe Warmer," *Down Beat* (July 25, 1968), 10; Feather, "Ellington's South African Protégé"; Rasmussen, ed., *Abdullah Ibrahim,* 10; Bruno Rub, liner notes, Bea Benjamin with Dollar Brand, *African Songbird.*

114. One of the last documented concerts they performed together was in Boswil, Switzerland, on April 28, 1973. She was featured on five songs—

two Ellington compositions, "Sophisticated Lady" and "Come Sunday," the spiritual, "Sometimes I Feel Like a Motherless Child," and two well-worn chestnuts in her repertoire, "I'm Glad There Is You" and "It Never Entered My Mind." See Rasmussen, ed., *Sathima Bea Benjamin*, 90.

115. Sathima Bea Benjamin, interview with author, March 5, 2004.

116. Z. B. Molefe, "A Hunger to Sing," found also in Rasmussen, *Sathima Bea Benjamin*, 48.

117. On Lincoln's life, work, and politics, see Farah Jasmine Griffin, *If You Can't Be Free, Be a Mystery: In Search of Billie Holiday* (New York: Free Press, 2001), 161–191; Eric Porter, *What Is This Thing Called Jazz? African American Musicians as Artists, Critics, and Activists* (Berkeley: University of California Press, 2002), 149–190.

118. Placksin, "To Me, Music Is Such a Direct Way," 17; Bea Benjamin with Dollar Brand, *African Songbird;* Rasmussen, ed., *Sathima Bea Benjamin*, 91; "African Songbird," South African Audio Archive, available at http://www.flatinternational.org/template_volume.php?volume_id=143#.

119. South African Democracy Education Trust, *The Road to Democracy*, 317–370.

120. "Sathima Writes," 72. She completed her petition for naturalization in New York in 1985. Petition for Naturalization, Sathima Ibrahim, #12343642, issued October 9, 1985, New York Southern District, available at http://search.ancestry.com/cgi-bin/sse.dll?h=2835027&db=nysound expet&indiv=try.

121. Sathima Bea Benjamin, interview with author, March 5, 2004.

122. Placksin, "To Me, Music Is Such a Direct Way," 17; see also Muller, "Sathima 'Beattie' Benjamin Finds Cape Jazz to Be Her Home Within," 32.

123. Placksin, "To Me, Music Is Such a Direct Way," 18.

124. Z. B. Molefe, "A Hunger to Sing"; also Rasmussen, *Sathima Bea Benjamin*, p. 47.

125. Benjamin, quoted in *Sathima's Windsong* (documentary film) by Daniel Yon, South Atlantic World Productions.

Coda

1. See Manthia Diawara's excellent critique of Afro-pessimism in: *In Search of Africa* (Cambridge, MA: Harvard University Press, 1998), 39–57; Isa-

belle Job, "The End of Afro-Pessimism?" *Conjuncture* (November 1997), 16–23; Ruth Mayer, *Artificial Africas: Colonial Images in the Times of Globalization* (Lebanon, NH: University Press of New England, 2002), 180–188.

2. The Cannonball Adderley Quintet, *Accent on Africa* (Capitol ST-2987); Hugh Masekela, *Introducing Hedzoleh Soundz* (Blue Thumb BTS-62); Pharoah Sanders, *Thembi* (Impulse! A AS-9206); Kuumba "Toudie" Heath and Mtume, *Kawaida* (O'Be Records OB-301); Mtume Umoja Ensemble, *Alkebu-Lan—Land of the Blacks (Live at the East)* (Strata-East SES-19724); and several LPs by Fela Ransome-Kuti and His Afrika 70, including *Fela Fela Fela* (LP HNLX5033), *Zombie* (Polydor PMLP 1003), *Upside Down* (Phase Four Stereo, London Records SP 44290), and *No Agreement* (Afrodisia DWAPS 2039). Other examples include Big Black, *Message to Our Ancestors* (MCA/Uni 73012), and *Lion Walk* (MCA/Uni 73033); Dudu Pukwana & Spear, *In the Townships* (Caroline C-1504).

3. Michael Veal, *Fela: The Life and Times of an African Musical Icon* (Philadelphia: Temple University Press, 2000), 152; Andrew Apter, *The Pan-African Nation: Oil and the Spectacle of Culture in Nigeria* (Chicago: University of Chicago Press, 2005). See also "In Retrospect: FESTAC '77," *The Black Perspective in Music* 5, no. 1 (Spring 1977), 104–105; Iris Kay, "FESTAC 1977," *African Arts* 11, no. 1 (August 1977), 50–51. The festival ran from January 15 to February 12, 1977. Nigeria was originally slated to host the event in 1970, but the civil war, political strife, and general disorganization delayed the event by several years.

4. On Fela's life and politics, see Veal, *Fela;* Tejumola Olanyian, *Arrest the Music! Fela and His Rebel Art and Politics* (Bloomington: Indiana University Press, 2004); Carlos Moore, *Fela, Fela: This Bitch of a Life* (London: Allison and Busby, 1982).

5. Veal, *Fela*, 153–154; John Collins, "Fela and the Black President Film—A Diary," in *Fela: From West Africa to West Broadway,* ed. Trevor Schoonmaker (New York: Palgrave, 2003), 69–70, 73; John F. Szwed, *Space Is the Place: The Lives and Times of Sun Ra* (New York: Pantheon Books, 1997), 341–342.

6. Randy Weston, with Willard Jenkins, *African Rhythms: The Autobiography of Randy Weston* (Durham, NC: Duke University Press, 2010), 112.

7. Ibid., 113.

8. Veal, *Fela,* 155–156; Dele Jegede, "Dis Fela Self!—Fela in Lagos," in *Fela,* ed. Schoonmaker, 86. Toward the end of her life, Fela's mother went by Funmilayo Anikulapo-Kuti, as Fela himself substituted Anikulapo for Ransome. On her life and work, see the excellent biography by Cheryl Johnson-Odim and Nina Emma Mba, *For Women and the Nation: Funmilayo Ransome-Kuti of Nigeria* (Urbana: University of Illinois Press, 1997).

9. Fela Anikulapo Kuti and Roy Ayers, *Music of Many Colors* (Celluloid CELL 6125).

10. Graham Haynes, *Nocturne Parisian* (Muse MCD5454 [CD]); *The Griots Footsteps* (Antilles 314–523–262–2 [CD]).

11. Craig S. Harris, conversations with the author between 2001 and 2009; see also http://www.craigsharris.com/bio/bio.htm.

12. World Saxophone Quartet, *M'Bizo* (Justin Time JUST 123); David Murray and the Gwo Ka Masters featuring Taj Mahal, *The Devil Tried to Kill Me* (Justin Time JUST224–2 [CD]).

Further Listening

This brief discography consists mainly of recordings by the four artists featured in the book, along with seminal discs by other musicians to which I refer throughout the book. The list is by no means comprehensive, nor is it intended to represent the vast output of African–jazz fusion or African-theme jazz recordings made during the 1950s and 1960s. Most of the LPs included here have been reissued on CD, but not all—notably, Kofi Ghanaba's early recordings are only available on LP from collectors because they have been long out of print. On most entries, I have provided the original label and catalogue numbers for the LP, and for the featured artists I have included the recording date in brackets. Anyone searching for more detailed discographical data may consult the Tom Lord Jazz Discography, www.lordisco.com.

Kofi Ghanaba (Guy Warren)

Africa Speaks, America Answers! Decca DL-8446. [1956]
Themes for African Drums, RCA Victor LSP-1864. [1958]
African Rhythms: The Exciting Soundz of Guy Warren and His Talking Drums,
    Decca DL-4243. [1959]
Emergent Drums, Columbia 33SX 1584. [1963]
Native Africa. Volume 1, KPM 1053. [1969]
Native Africa. Volume 2, KPM 1054. [1969]
Afro-Jazz, EMI/Columbia SCX-6340. [1969]
The African Soundz of Guy Warren of Ghana, EMI Records Fiesta FLPS-1646.
    [1972]

The Divine Drummer—Odumankuma, Retroafric 16CD. [1978]
That Happy Feeling, Safari Records and Tapes SAF A1 [Accra]. [1979]
Ghanaba! Live at the Arts Centre, Accra!! Safari Records and Tapes SAF A2 [Accra]. [1987]

Randy Weston

Cole Porter in a Modern Mood, Riverside RLP-2508. [1954]
The Randy Weston Trio with Art Blakey, Riverside RLP 2515. [1955]
Get Happy with the Randy Weston Trio, Riverside RLP 12-203. [1955]
Jazz A La Bohemia, Riverside RLP 12-232. [1956]
With These Hands, Riverside RLP 12-214. [1956]
The Modern Art of Jazz, Dawn DLP-1116. [1956]
Piano A-la-mode, Jubilee 1060. [1957]
Little Niles, United Artists UAL 4011. [1958]
Randy Weston Trio and Sextet: From 52nd Street to Africa, Fresh Sound Records FSR-CD 433. Originally released on a joint LP with the Lem Winchester Quartet, *New Faces at Newport,* Metro Jazz E 1005. [1958]
Uhuru Afrika, Roulette Records SR65001. [1960]
Music from the New African Nations Featuring the Highlife, Colpix CP 456. [1963]
African Cookbook, Atlantic SD 1609 [1964]
Berkshire Blues, AL 1026. [1965]
Blue Moses, CTI 6016. [1972]
Tanjah, Polydor PD5055. [1973]
Blues to Africa, Freedom (E)FLP40153. [1974]
African Nite / Nuit Africaine, LP Owl 01. [1975]
African Rhythms, Chant Du Monde LDX 74602. [1975]
The Healers, LP Cora 02. [1980]
The Spirits of Our Ancestors, Verve / Gitanes 511 857-2. [1991]
Marrakech in the Cool of the Evening, Verve / Gitanes 521 588-2. [1992]
The Splendid Master Gnawa Musicians of Morocco, Verve / Gitanes 521 587-2. [1992]
Volcano Blues, Verve / Gitanes 519 269-2. [1993]
Earth Birth, Verve / Gitanes 537 088-2. [1995]
Saga, Verve / Gitanes 529 237-2. [1995]
Khepera, Verve / Gitanes 557 821-2. [1998]
Spirit! The Power of Music, Verve / Gitanes 543 256-2. [1998]

Ancient Future/Blue, Mutable 17508-2. [2002]
Zep Tepi, Random Chance 7020267. [2005]
The Storyteller, Motéma Music Mtm-51. [2010]

Ahmed Abdul-Malik

Jazz Sahara: Ahmed Abdul-Malik's Middle Eastern Music, Riverside RLP 12-287. [1958]
East Meets West: The Musique of Ahmed Abdul-Malik, RCA Victor LSP-2015. [1959]
The Music of Ahmed Abdul-Malik, New Jazz 8266. [1961]
Sounds of Africa, New Jazz 8282. [1962]
The Eastern Moods of Ahmed Abdul-Malik, Prestige PR16003. [1963]
Spellbound, STLP 8303. [1964]

Sathima Bea Benjamin

A Morning in Paris, Enja (G)ENJ-9309-2 [CD]. [1963]
Boswil Concert 1973 (Abdullah Ibrahim [Dollar Brand], featuring Bea Benjamin), LP Columbia SAKB473. [1973]
African Songbird (with Dollar Brand), The Sun As-Shams GL 1839. [1976]
Sathima Sings Ellington, LP Ekapa EK001. [1979]
Dedications, LP Ekapa EK002. [1982]
Memories and Dreams, LP Ekapa EK003. [1983]
Windsong, LP Ekapa EK006. [1985]
Love Light, LP Ekapa EK008. [1987]
Southern Touch, Enja ENJ-70152 [CD]. [1989]
Cape Town Love, Ekapa SA001 [CD]; Booktrader Records BOOK-8. [1999]
Musical Echoes, Ekapa SA002. [2002]
Song Spirit, Ekapa SA003. [previously released material, 1963–2002]

Miscellaneous Recordings

The Cannonball Adderley Quintet, *Accent on Africa,* Capitol ST-2987).
Big Black, *Message to Our Ancestors,* MCA / Uni 73012.
Art Blakey and the Jazz Messengers, *Ritual,* Pacific Jazz EP 4-54.
Art Blakey and the Afro-Drum Ensemble, *The African Beat,* Blue Note BLP 4097.

Art Blakey, *Orgy in Rhythm. Volumes 1 and 2,* Blue Note 56586.

John Coltrane, *Africa/ Brass,* Impulse! A-6.

John Coltrane and Wilbur Harden, *Dial Africa,* Savoy SJL 1110.

Kuumba "Toudie" Heath and Mtume, *Kawaida* (O'Be Records OB-301.

Abdullah Ibrahim [Dollar Brand], *Duke Ellington Presents the Dollar Brand Trio,* Reprise R96111.

———. *Dollar Brand Plays Sphere Jazz,* Gallo Continental ZB 8047.

———. *Blues for a Hip King,* Kaz CD 104.

The Jazz Epistles, *Jazz in Africa. Volume 1,* Continental CON-T 09.

———. *Jazz in Africa. Volume 2,* Continental CON-T 10.

Fela Anikulapo Kuti and Roy Ayers, *Music of Many Colors,* Celluloid CELL 6125.

Fela Ransome-Kuti and His Afrika 70, *Fela Fela Fela,* LP HNLX5033.

———. *Zombie,* Polydor PMLP 1003.

———. *Upside Down,* Phase Four Stereo, London Records SP 44290.

———. *No Agreement,* Afrodisia DWAPS 2039.

Herbie Mann, *Herbie Mann at the Village Gate,* Atlantic 1380.

———. *Gone Native,* Savoy MG12175.

Herbie Mann and the Afro-Jazz Sextet, *The Common Ground,* Atlantic LP1343.

Hugh Masekela, *Introducing Hedzoleh Soundz,* Blue Thumb BTS-62.

Todd Matshikiza and original cast, *King Kong: An African Jazz Opera,* Gallo CDZAC51R [2003]. [orig. 1961]

Mtume Umoja Ensemble, *Alkebu-Lan—Land of the Blacks (Live at the East),* Strata-East SES-19724.

Oliver Nelson, *Afro-American Sketches,* Prestige PR-7225.

Michael Babtunde Olatunji, *Drums of Passion,* Col CS9307.

Max Roach, *Freedom Now Suite—We Insist,* Candid CJM-8002.

Horace Silver, *Horace Silver Trio and Spotlight on Drums: Art Blakey—Sabu,* Blue Note 1625.

Acknowledgments

I'm amazed by how many people had a hand in this small book. Foremost, of course, are the musicians who are the subjects of *Africa Speaks, America Answers:* Randy Weston, Kofi Ghanaba, and Sathima Bea Benjamin generously shared their stories, papers, and music with me; they opened their homes and gave me hours of their time. Weston, who I've known since 1998, and his lovely and brilliant wife, Fatou, have engaged me in a decade-long conversation that has been truly inspiring. His performances, whether solo piano or with the entire African Rhythms ensemble, have shaped this book almost as much as his words. Over the years, members of Weston's band—notably T. K. Blue, Alex Blake, the late Benny Powell, and especially percussionist Neil Clarke—have provided crucial insights and encouragement. Clarke knows more about the African drum in America than anyone I've ever encountered, and his own forthcoming book will turn conventional knowledge completely on its head.

Sathima Bea Benjamin always found time to share her precious recollections, and every time I heard her sing she demonstrated her music's extraordinary emotional depth. Kofi Ghanaba not only invited me to Ghana to spend a couple of weeks with him, but his manager, Arnold Merz, arranged lodging in Accra, shared rare recordings, and facilitated my trip. John Collins, Ghanaian popular music's leading historian, shared material from his own collection, helped me navigate Accra, and introduced me to Juma Santos, who had a wealth of information at his fingertips. But no one in Ghana was more generous and giving than Gye Nyame Hossana Ghanaba (Mawuko), Kofi's youngest daughter. She was my guide, facilitator, translator, driver, confidante, nurse, and to this day is one of my dearest friends.

Without Henry Louis Gates, Jr., this book would not exist. His gracious invitation to deliver the Nathan I. Huggins Lectures gave birth to this project, and the intellectual atmosphere at Harvard University's W. E. B. Du Bois Institute fed and challenged my incipient ideas. Faculty, fellows, and visiting scholars who attended the lectures offered a wellspring of ideas, criticisms, and suggestions—notably Emmanuel K. Akyeampong, Larry Bobo, Glenda R. Carpio, Jacquelyn Dowd Hall, Evelyn Brooks Higginbotham, Tera Hunter, Abiola Irele, Robert Korstad, Ingrid Monson, Marcyliena Morgan, Ronald Radano, Tommie Shelby, and many others. And without Harvard University Press, this book would not have seen the light of day. Joyce Seltzer poked, prodded, and cajoled until she magically had a manuscript in her in-box, and then she went to work on making a mess of ideas cohere into a book. I'm also grateful to her able assistants, Jeannette Estruth and Brian Distelberg, and to my excellent copy editor, Kate Brick.

Many colleagues heard me speak about all or part of the manuscript, and some read it at various stages. I'm indebted to all, particularly the Center for Jazz Studies at Columbia University, the Jazz Study Group, New York University, as well as some independent writers. They include Hishaam D. Aidi, May Alhassen, T. J. and Lois Anderson, Dwight Andrews, Sylvia Chan-Malik, Jayne Cortez, Stanley Crouch, Danny Dawson, Manthia Diawara, Brent Edwards, Melvin Edwards, Steve Feld, Krin Gabbard, Kevin Gaines, Kyra Gaunt, John Gennari, Maxine Gordon, Sandra Jackson-Dumont, Farah Jasmine Griffin, Monica Hairston, William Harris, Seton Hawkins, Ellie Hisama, Eugene Holley, Jr., Michael Honey, Vijay Iyer, Travis Jackson, Loren Kajikawa, Deborah Kapchan, Helene Neveu Kringelbach, George Lewis, George Lipsitz, Noel Lobley, William Lowe, Jacqui Malone, Timothy Mangin, Herbie Miller, Ingrid Monson, Fred Moten, Dawn Norfleet, Jack O'Dell, Robert O'Meally, Brett Pyper, Guy Ramsey, Julius Scott III, Nikhil Singh, D. L. Smith, Louis Chude Sokei, John Szwed, Jeff Taylor, Greg Thomas, W. S. Tkweme, Sherrie Tucker, Penny Von Eschen, Chris Washburne, Salim Washington, and my very old friend Eric Wright. I offer special thanks to those whose influence on this work has been enormous and whose presence is now sorely missed: the late Ted Joans, Manning Marable, Sekou Sundiata, Mark Tucker, and Clyde Woods. Musicians Chief Bey, Richard Davis, Johnny Griffin, Craig Harris, Fred Ho, Hugh Masekela, René McLean, and Simon Shaheen shared invaluable memories and interpretations of the music, and filmmakers Glenn Ujebe Masokoane *(Blues for Kippie)* and Dan Yon *(Sathima's Windsong)* generously shared early cuts of their films.

Zvi Ben-Dor Benite not only translated Arabic lyrics but schooled me in Arab poetry and music. Lynda Wright transcribed about half of my interviews, enhancing the text with additional information. As always, I benefited from terrific research assistants—Elleza Kelley, Harald Kisiedu, Russell Marlborough, and Kendra Tappin—and outstanding archivists, especially Jo-ellen El Bashir, Curator of Manuscripts, Moorland Spingarn Research Center; the entire staff at the Institute of Jazz Studies, Rutgers University (especially Ed Berger, who had developed a personal friendship with Ahmed Abdul-Malik); Howard Dodson, James Briggs Murray, Diana Lachatanere, and the staff at the Schomburg Center for Research in Black Culture; the various staff at the National Archives; and Reuben Jackson and the staff at the Smithsonian Institution Jazz Archives, Museum of American History, Washington, D.C.

Several parties deserve thanks for permitting me to use photographs and song lyrics within my book. Kim Stewart of Chuck Stewart Photography and Cynthia Sesso of CTS Images both worked swiftly and exuberantly to supply valuable photographs. Special thanks to Gye Nyame Hossana Ghanaba (Mawuko) for allowing me to reproduce photographs held in her father's estate, and for granting permission to reproduce lyrics from "The Highlife" (Kofi Ghanaba, 1956). Arnold Rampersad put me in touch with Craig Tenney of Harold Ober Associates, who generously granted permission to reproduce Langston Hughes's lyrics from "African Lady" and "Uhuru Kwanza" (copyright © 1960 by Langston Hughes, copyright renewed 1988 by George Houston Bass; reproduced by permission of Harold Ober Associates, Inc.). Finally, I'm grateful to Sathima Bea Benjamin and Ekapa Records for granting permission to reproduce lyrics from "Africa" (1974), "African Songbird" (1975), and "Music" (1974). Permissions have been granted for nonexclusive world rights, all editions.

I've had many opportunities to share work in progress and receive critical feedback from colleagues all over the world. Thanks to my old friend Sidney J. Lemelle, I had the honor of delivering the Ena H. Thompson Lectures at Pomona College, where I presented an early version of the entire project. Likewise, I've shared parts of the work as it developed through the following forums: St. Claire Drake Lecture, Stanford University; Ioan Davies Memorial Lecture, York University, Toronto; Paul Lyons Memorial Lecture, Stockton College; Shirley Kennedy Memorial Lecture, University of California, Santa Barbara; Solomon Katz Distinguished Visiting Lecture in the Humanities, Simpson Humanities Center, University of Washington; Walker Ames Lecture, University of Washington, Tacoma; Provost Lecture Series, State University of New York, Binghamton; Department of Ethnomusicology, University of Oxford; The Queen's College, Belfast, Northern Ireland; American Studies Center of the University of the Ryukyus, Okinawa, Japan; Washington University in St. Louis; Lewis and Clark College, Portland, Oregon; University of California at Los Angeles; University of Maryland (College Park and Baltimore); and the University of Michigan, Ann Arbor. Special thanks to those colleagues who arranged these talks, notably Kosuzu Abe, Robert Chase, Barbara Crow, Robert Gregg, Loren Kajikawa, Brian Kelly, George Lipsitz, David McNally, Katsuyuki Murata, and Martin Stokes, to name a few.

Finally, I'm indebted to Diedra Harris-Kelley, who initially suggested I deliver three lectures on Romare Bearden and music, but after many hours of conversation helped guide me to *Africa Speaks*. I thank my entire family—in-laws and outlaws—particularly my siblings and our extraordinary mother, Ananda Sattwa, who taught us that music knows no national boundaries. And I thank my children: Elleza Kelley, my researcher, linguist, pop music encyclopedia, and MC of GP, for actually working on this book; Azizi Hamilton, master-in-the-making of the djembe and dundun whose love of the drums infected me; and our newest addition, Sekou Amir Kelley-Hamilton, who at six months rocks in time to Angélique Kidjo's "Battu" and has already begun to work out on his little Schylling piano (he can even play with his teeth!).

Last but not least, much gratitude to LisaGay Hamilton, my beautiful and talented partner to whom this book is dedicated. She is the only other person who has genuinely lived with this book, talked about it daily, heard the music, read my prose, and on many occasions kept me from walking away from the whole enterprise. And she improved the text immeasurably by asking one single question, over and over again: "So, what is this book about?"

Index